A Programmed Course in Conflict-Resolution and Anger Control

Toward Nonviolence and Harmony in Human Relations

Joseph M. Strayhorn, Jr., M.D.

Psychological Skills Press
Wexford, Pennsylvania

Published by:
Psychological Skills Press
263 Seasons Drive
Wexford, Pennsylvania 15090
 www.psyskills.com

Author's email: joestrayhorn@juno.com

10-Digit ISBN: 1-931773-11-4
13-Digit ISBN: 978-1-931773-11-9

Contents:

Lists and Charts on Anger Control

Tasks for Anger Control

1. Goal-setting
2. Internal sales pitch
3. List of choice points
4. Learning the terms for:
   - steps in fantasy rehearsal
   - types of provocations
   - goals or motives
   - types of thoughts
   - alternative emotions
   - behaviors
   - responses to criticism
   - conflict-resolution steps
5. The Twelve-thought Exercise and the Four-thought Exercise
6. Learning relaxation and emotional control
7. Decisions
8. Fantasy rehearsals and role-plays
9. Self-monitoring
10. Celebrations exercise
11. External rewards
12. Reading and reminding

The STEBC of Fantasy Rehearsal

Situation: Vividly imagine and describe the situation.
Thoughts: Tell what thoughts you'd like to have.
Emotions: Describe how you'd like to feel while responding.
Behaviors: Imagine yourself doing the best possible response.
Celebration: Take pleasure in the fact that you've handled the situation well.

Mnemonic: These are the STEBC ("STEPS") you go through.

Types of provocations

Conflicts
  Refusals of your requests
  Arguments over scarce resources
  Commands, or orders to do something you don't want to do
  Orders in a harsh and bossy tone
Harmful acts
  Physical threats, physical violence, harm to property
  Thefts
Criticism and Disapproval
  Irritated or disparaging tones of voice
Frustrations
  Things happening in an unwanted way
  Promises broken
  Someone else gets what you want
  Starting to lose a competition
  Being treated unfairly
  Frustrations that raise the level of irritation so that something else becomes the straw that breaks the camel's back

Some triggers to non-angry aggression:

Power: Using violence to get something from the other person
Boredom and stimulus seeking
Dominance hierarchy: The wish to prove oneself "higher on the pecking order"
Sadistic urges: Enjoying making the other person feel bad

The Twelve-thought Exercise

1. Awfulizing: "This is a very bad and dangerous situation." "This is terrible."
2. Getting down on yourself: "I did something wrong and bad. I failed."
3. Blaming someone else: "That person did something bad. That person is causing bad things to happen."
4. Not awfulizing: "This isn't the end of the world. It may be unpleasant, but I can take it. I can handle it."
5. Not getting down on yourself: "I may have made a mistake, but I don't want to spend energy punishing myself."
6. Not blaming someone else: "That person may have done something I don't like, but I want to spend my energy in ways other than thinking how bad he is."
7. Goal-setting: "Here's what I want to accomplish in this situation . . ."
8. Listing options and choosing: "I could do this, or this, or this . . .I think that this is best to do."
9. Learning from the experience: "Next time a situation of this sort comes up, I'll do this."
10. Celebrating luck: "Here's something good about the situation I'm in: . . ."
11. Celebrating someone else's choice: "I'm glad that this person did this: . . ."
12. Celebrating your own choice: "Hooray, I'm glad I . . ."

The Four-thought Exercise

- Not awfulizing: "I can handle this."
- Goal-setting: "My goal here is not to teach the other person a lesson, but to make things come out well for me." "Here's an opportunity for me to have a great success at anger control!"
- Listing options and choosing: "I could ignore him. I could ask the teacher for help. I could calmly say to him what I want. I could try to leave him."
- Celebrating your own choice: "Hooray! I stayed cool and made a wise decision!"

Mnemonic: Not Gonna Lose Cash.

Menu of GOALS OR MOTIVES for Anger Control Choice Points

Motives that are not useful:

revenge (to get even with the other person, regardless of whether this accomplishes anything)
sadism (taking pleasure in the other person's discomfort or pain)

Motives that are sometimes useful, but you should think twice about them:

dominance (to set or break a precedent of who is or isn't boss)
defense (to keep the other from taking advantage of you)
punishment (to give an unpleasant consequence in order to discourage a behavior)
stimulus-seeking (to get some excitement going)

Motives that often lead to peace and nonviolence:

avoiding harm (making sure no one is hurt)
self-discipline (creating for yourself a "self-discipline triumph")
problem-solving (finding the best way to work things out)
empathy and understanding (putting yourself in the other's place)
kindness or friendship (being ethical, developing a good relationship)

Mnemonic for the last set: ASPEK

Emotions for Provocations, Other Than Anger

Determination: "I'm determined to show myself I can handle this really well."
Curiosity: "What's going on with the other person? Can I understand the person better?"
Cool and calculating: "What are the possible responses? What is the best one?"
Sympathy: "The person has had a rough time."
Humility: "I'm not perfect either." or "Let me cure my own faults before feeling too righteously indignant about other people's."
Pride: "Hooray for me, I'm handling this situation really well!"

Mnemonic: DC current sends him power.

Behaviors for Provocations, Other Than Aggression

- Ignoring the person who is provoking you.
- Differential reinforcement.
- Assertion: calmly saying what you want.
- Conflict-resolution: trying to do a "joint decision" conversation.
- Criticism responses: practicing one of our types of responses to criticism.
- Relaxation: using a relaxation technique to calm yourself.
- Rule of law: appealing to a law or an authority.
- Away from the situation, temporarily – or permanently.
- Apologizing.
- Friendliness: kindness, cheerfulness, humor.
- Force – of a nonviolent nature.
- Tones of voice: low volume, tempo, and pitch, positive if possible.

A mnemonic using the first letters of these phrases is Ida <u>Craft</u>. The underlined letters are used twice.

Guidelines for Conflict Resolution

1. Defining. Each person defines the problem from his or her point of view, without blaming, and without telling what the solution should be.
2. Reflecting. Each person reflects to let the other person know he understands the other person's point of view.
3. Listing. They list at least four options.
4. Waiting. They don't criticize the other's options till they've finished listing.
5. Advantages. They think and talk about the advantages and disadvantages of the best options.
6. Agreeing. They pick one to try.
7. Politeness. They don't raise their voices or put each other down or interrupt.

Mnemonic: Dr. L.W. Aap

Ways of Responding to Criticism

1. Thank you
2. Planning to ponder or problem-solve
3. Agreeing with part of the criticism
4. Asking for more specific criticism
5. Reflection
6. I-want statement
7. Silent eye contact
8. Explanation or debate, done rationally
9. Criticizing the critic

Mnemonic: T-Paarisec.

Sources of Nonpunitive Power

1. reciprocity
2. money
3. competence in valued skills
4. work capacity
5. friendship
6. modeling
7. prestige and social status

8. walk-away power
9. assertion
10. verbal persuasion
11. leadership
12. leadership jobs
13. decision-making skill
14. ethics
15. tolerance of others' hostility to you
16. organizing groups
17. the law
18. clear goals

Things To Say To Create a Good Emotional Climate

Expressing gladness that the other person is here:

Good morning! Good afternoon! Good evening! I'm glad to see you! It's good to see you! Welcome home! Hi! I'm glad you're here!

Expressing gratitude and appreciation:

Thanks for doing that for me! I really appreciate what you did. I'm glad you told me that! Yes, please! That's nice of you to do that for me! This is a big help to me. Thanks for saying that!

Reinforcing a good performance of the other person:

You did a good job! That's interesting! Good going! Good point! Good job! Congratulations to you! You did well on that! That's pretty smart!

Positive feelings about the world and the things and events in it:

Wonderful! That's really great! Wow! Hooray! I'm so glad it happened like that! Sounds good! Look how beautiful that is!

Wishing well for the other person's future:

I hope you have a good day. Have a nice day! Good luck to you! I wish you the best on (the thing you're doing).

Offering help or accepting a request for help:

May I help you with that? I'd like to help you with that. I'll do that for you! I'm going to do this job so that you won't have to do it! Would you like me to show you how I do that? I'd be happy to do that for you! I'd love to help you in that way!

Positive feelings about oneself:

I feel good about something I did. Want to hear about it? Hooray, I'm glad I did this!

Being forgiving and tolerating frustration:

That's OK; don't worry about it. It's no problem. I can handle it. I can take it. It's not the end of the world.

Expressing interest in the other person:

How was your day today? How are you? How have you been doing? How have things been going? So let me see if I understand you right. You feel that _____. So in other words you're saying _____. I'd like to hear more about that! I'm curious about that. Tell me more. Uh huh . . . Yes . . . Oh?

Consoling the other person:

I'm sorry you had to go through that. I'm sorry that happened to you.

Apologizing or giving-in:

I'm sorry I said that. I apologize for doing that. I think you're right about that. Upon thinking about it more, I've decided I was wrong. I'll go along with what you want on that.

Being assertive in a nice way:

Here's another option. Here's the option I would favor. An advantage of this plan is . . . A disadvantage of that option is . . . Unfortunately I can't do it. I'd prefer not to. No, I'm sorry, I don't want to do that. It's very important that you do this.

Humor:

Saying or doing funny things, retelling funny things, or laughing when the other person is trying to entertain you by being funny. But avoiding sarcasm or making fun of the other person.

Chapter 1: What We're Trying To Do, and Why

1. This book aims to help people get along better and live in happiness and peace with one another. It envisions a world where people no longer try to kill, hit, or hurt one another. But even beyond nonviolence, it is aimed at helping people to have good, satisfying relationships with one another, despite the conflicts that arise in every relationship. This book attempts to help people deal better with the sorts of situations that make people angry, and to be expert at handling those situations.

The purpose of this book is to help people

A. get rid of all anger,
   or
B. deal better with the sorts of situations that make people angry?

2. In this book we will be talking a lot about the "sorts of situations that make people angry." We will be talking about them so much that we need a shorter way of referring to them. The word we will use is *provocations*. A provocation is anything that happens to you that might tend to make you angry. When someone hits you or calls you a name, those are provocations. When your car or your computer won't work or when you can't find your glasses, those are provocations too. If your friend says, "Let's play basketball," that can be a provocation, if you don't like basketball or feel like playing basketball.

The situations that tend to make people angry are called, in this book,

A. provocations,
or
B. trigger situations?

3. Many people don't have big problems with losing their temper. But all people disagree with at least some other people. All people need to work out those disagreements somehow or other. Everyone needs to get along well with some other people. The material in this book is relevant for everyone. The author feels that the people who should study nonviolence, anger control, and conflict resolution are

A. only those people with big problems in this area,
or
B. everyone?

4. Part of the title of this book is the phrase "anger control." Does good anger control mean never feeling angry? Our abilities to feel angry evolved for a reason. Anger, like fear and guilt and

other negative emotions, sends us very important signals about what is going on in our world. The feeling of anger is often a signal that we have a problem with something that someone else is doing. Perhaps the other person is trying to take advantage of us. Or perhaps the other person is doing something without realizing that it causes us harm. The feeling of anger can remind us to solve our problems with other people, rather than simply letting the problems continue.

What's an example of the idea of this section?

A. A woman notices herself feeling angry over the disrespectful way her children talk to her. She realizes she needs to do something about this problem.
or
B. A woman gets so angry at her child that she hits the child very hard.

5. Suppose a kid in school finds that another kid has stolen her lunch. She feels angry. She thinks, "I don't want to let this kid get away with this!" She feels determined to do something about it, rather than just to be passive and take it without doing anything. She thinks carefully about what she wants to do.

This is an example of

A. anger as a signal that there is a problem between people that needs to be solved,
or
B. someone who didn't feel any anger, and realized there was a problem anyway?
A.

6. On the other hand, suppose the girl in this example had felt so angry and out of control that she could NOT think carefully about what to do, so had no choice but to attack the other kid and try to hurt her as much as possible. Then she might hurt someone badly, get badly hurt herself, get kicked out of school, or cause something else bad to happen.

This illustrates the point that:

A. One should not feel anger.
or
B. It's not good to feel so angry that you can't control what you are doing.

7. The goal of anger control, then, is not to get rid of all anger. But it is to always keep the ability to *think carefully about what to do* in the situations that cause us anger. Sometimes we might decide to punish the other person. But there are several other types of options, and one of the purposes of this book is to learn what those other options are.

Which of the following examples illustrates what this section advises?

A. A man's car is dented by someone else. The man thinks carefully about the steps to take in dealing with the other person and getting the car fixed.
or
B. A dog jumps up on a man, and the man, without thinking, hits the dog to punish her.

8. Punishing means doing something unpleasant to someone in order to discourage the person from continuing to do something. Anger is the urge to punish someone. When someone does something we don't like, punishment is one way of trying to get him or her to stop. For example, a bully teases and picks on another kid. The kid gets mad, and hits the bully really hard. Suppose that this punishment causes the bully to leave the kid alone. The kid has learned from this that hitting and punishment and anger work. Because punishment sometimes works, most of us get the urge to punish when we are being harmed – in other words, we feel angry.

Which is an example of punishment?

A. washing out someone's mouth with soap when the person has said a swear word,
or
B. challenging someone to a wrestling match, just to see who can wrestle better?

9. But punishment is only one way of influencing another person's behavior. It is often not the best way. There are many problems with punishment. One of the big problems is called the "vicious cycle of punishment." Here's how this happens: the person who is punished, instead of stopping hurtful behavior, does something hurtful to punish the other person for punishing him!

Suppose one person bumps into a second. The second gets mad, and punishes the first by hitting him. This punishment makes the first one madder, and the first then hits the second one hard enough to hurt him badly. But the second one, determined to punish the first, gets a chain and hits the first one really hard with it. The second gets a knife or gun to punish this action. Where does it stop? Sometimes this vicious cycle stops only when one of the people has killed the other. Very many people die because of this vicious cycle of punishment.

When people get into a vicious cycle where each punishes the other for punishing him,

A. sooner or later they always come to their senses,
or
B. sometimes the cycle ends only with death or severe injury?

10. When people rely only on punishment to influence each other, another problem arises. What develops has been called the "law of club and fang." The law of club and fang means that whoever is more powerful at hurting the other person gets his way. The less powerful have to live in fear of the more powerful. The most powerful people have their way – for the moment.

The law of club and fang means that:

A. Each person is treated fairly.
or
B. "Might makes right."

11. No matter how big and strong someone is, all it takes is one gunshot (even from someone who is small and weak) to end his rule. Thus the person who controls others by fear needs to live in constant fear of violence.

The law of club and fang is the main law in some communities of drug dealers. One person rises to power, only to be replaced after the next drive-by shooting. It is a depressing and deadly way for human beings to exist. In a place where the law of club and fang is the only law, life can be described as "nasty, brutish, and short."

Mr. X feels that he can bully other people all he wants, because he is the strongest and quickest person around.

What problem with his reasoning was brought out in this section?

A. He will get old some day and someone else will be stronger and quicker.
or
B. When guns are involved, it doesn't matter how strong you are.

12. As people learn to think more about the way people live with one another, they start to use the word *society* more often. This word refers to the "totality of the social relationships of a group, or of the world." If you look at the way lots of people act toward one anotherother and get along with one another, how good is what you see? If you see lots of happiness and good will between people, you see a better society. If you see lots of unhappiness and fighting and killing, you see a worse society.

The word *society*, as we are using it now, refers to

A. an expensive party given by rich people,
or
B. what the relationships of people in a large group are like?

13. Much of world history, is the story of the law of club and fang. Just about every group that could get at other groups had wars with other groups!

Most scientists believe that, during the many centuries before history was recorded, life was no more peaceful: people banded together in tribes that often fought one another. When food was scarce, people probably fought over it, and the winners survived. People stayed alive by hunting animals and fighting predators. Violence and fighting skills were much more useful for our prehistoric ancestors than they are for most of us. However, even today, in some locations and subcultures, fighting is an important survival skill.

According to this view, the ability to be violent

A. is just as useful as it ever was, or
B. has become less and less useful as human beings have become more civilized?

14. The law of club and fang has dominated much of human history. But as human society improves, and as people become more *civilized*, we move away from the law of club and fang. We come up with new ways of dealing with disagreements between people. We can talk and think calmly about those disagreements, and often find a solution that both people will accept. We can make rules and laws about what is right and wrong. We can create authorities and enforcement systems that make sure that people will have to treat one another fairly, whether they are strong or weak. We can influence other people's behavior by persuading, teaching, and reasoning, by giving rewards, by showing the other person examples, and by other peaceful ways. As human society becomes more civilized, we come to rely on ways of influencing one another other than punishment.

What does the word "civilized" mean, as used in the section above?

A. able to use methods other than violence to deal with disagreements, or
B. having big buildings and cars rather than living in huts and riding donkeys?

15. The ability and the urge to fight probably developed in the human brain over many centuries. Fortunately, human beings also have developed great ability to learn and to make decisions. We can learn to choose carefully when to fight and when not to. By work and practice, people can learn to play music, do mathematics, read books, or use computers in ways that our primitive ancestors could not have dreamed of. Similarly, by work and practice, we can cultivate nonviolence skills that would have been out of the question for our primitive ancestors.

The author's attitude is that:

A. The brain is meant to be aggressive, and there's nothing we can do about that.

or

B. We can learn nonviolence skills that let us choose when to use anger and fighting, and when not to.

Good Decision Making Is the Goal

16. Too much anger gets in the way of solving our problems with other people. Too much anger makes us fix our minds only on punishing the other person and blinds us to other solutions to the problem. When people lash out at one another in anger, they move away from civilized society and toward the law of club and fang.

What's an example of the problem with "too much anger" that was just named?

A. A man feels so angry at his wife that he screams at her and hits her, when she would have been glad to do what he wanted if he had only asked her politely.

or

B. A person is feeling angry, and can't concentrate on solving his math problems for that reason.

17. Now let's return to the question, what is the goal of anger control? It's not to cease to feel anger. Instead, it's to be able to think clearly at all times about the best solutions to problems, without allowing anger to disrupt the thought process. It means that we can make choices based on what will make things turn out best for ourselves and others. It means that we do what we predict will make things turn out best.

What's the main point of this section?

A. Sometimes we predict what we think will happen, and we are wrong.

or

B. We want to predict which way of handling a situation will make things turn out best, and choose that action.

18. Here's one thing we do when we think clearly about what to do. We see and hear what is going on in a situation, and we try to understand what is happening, coming to conclusions that are supported by evidence. We don't assume that people want to harm us unless there is good evidence for this.

For example, someone sees us and starts walking toward us. What is he doing this for? If we assume that he wants to rob and kill us, we will be much more likely to want to hurt him. On the other hand, if we assume he is lonely and wants to socialize, or that he is lost and wants to ask directions, or that he has a message he wants to bring us, we are more likely to be friendly to him.

What's the main point of this section?

A. We'll be less likely to hit or yell at people if we don't assume they're out to get us.
or
B. We should always assume the worst of people, because then we'll protect ourselves if we need it.

19. Another thing we do when we think clearly is to list peaceful, friendly, nonviolent options for the situation. We should consider these responses first, and use violence only as a last resort.

A person's boss yells at him and puts him down constantly. What's an example of his following the advice of this section?

A. He thinks about the following options: going to the boss's boss, talking to a lawyer, quitting the job, saying he will quit if the harassment doesn't stop, and talking with his boss calmly about the problem.
or
B. Without thinking, he yells at the boss and shoves him, and gets fired.

20. Another thing we do is to predict accurately the consequences of the options we are considering. Before we do something unfriendly or violent, we think very carefully about what the results will be. We compare those results to those of any other actions we could take.

What's an example of the type of thought process that this section advises?

A. "If I yell at him, he will feel threatened and angry. If I speak softly to him, we may be able to work something out."
or
B. "In the past, human beings had no choice but to use the law of club and fang; now they have more peaceful options."

21. Another thing we do when we think clearly about our actions is to take other people's feelings into account. We put a large value on making other people happier, and avoiding making other people unhappy. In other words, we don't make our decisions from a selfish point of view. We try to be kind.

Which thought is an example of what this section advises?

A. "I want to increase other people's happiness, as well as my own."
or
B. "I look out for myself only. Other people are not my problem."

22. We also think about what will make things turn out well in the long term, not just right now. We think about how our actions will affect our long-term relationships with people, not just what we will get right away or how we will feel in the next few moments.

Which thought is an example of what this section advises?

A. "Right now I might feel like yelling and swearing at him, but in the long run, this would hurt our friendship."
or
B. "I swore at him and felt better for doing it, so it must have been a good thing to do."

23. In summary, we make our choices based on what will make ourselves and others happiest in the long run. We calculate as well as we can what's the best action we can take, of all those that are available to us. If the feeling of anger is so great that it interferes with deciding on and carrying out such choices, then we need to feel less anger.

Another way of saying this is that:

A. You should never try to change a feeling.
or
B. The first priority is to make good choices. If feeling too much anger leads us to bad choices, then we need to reduce that anger.

The Methods of This Book Are for Us All

24. Almost all people can benefit from learning better methods of dealing with provocations, even those of us who never hit or yell at anybody.

Suppose a woman is very bothered by several things that her husband does. She does not talk with him about these problems because she does not want to get angry or make him angry. But over time her smoldering resentment builds up to the point where she is never cheerful with him, does not feel affection toward him, and feels bad when he is around her. Even though she has never screamed or hit, the way she is handling provocations is causing a very bad outcome.

The person in this example is

A. doing just what this book advises, because she is not yelling or hitting,
or
B. not achieving what this book hopes to help you achieve, which is a good outcome when provocations arise?

25. The alternative to screaming and hitting is not holding anger inside and feeling miserable. It is dealing rationally with the provocation. Many times this means sitting down and having a calm conversation with the other person about the problem. Sometimes it means getting out of a relationship and avoiding the other person. Sometimes it means taking the problem to a higher authority, such as a judge, and letting that person decide what should be done. Sometimes dealing rationally with a provocation means deciding that it is too little to

bother with, and forgetting about it. And there are other options, as well. Hardly any of us always chooses the best option for each provocation that comes our way. The goal of this book is to help us choose the best options for provocations that we can, as often as we can.

One of the ways for rationally dealing with provocations that was NOT mentioned in the last section was

A. pounding on a pillow to get your anger out,
or
B. having a calm discussion to seek the solution to the problem?

The "Catharsis Theory" of Anger Does Not Work

26. People used to think that you had only two choices about anger: to hold it inside or to "let it out," or express it. At one point in history it was thought that you should let out your anger so that it would not stay inside. This idea is called the "catharsis" theory. The word *catharsis* means getting something out from you. The catharsis theory was that getting anger out by yelling or screaming or some other means would make you less angry.

Which of the following two statements does *not* go along with the "catharsis" theory of anger?

A. If you don't let anger out, it will stay inside you until you let it out.
or
B. If you act less angry, you'll feel less angry.

27. We now know that the catharsis theory of anger was harmfully incorrect. Anger is not something that you "have"; it's more like something that you "do." If we anger ourselves, we can un-anger ourselves. We can learn to turn up or down our own level of anger. We can choose how much anger we want to feel. In other words, we can control anger if we learn how.

The point of this is that:

A. We can never control an emotion. We can only control our behavior.
or
B. We can learn to control both our emotions and our behavior.

28. People have also discovered that expressing anger does not necessarily "get it out." There have been lots of experiments that have shown that yelling angry words, talking about your dissatisfaction, having fantasies of fighting, hitting things, and doing other aggressive behaviors tend to make us more angry, not less angry.

In other words,

A. If you scream and curse at someone, you'll feel more friendly to him because you've let your anger out.

or

B. If you scream and curse at someone, you'll likely feel more angry at that person, not less.

29. One experiment was done with young children. Some were given toy weapons such as guns and swords to play with. Others were given toy boats and planes. The children who played with the weapons did more pretending about violent behavior than the children who played with boats and planes. If the catharsis theory were right, then we would expect those kids to get their anger "out of their system" by their pretend play, and to hit and kick one another less often than the other group. But, instead, the opposite was found. The group that did the pretend play about fighting did *more* real-life fighting, not less.

A summary of this is that:

A. Pretend fighting led to more real-life fighting.

or

B. Fighting in imagination removed the urge to fight from people's systems.

30. Another experiment was done with adults who had been laid off from their jobs. Each of them had a talk with someone. But in this experiment, some of them were encouraged to talk about their angry feelings about getting laid off, whereas others were not. If the catharsis theory were true, those who had a chance to "talk out" their angry feelings would be less angry. But the opposite was found: they were more angry.

The conclusion of this experiment was that:

A. Talking about your anger will make you less angry.

or

B. Talking about your anger sometimes makes you more angry.

31. Researchers have done surveys of families. They have asked people how often they yell at one another in anger. They have also asked people how often they hit one another. If the catharsis theory were true, you would expect that the families who yelled at one another more would have ways of "draining off" their anger so that they would hit one another less. Instead, researchers find just the opposite: in families where people yell at one another more, they also tend to hit one another more.

The point of this study is that:

A. People who yell at each other get their anger out of their system, so they hit one another less.

or

B. People who yell at one another hit one another more.

32. Many studies like this have taught us that the catharsis theory just doesn't work. Instead, we should think about the "practice theory" of anger. If we practice acting angry by yelling, we're more likely to act angry by hitting. If we practice anger by thinking about how badly we've been mistreated, we're more likely to keep feeling angry. If we practice anger by pretending to do angry fighting, we are more likely to do angry things in real life.

Which theory would predict that the more someone screams, yells, and hits, the more angry the person tends to feel?

A. the practice theory,
or
B. the catharsis theory?

33. It shouldn't surprise us too much that yelling or fighting usually doesn't make us less angry. Let's think about other emotions, such as joy and happiness. If we laugh and smile and joke around and have fun with people, does that "get our happiness out" so that we are left with sadness? No – being able to express our joyous feelings usually increases them. If acting happy doesn't make us sad, then why should we expect that acting angry should make us mellow?

Suppose that someone notices the nice things that other people do and tries to say, "Thank you." Which of the following is more likely?

A. The person would probably feel very ungrateful, because he got his grateful feelings out by saying thank you.
or
B. The person would probably feel more grateful, because he has practiced the types of thoughts and behaviors that go along with gratitude.

34. When people yell angry words at people and call them bad names, that's called *verbal aggression*. When you hurt someone else's body, that's called *violence*. The two of these tend to go together.

Which is closer to what we observe?

A. The more verbal aggression, the more violence.
or
B. The more verbal aggression, the more people reduce their wish for violence.

35. How do we "do anger"? What do we do when we are angry, and how can we stop doing it so we can get less angry?

We do several things when we are angry. We say things to ourselves that blame someone else: things such as, "that terrible person, he shouldn't be doing this, who does he think he is? . . . " and so forth. We say things to ourselves about how bad the situation is: "This is terrible; I'm not going to take this off anybody!" We tense our muscles. We might clench our jaws and our fists. We get our adrenaline pumping by turning up a certain part of our nervous systems. We speak loudly, fast, and with lots of changes of pitch. We are more inclined to scream at people than to listen to them. We think about ways of punishing the other person and not about ways of making people happier in the long run. We might yell angry words to the other person, or try to hurt the other person.

The paragraph above seems to say that:

A. Anger is a pure feeling that has nothing to do with thoughts and behaviors.
or
B. Anger is a feeling that is very strongly related to thoughts and behaviors that we can choose to do or not to do.

36. All the behaviors we just listed are things that we can control. We can choose how much we want to do them. If we decide that this batch of angry behaviors does us harm, we can practice doing the opposite of them. We can practice speaking softly and slowly. We can practice thinking that the situation is not awful and that spending time blaming the other person is not our best use of energy. We can consciously relax our muscles. We can leave the other

person for a while so that we can think silently by ourselves. Or we can listen to the other person rather than screaming at him. We can think about ways to solve the problem rather than ways of punishing the other person. We can remind ourselves that our cherished values are nonviolence and justice, rather than the power to hurt or kill. We can speak words aimed at finding the best solution to the problem. This is how you "do" anger control, conflict resolution, and nonviolence instead of doing anger.

A good title for the paragraph you just read would be:

A. "How to 'do' nonviolent thought and action."
or
B. "All feelings are good."

37. If we really want to achieve good anger control and conflict resolution and nonviolence, we need to practice doing these things very often. We need to practice them while imagining or pretending that we are in the types of situation that would make us angry. That way, we build up the habit of handling those situations in they way we would like to. Using our imaginations to practice what we would like to do is called *fantasy rehearsal*.

Which thoughts sound like those of someone who is doing a fantasy rehearsal of anger control?

A. "He has criticized the story I wrote. I can learn something from this. I don't have to agree with him. But I can speak softly to him, and be true to my ideals of nonviolence. I'm relaxing . . .
or
B. "I don't feel like reading this any more, so I won't."

Denying Anger and Denying Provocations

38. There is something good to be said for the feeling of anger: it signals us that a provocation has occurred. Sometimes it's important not to try to convince ourselves that there is no provocation, when provocations are present.

Suppose that a man jokingly makes insulting and demeaning remarks about his wife, in the company of other people. But she has always been taught not to get angry or to "make waves" of any sort. She smiles at his remarks and doesn't feel angry. But over time, she finds herself not wanting to be with him and wanting to get out of the relationship, without knowing exactly why.

It's good to be able to feel anger at least strongly enough to know a provocation when you see and hear it. When the woman finally gives herself permission to say to herself, "I don't like these remarks, at all," she takes her husband aside and tells him to stop making them. He does so, and the relationship is much improved.

The moral of the story is that:

A. It's good to be able to recognize when provocations are occurring, and thus anger can sometimes be a useful signal.
or
B. You are always better off not thinking the thoughts that make you angry.

Types of Anger Provocations

39. It's good to have in mind the words for different types of provocations, because when we learn the art of anger control, we learn to handle these provocations better.

One type of situation is called conflict. When we are in a conflict situation, we have wishes that are at odds with someone else's wishes. For example, I want to play music, but another person wants silence. A husband wants to take an expensive vacation, but his wife wants to save the money for later. Two people both believe they have the right to go first in using a computer. A parent commands a child to clean up the house, but the child thinks that someone else should do it. A teacher commands a student to stop talking to a friend; the student thinks the teacher should use a more polite tone of voice.

Which of the following is a conflict?

A. It starts raining when I wanted the weather to be sunny.
or
B. Two people both want the last piece of pie that is left.

40. A second type of provocation is a harmful act by someone else. The other person may do damage to our bodies, our property, or our reputation. For example, in the hall, a kid pushes another kid into a locker. Someone backs his car and hits our parked car. A kid hits his brother. Someone spreads bad rumors about someone. Someone tears our homework paper. A nation drops a bomb on another nation's ship.

These harmful acts can be accidental or done on purpose. Obviously, if we believe that the harmful act is an accident, we will be less angry than if we believe the other person was purposely trying to harm us.

If what was just said is true, which of the following acts will make us angrier?

A. Someone fails to stop soon enough and runs into the rear end of our car at a traffic light.
or
B. Someone puts fireworks in our mailbox to watch it explode.

41. A third type of situation is criticism or disapproval. A boy walks down the hall, and another boy says, "Hey, you dork!" A teacher says to a student, "You didn't work on this homework assignment as much as you should have!" Someone drops something, and someone else says sarcastically, "Nice coordination you've got there!"

Which is an example of criticism or disapproval?

A. A student is reading a book after finishing an assignment. The teacher, in a kind voice, says, "I'm sorry, but we have to start something new, and you're going to have to finish up reading the book."
or
B. A student is reading a book after finishing an assignment. The teacher frowns at him and says, "What do you think you're doing?"

42. A fourth type of situation is called a frustration. In a frustration situation, we don't get what we want. Something unwanted happens. For example, I am writing, using a computer, and the power goes off; I lose my last half-hour's work. Someone promises to pay me for something, but the person has no money at the time and has to put off the payment until later. A waitperson at a restaurant spills water on me.

Which of the following is a frustration?

A. I expect someone to pay back some money he owed me, but he says, "I don't have the money."

or

B. I give someone some money, not expecting to get paid back, and feel good when the person can use it.

43. Conflict, harmful acts, criticism, and frustration: these are four major types of situations that make us mad. We call all these types of situations provocations. They all tend to provoke anger in us. But if we practice, we can learn to handle these situations very skillfully. We can learn to handle them in ways that make things come out best. We can decrease our own pain and the pain of other people.

What word includes conflicts, harmful acts, criticism, and frustrations?

A. provocations,

or

B. hurts?

44. What does it mean to handle conflicts, harmful acts, criticism, and frustrations expertly? First, we don't get very upset over very little things. There are little conflicts, acts of very slight harm, little criticisms, and little frustrations. Many of these unimportant situations can be handled simply by ignoring them and going happily on our way.

Which of the following provocations do you think is best handled by simply ignoring it and going on your way?

A. A two-year-old child you don't know sticks his tongue out at you as you walk past him in a grocery store.

or

B. Someone in your family uses very abusive language toward you, day after day.

45. Here's a second meaning of expert handling of provocations. No matter how big or little the provocation is, the expert can keep his head. This means that he keeps cool enough to think about what action will make things come out best.

What's an example of someone's keeping his head?

A. When insulted, he thinks for a while about how to respond. He decides that, in this case, the best response would be to ignore the other person, and he does so.

or

B. When insulted, he "loses it" and starts screaming at the other person. Later he says, "I can't help it. It's something I can't control."

46. Third, the expert is skilled at choosing and using the techniques that make things come out best. The expert is skilled at choosing when and how to protect himself, talk to the other person,

recognize just and fair solutions, and appeal to the rule of law when necessary.

Which words provide an example of a technique that will make things come out best?

A. "You're just a stupid idiot."
or
B. "Let's see if you think this would be a good solution to the problem."

Causes of Non-angry Violence

47. If you are going to reduce violence and aggression in the world, it's good to understand as well as possible what causes people to be aggressive and violent. Anger in response to provocations is not the only cause.

The reason to understand the causes of aggression and violence is that:

A. It's just an interesting and fun subject.
or
B. We need to understand the causes in order to reduce aggression and violence.

48. Sometimes people do violent or aggressive things to people they are not angry at. Let's think about four causes of this type of violence.

The first is violence aimed at getting something. For example, someone knocks someone down on the street to steal money from him. The mugger is not angry at the victim; he just wants what the victim has. The motive for the violence is *power*. Violence is often used to make someone else do something.

What's another example of violence aimed at getting something?

A. A person is jealous of how much better-looking someone else is, and in a fit of anger, he hits the other person.
or
B. A general in an army orders a pilot to bomb some enemy soldiers in order to get an advantage in a war.

49. The second cause of non-angry violence is boredom and stimulus-seeking. For example, suppose there is a boy who tends to get bored easily and who enjoys excitement and high emotions. He walks past his brother, who is reading, and slaps the brother on the side of the head. He does this just to get a loud and angry response from his brother.

What's an example of non-angry verbal aggression that someone does out of boredom and stimulus-seeking?

A. A kid starts chanting, "Ricky is stupid, Ricky is stupid," while riding on the bus, hoping that Ricky will entertain him by getting mad.
or

B. A drug dealer says to another drug dealer, "You sell drugs in my territory, and you're going to find yourself hurting bad."

50. The third cause of non-angry violence is to prove dominance. Proving dominance means showing that you are more powerful than someone else. For example, one high-school kid trips another one. He knows that he is bigger and stronger enough that the guy he trips won't fight back. He trips the kid just to prove that he is more powerful; it gives him pleasure to show this to himself and to other people.

What does the word "dominance" mean?

A. who gets to be boss, who's more powerful, who is the "top dog,"
or
B. who is more intelligent?

51. The fourth cause of non-angry violence occurs when someone actually enjoys seeing or producing someone else's suffering. This is, of course, a very bad reason to do harmful things, and it is a very big problem whenever it exists. Urges to hurt someone else for the pleasure of it are called *sadistic*. Everyone should earnestly wish for a society where no one has sadistic urges.

Which of these thoughts is *least* likely to be present in someone with sadistic urges?

A. I feel sorry for anyone who is hurt.
or
B. I enjoy watching fights.

52. When you read about non-angry violent acts, do they seem even more unjust and unfair and wrong than violent acts carried out in anger? The law often makes a distinction between violence carried out "in cold blood," meaning without anger, and violence carried out "in the heat of the moment," meaning with a lot of anger. Violence in cold blood tends to be punished more severely. The exception to this is the violence of warfare and law enforcement, which are examples of power-motivated violence.

Which person would you expect to regret an act of violence more?

A. someone who carefully planned a hurtful act in order to get something,
or
B. someone who impulsively hit someone while very angry?

Why Are Violence, Inexpert Conflict-Resolution, and Poor Anger Control Humanity's Biggest Problems?

53. A famous example of violence and very poor handling of conflict occurred in the U.S.A. on September 11, 2001, when terrorists hijacked airplanes and crashed them into the Pentagon, a field in Pennsylvania, and the World Trade

Center Towers in New York City. Nearly 3,000 people were murdered by these terrorists. Such terrorism is just one piece of evidence that human beings all over the world need to learn to pursue their goals by nonviolent, reasonable, thoughtful ways.

In this paragraph the author cites these attacks as evidence that

A. People all over the world need to learn nonviolence.
or
B. More terrorists need to be killed.

54. How does the violence that U.S. citizens did to each other in 2001 compare to that done by terrorists? For the year 2001, more than five times as many U.S. citizens were killed by their fellow citizens as were killed by the terrorists! U.S. residents have killed one another in similar numbers during each year before and after the 2001 terrorist attacks.

How many serious violent attacks per year do U.S. citizens make on one another, counting not only killings, but also serious injury and attempts at serious injury? According to the U.S. Bureau of Justice Statistics, the number of serious violent crimes in 2001 was over two million! If U.S. citizens could learn to stop attacking and killing one another, we would prevent many times more deaths and injuries than those

caused by the worst terrorist attack in U.S. history.

The conclusion this argument points to is that:

A. Thousands of lives could be saved if people in the U.S. could learn to be nonviolent with one another.
or
B. Violence is especially bad when the victims did nothing to provoke it.

55. Many killings are provoked by little things. One killing, according to a newspaper report, occurred when one person parked in a parking space that the other person had been saving for his own. Another death occurred because two people were waiting to use a phone, and each felt that he should be first. Can anybody think that these issues make enough difference for someone to die for? But deaths occur for such stupid reasons when people are not good at anger control, conflict resolution, and nonviolence.

The point of this section is that:

A. The issues that people kill one another over are almost always very important problems.
or
B. With low skills of anger control and conflict resolution, people often kill one another over very unimportant issues.

56. When someone dies a violent death, the friends and relatives of that person are greatly harmed. Children grow up without parents. Friends and spouses and parents suffer from grief, nightmares, and stress.

The point of this section is that:

A. Violence hurts not only the victim, but also the victim's friends and relatives.
or
B. The effects of violence do not spread to people other than the victim.

57. The major reason violence is the biggest threat to humanity is the existence of nuclear weapons. These weapons are powerful enough to destroy all human life on this planet. Nothing else – no disease, no natural disaster – threatens the continued existence of the human race as much as highly advanced nuclear weapons, combined with our very limited skills in anger control, conflict resolution, and nonviolence.

Which does the author feel threatens the human race more?

A. a very bad disease,
or
B. nuclear war?

58. For this reason, if human life on this planet is to survive, we need to move forward quickly with the task of studying nonviolence. We need all people, the world over, to study nonviolence and to cultivate nonviolence habits. We need people to do the sort of thing you are doing right now!

One way the author just mentioned to reduce the chance of nuclear war is for

A. people to study nonviolence and conflict-resolution,
or
B. one country to make sure that no other countries have nuclear weapons?

The Myth of the Violent Hero

59. Video games, movies, and television shows often entertain us with the image of what we may call the "violent hero." James Bond is an example of such a character, and there are many, many others. This character (usually a man) battles evil people who attempt to kill or hurt him. But the evil ones always fail. Their bullets and knives always seem to miss our hero. Our hero always defeats the people he fights. The viewers tend to admire this character for his strength, courage, and skill. Many people who watch get the idea that violence and fighting are very romantic, admirable, and courageous things to do.

The "violent hero" tends to be a character the filmmaker expects people watching a movie will

A. admire,

or

B. feel sorry for?

60. There's another interesting thing about the violent hero of movies. He takes part in fistfights in which he gets hit really hard in the head. He gets knocked unconscious regularly. He sometimes receives knife or gun injuries. But none of these injuries seem to do him any permanent damage. He always fully recovers, and usually recovers very quickly.

The author seems to suggest that the violent hero doesn't get killed or permanently injured because

A. he is so tough and strong,

or

B. he is a fictional character and not a real one?

What Really Happens to Aggressive People

61. The myth of the violent hero entertains many people, but you should not mistake it for truth. People who participate in fights tend not to become heroes – they tend to get killed. Even more often than they get killed, they receive severe injuries that stay with them for the rest of their lives. One very hard blow on the head can sometimes destroy part of their brain functioning; they can find it hard to learn for the rest

of their lives. Or a single hard blow on the head can give them a seizure disorder that they never recover from. Other fighters lose the use of arms or legs and become paralyzed. Some are blinded in one or both eyes.

The point of this section is that people injured in fights

A. often never fully recover,

or

B. usually get well without permanent effects?

62. Doctors who take care of injured people realize how wrong the violent hero myth is. Many injuries leave people permanently disabled. People who are injured by bullets or knives that strike "only" in the arm or leg can lose much or all use of that arm or leg. They can get pain that doesn't go away.

The point being made is that most injuries in real life are

A. bigger problems than in movies,

or

B. smaller problems than in movies?

63. People think of sports heroes as being so tough that their bodies can withstand any sort of blows. But the human brain, our joints, and our other organs are delicate instruments. It is easy to injure them permanently. Mohamed Ali, one of the most famous boxers of all time, suffered permanent

brain damage which probably resulted from boxing. Many studies have shown that brain damage is not unusual for boxers. Getting hit hard in the head is not good for the brain! Joe Namath, a famous football quarterback, had his knees so damaged by playing football that he will suffer pain and disability for the rest of his life. People's bodies are not made for getting hit hard over and over. Permanent injury is very likely to occur when they do.

The point being made here is that:

A. People who don't recover from sports injuries just weren't tough enough.
or
B. Even tough and strong sports heroes get permanent injuries from blows to their bodies.

What Happens to Aggressive Children Who Don't Learn Nonviolence Skills?

64. Much scientific research has been done, looking at groups of children who are identified as hitting or kicking often. What happens to them as they grow up? Some of them stop being aggressive and do fine. But, as a group, aggressive children don't do well. They tend to get rejected by other children their own age. They are less successful at school. They finish fewer years of education. When they grow up, they have trouble getting hired for jobs, and they lose their jobs more often. They are more likely to be

unemployed for long periods of time. For these reasons, they don't make as much money, and many of them always seem to be short of money. They have more trouble with drinking alcohol. They get into trouble with the law more often and wind up in prison more often.

Which group makes more money over the course of their lives?

A. aggressive children,
or
B. non-aggressive children?

65. Is all lost for an aggressive child? No; people can learn the techniques of nonviolence, anger control, and conflict-resolution if they want to, and are willing to work at it enough. But it helps people get motivated to learn the skills of nonviolence if they realize that people who lose their tempers and hurt people tend to be the losers of our society, not the winners.

The point of this section is that:

A. Once someone is aggressive, he or she can never change.
or
B. Aggressive people can change, and if they do, they are more likely to be "winners" and less likely to be "losers" in life.

Aggressive Men and Their Relationships with Women

66. In the "myth of the violent hero," women find the powerful, brave, aggressive hero very attractive. Some real-life women are unlucky enough to be attracted to very aggressive men. Many of these women unfortunately find out that aggressive men are often aggressive toward their wives as well as toward other people. The wives of such men are more frequently depressed and are more likely to separate from their husbands than are the wives of nonviolent men. And the wives of aggressive men are more likely to get hurt or killed by their husbands.

Why do you think that the wives of aggressive men leave their husbands more often?

A. because they don't like getting yelled at and hit,
or
B. because they find themselves attracted to even more aggressive men?

67. People who watch a lot of "violent hero" movies may be surprised to hear about an experiment that some scientists did. This experiment showed that women tend to find men more attractive if they are kind and giving than if they were more selfish. In the experiment, men were put in the company of some women on several occasions. The experimenters coached the men to act unselfish on some occasions and selfish on other occasions. On some occasions, they talked about helping others and volunteered to do a boring task, rather than letting someone else do it. On other occasions, they did the opposite. The men were rated more highly by women as being desirable for friendship and dating when they acted unselfish. They were even rated as more physically attractive!

The conclusion of this study was that:

A. Women like men who "look out for number one."
or
B. Women like kind men.

Aggressive People's Relationships with Their Children

68. Aggressive people tend to be aggressive toward their children as well as toward other people. Injuring children is called child abuse, and children of abusive parents tend to develop problems more often than the children of non-abusive parents. One of those problems is that they tend to grow up to abuse their own children. People who have been hit or hurt a lot as children usually need to work at anger control even more than other people do.

This paragraph reports that:

A. Aggressive people are almost never aggressive to their own children.
or
B. Aggressive people tend to be aggressive to their children and cause

these children lots of problems in that way.

Hitting and Hurting People Are Against the Law

69. Some people who hit people often are surprised to learn that hitting other people is against the law. The crime is called *battery* when someone physically hurts someone else. It is even against the law to try to hurt someone else, or to threaten to do so: this crime is called *assault*. The more injury is done to another person, the more likely someone is to be arrested and tried for assault and battery. It is called *aggravated* assault and battery when someone hurts someone badly. This results in longer prison terms and higher fines.

The main point of this section is that hitting or hurting another person, or even trying or threatening to do this, is

A. wrong but not against the law,
or
B. against the law?

70. Violence by adults has for a long time been taken more seriously than violence by children. Adults who hit each other are much more likely to be charged with assault and battery than are children. But violence by children is gradually being taken more and more seriously, as there are more and more

times when children seriously hurt other people.

Who is more likely to be charged with assault and battery?

A. a four-year-old kid who hits another at a preschool,
or
B. an adult who hits his neighbor in an argument?

71. If someone hurts someone else, there are two types of penalties that are possible. The first is criminal penalties: having to go to jail or pay a fine. The second is called civil penalties. These are payments that the violent person has to pay to the victim or to the victim's family, to try to make up for the damages that were done. These payments get made as a result of the violent person's getting sued and being found responsible for the damages that were done.

What do we call the payments a violent person has to make to the victim or the victim's family if he is sued and found liable for injuries?

A. criminal penalties,
or
B. civil penalties?

The Costs of Violence

72. Social scientists have tried to answer the question, "How much

money could we save if people were not violent to one another?" When they try to figure this out, they add up several types of costs. One is the cost of hospital stays and medical care for people who are hurt. Another is the years of work lost by people who have been hurt or killed. Another is the cost of policemen, judges, prison guards, parole officers, and so forth, to try to deal with violent criminals. Another is the mental health care of victims of violent crime, whose minds are affected as well as their bodies. When you add up all these figures, the yearly total for the U.S., according to some estimates, is about $300 billion!

The point being made is that:

A. Violence wastes lots of money in our society.
or
B. Violence does not affect people with respect to money.

73. The $300 billion just mentioned does not count the U.S. defense budget, which is another cost that would go away if the whole world were totally nonviolent. How much money would be saved if it were not necessary to fight wars and prepare for fighting wars? In recent years the amount of money spent on this is at least $400 billion per year. This does not count additional charges for the war in Iraq. It also does not count money spent on the Homeland Security Department, which is also used

in protection against violence. If we add these to the number estimated previously, we get almost a trillion dollars a year!

The author thinks that the amount of money wasted by violence is

A. huge,
or
B. not very big?

74. What could people do with the huge amounts of money now spent trying to deal with the violence problem? We could make sure that everyone on the earth has clean water and sanitary places to live. We could feed all hungry people. We could make huge progress in curing diseases. We could educate all people on the Earth who are willing and able to be educated. We could make sure that the opportunity to do useful work is available to all. With cooperation, we could virtually eliminate poverty from the Earth.

What point is made by this paragraph?

A. The money wasted on violence could be used to do great things for people.
or
B. Violence creates jobs for jail guards, judges, gun-makers, and lots of other people.

75. The idea that I am expressing now was expressed well by Dwight David Eisenhower, who was the general in

charge of the U.S. forces in Europe during World War II and later President of the U.S. Here is the way he put this idea:

"Every gun that is made, every warship launched, every rocket fired, signifies in the final sense a theft from those who hunger and are not fed, those who are cold and are not clothed. This world in arms is not spending money alone. It is spending the sweat of its laborers, the genius of its scientists, the houses of its children.

"This is not a way of life . . . Under the cloud of war, it is humanity hanging itself on a cross of iron."

The person who pointed out how much of human effort is wasted on war and weapons was a

A. general in the military,
or
B. college professor of peace studies?

76. There is another cost of violence that can't be measured well in dollars. This cost is how much people's lives have been made worse by having to fear getting hurt or killed by another person. Millions of kids fear going to school, because they know that they will be bullied there. Millions of people are afraid to walk around in their neighborhoods, for fear that they will be caught in gunfire or mugged. There are many neighborhoods where pizza companies and cab companies will not

send drivers, for fear of the high violence that takes place there. Millions of people will not let their children run around outside without watching them, for fear of violent crime. Thus violence not only costs money: it makes life unhappy. It causes fear that has effects far beyond the actual numbers of people who are hurt or killed.

The point made here is that:

A. Violence wastes lots of money.
or
B. Even more important than the money wasted is the fact that violence makes life less happy.

77. The more one works with individuals who have fear problems, the more one realizes that unkind and cruel behavior is at the heart of most fears. For example, a therapist sees one person who is afraid of going to school, another who is afraid of going to bed alone at night, a third who is afraid of public speaking, and a fourth who is afraid of vomiting. These sound like very different fears. But the more the therapist listens to the people, the more he finds that the first is really afraid of being bullied at school. The second is really afraid of mean people attacking him at night. The third is really afraid that people will ridicule and humiliate him after his speech. And the fourth is afraid of being rejected and made fun of if he vomits. What seems like four very different fears is really the common fear

of the cruelty of our fellow human beings.

The author's observation has been that:

A. Each fear is totally different from every other.
or
B. Many seemingly different fears are really the fear of being treated in a mean away.

78. For the people who have been victims of violence, there are often lingering effects called posttraumatic stress. After having been mugged, beaten up, knifed, or threatened, people often have recurrent nightmares about the event. They find themselves getting really scared when things remind them of what happened. The memory of the scary thing flashes back into their minds. Not just lives and dollars, but the quality of life is affected.

People who have been victims of violence

A. usually don't suffer long-term effects,
or
B. often suffer long-term psychological effects called posttraumatic stress disorder?

Nonviolence Is a Job for Everyone

79. Everyone, not just a few people, should study anger control, conflict resolution, and nonviolence. Even the people who have never hit anyone, and who have never even raised their voices at anyone, will benefit from studying this subject. Why? One reason is that all of us experience provocations. We all experience frustrations, conflicts, criticisms, and harmful acts. Devoting lots of thought to how to handle these situations well will be helpful to anyone.

What is the point of this paragraph?

A. Many people are actually violent.
or
B. All people need to deal with provocations.

80. Here's another reason we're all in this business together. The violence or angry words of one person are the provocation for the next person. When people are hostile, they often provoke several other people to hostility. And those several other angry people often provoke still other people. Thus hostility spreads from person to person.

But in the same way, kindness and good will can spread from one person to another also.

How do kindness or aggression spread from one person to another?

A. Being treated kindly makes us feel like treating others kindly; being treated

meanly makes us more likely to get angry at other people.
or
B. Being treated kindly or meanly by one person has no effect on how you want to treat other people.

81. Let's think about the phrase "emotional climate." The phrase means: how do the people in a certain group feel about one another: how much do they feel angry, suspicious, and wanting revenge, and how much do they feel loving, cheerful, compassionate, and kind?

When you are with your family, a friend, a group of classmates, a group of people at work, or any other people, your hostility or kindness affects the way other people in the group feel.

The emotional climate of a group is

A. what the people in the group feel about the weather,
or
B. how friendly or unfriendly people in the group feel toward one another?

82. The kindness, cheerfulness, and enthusiasm of one person can dramatically affect the emotional climate of a family or a small group of friends. Try it some time. Try to speak with tones of kindness, approval and enthusiasm as much as you can. Try to do as many helpful and kind acts as you can. See what the effect is on the group

you are in. If your experience is like mine, it is very likely that the mood of the group will be lifted, and other people will speak to one another in more positive tones. You will have changed the emotional climate of the group for the better.

You are hearing the prediction that:

A. If you try to speak in very kind, enthusiastic tones, you can change the emotional climate of just about any group you are in,
or
B. No one person can change the emotional climate of a whole group of people.

83. If you can change the emotional climate of a group, just in a few minutes, imagine how much you can affect the emotional climate of the people you come into contact with over the course of a lifetime. Those people, in turn, affect other people, and so on. Even though there are now six billion people on this earth, it's likely that over a lifetime, each of us can have a significant effect on the emotional climate of humanity!

This paragraph suggests that:

A. No one can change the world.
or
B. Each of us can change the world at least a little bit.

84. An emotional climate of friendliness, kindness, cheerfulness, and approval is where violence and hostility are least likely to take place. You can contribute to that sort of emotional climate.

The point of this paragraph is that creating a positive emotional climate

A. reduces the chance of aggression and violence,
or
B. doesn't have anything to do with aggression and violence?

The Spectrum from Kindness to Violence

85. Let's think more about the question of this chapter: what, through the methods of this book, are we trying to do? Let's think about a spectrum of ways that people can act, from most friendly to most violent.

1. Cheerful kindness. Being friendly, cheerful, approving, humorous, complimentary, helpful, and enthusiastic.
2. Tolerance. Having a "live-and-let live" attitude to the other person; you let the person do what he wants without needing to influence it.
3. Modeling and differential reinforcement. You influence the other person, and change his or her behavior, but by non-aversive means, such as showing the person positive examples (modeling) or paying positive attention to the good things the other person does and ignoring the undesirable things (differential reinforcement).
4. Constructive criticism, polite negotiation, or appeal to the rule of law. When the other person's behavior causes you a problem, having friendly, constructive criticism, meant to help the other person act better, in ways that are also helpful to the person himself. OR doing some rational negotiation with someone about a problem, speaking directly, but in a polite way. OR appealing to an authority to enforce "the rule of law" about what is fair and just.
5. Mild verbal anger. Showing some signs of anger or irritation to the other person, verbally.
6. Strong verbal anger. Raising the voice, using tones of voice that communicate greater anger.
7. Nonviolent physical force. Physical force without trying to hurt the other. For example, physically taking a violent person to a room where he can be by himself.
8. Non-weapon violence in self-defense. For example, hitting someone back who has hit you.
9. Using weapons for physical violence. Using knives, guns, bombs, or other weapons to hurt or kill.

As you go down this list, the ways of acting get

A. more abstract,
or
B. more aggressive?

86. It's impossible to make an exact order that applies to all situations. If I'm dealing with a small child who doesn't want a diaper changed, it's much more appropriate to use nonviolent physical force (that is, gently pick up the child and take the child to change the diaper) than to use either strong or mild verbal anger. If I'm a doctor, I'd rather have someone use verbal anger toward me than to appeal to the rule of law by suing me.

The point of this paragraph is that:

A. Although the list we made earlier generally goes from less aggressive to more aggressive, it depends upon the specific act.
or
B. The list we made earlier is a totally reliable way to determine which acts are more aggressive than others.

87. The goal is to stay close to the beginning of this list, using the kinder and gentler ways of dealing with people, unless there is a very good reason not to. In other words, we want to use the least hurtful, aggressive and violent behaviors that we can, and still

deal effectively with the provocations we experience.

It is a worthy goal to

A. practice all nine ways of acting to other people,
or
B. stay close to the nonviolent and kind end of the spectrum, unless there's a very good reason not to?

Competition and Cooperation, and Why It's Important Not To Get Stuck in the Past

88. People sometimes compete with one another, and sometimes cooperate. When two people are in a boxing match, an angry argument, a presidential debate, or on opposite sides in a war, they are trying to defeat each other. They are competing. If I'm competing, I don't want the other person to get what he wants, because that's the opposite of what I want. Our wants are incompatible.

When two people are raising children together, or building a house together, or dancing with each other, having an entertaining conversation with each other, or singing harmony with each other, they share the same goal. They are cooperating. If I'm cooperating, I want the other person to get what he wants, because I want the same thing.

The main idea of this section is that:

A. Candidates in a presidential debate are feeling competitive with each other.

or

B. In competition, two people work against each other, and in cooperation, they work toward a shared goal.

89. One very important mixture of cooperation and competition is trade, or exchange. For example, I sell a house to someone. The other person wants the house more than she wants the money I'm paid; I want the money more than the house. We put together a deal that will make us both better off. In that sense, we are cooperating on constructing a deal that we can both accept. There's a competitive element, because I would prefer the price of the house to be higher, and she would prefer it to be lower.

Similarly, if I have a store, my customers and I are involved in exchange. The relationship is cooperative, because in order to stay in business, I have to give both myself and my customers a good enough deal. Less obviously, when two people are in love or married, they are involved in an exchange in which each person meets some wishes of the other, with the expectation that the other will meet some wishes in return. Sometimes the competitive part of the exchange beats the cooperative part, and the relationship breaks up.

The main idea of this section is that:

A. People selling houses want the price to be as high as possible.

or

B. Exchanges are both cooperative and competitive, and if both people get their wants met well enough, (that is, if there is enough cooperation) the relationship lasts.

90. Many times people get trapped into relating with the people of the present as if they were the people of the past. For example, they compete with people who would have been happy to cooperate with them, because they have gotten into the habit of viewing people as their opponents.

For example, a boy grows up in a neighborhood and a school where he is constantly picked on and bullied. He learns to be suspicious of everyone and to defend himself aggressively.

Now the boy is a man, and someone comes along who would like to be friendly. But the man assumes that the other person is out to get him. The man is suspicious and hostile. The other person doesn't like this, and says some angry words in reply before moving on to someone else. The man thinks, "I was right. He just wanted to be mean to me, like everyone else."

The main idea of this section is that:

A. Sometimes people relate to other people in ways they've learned with people in the past, and those ways aren't appropriate for people in the present.

or

B. You should not be suspicious of people, because they aren't interested in taking advantage of you.

91. People can sometimes be too trusting, rather than not trusting enough, when they relate to people of the present as if they were people of the past. For example, a girl is raised by loving caretakers who have her best interest in mind, and she also relates to pleasant and generous friends. Later, she moves to an unfamiliar city and entrusts herself to a "con man," who is only out to take advantage of her.

The main idea of this section is that:

A. It is not good to trust strangers.

or

B. People who have been treated very well sometimes can be too trusting and can be taken advantage of; they too are relating to people in the present as if they were the people of the past.

92. We call it "paranoia" when people have a false idea that others are out to get them. One person has suggested calling it "narapoia" when people have a false idea that someone is out to help them.

Obviously, there are times when people want to take advantage of you, and times when people want to help and cooperate. Our job is to try to see each encounter with a person as it is in the present, undistorted by past experiences with other people. We want to be neither paranoid nor narapoid!

The main idea of this section is that:

A. Our job is to make correct judgments about others, rather than to assume that people are the people of our past.

or

B. The only way we know anything is from our past experience.

93. How do we make accurate judgments of people? We gather data. We listen to them talk. We encourage them to talk about themselves. We watch what they do. We get to know them. We observe them enough to know what they want.

If we are making accurate assessments of people, we come to appreciate how different from one another people are. We find that many are to be trusted in some ways and not in others. If we think that everyone we meet is the same type of person, we are probably distorting our views of other people based on our past experience.

The point of this section is that:

A. First impressions are usually correct.

or
B. To get to know a person, you gather information from what the person says and does.

94. Here's another way in which past relationships can distort present ones. People who have grown up indulged, being given what they want, can find themselves with anger control problems. Why? Because they have come to expect that people *should* treat them with the same degree of respect and generosity they received in the past. They have developed unrealistically high expectations of how people should act toward them. They have too high a sense of entitlement; they are spoiled. When other people don't do what they think they *should*, they get very angry.

The point of this section is that:

A. When people are treated badly, they get into the habit of aggressively defending themselves.
or
B. When people have been indulged, they can feel lots of anger over not getting what they feel they deserve.

95. How do we make accurate judgments about what people *should* and *should not* do to each other, and what is reasonable to expect from other people? We study the question. We observe people in relationships. We observe the types of exchanges made by people who are happy with each other.

We keep an open mind, and find out what people are willing to do for us and what they aren't, in exchange for what we give them. We experiment to find out how much giving and taking are necessary for happy relationships.

This section is about

A. figuring out how much is reasonable to expect from another person,
or
B. figuring out what sort of sales pitch to use when trying to make a deal with someone?

96. It's sometimes very hard to overcome past influences. If you have been mistreated and victimized over and over, it can be very hard to believe that people can actually be cooperative and friendly. If you have been overindulged for many years, it can be hard to believe that people are not here to serve you in the way you think they *should*. It often takes a lot of work to overcome the distortions that past relationships give to those of the present.

This section says that:

A. All you have to do is to keep in mind the difference between the past and present, and this should straighten out any relationship difficulties.
or
B. It sometimes takes a lot of work to get clear views of present relationships, undistorted by those of the past.

Conflict-Resolution and Anger Control Are Important for Society and Individuals

97. The human race has been on this planet for millions of years. The progress in science and technology over the last few hundred years has been amazing. Progress seems to be getting faster all the time.

But the human race still hasn't made enough progress to end violence. Will the human race see an end to violence in the next couple of centuries? I believe that it can. I believe that we already know a great deal about how to end violence, and a large part of what we need is simply teaching people the principles presented in this book.

On the other hand, it is entirely possible that the human race can kill itself off entirely. This could happen through the most violent event possible, a nuclear war.

We are faced with a challenge that could not be more dramatic. Can we learn the principles of nonviolence fast enough to keep humanity from destroying itself?

One of the ideas in this section is that:

A. Violence will always be a big problem for the human race.
or

B. It is possible that violence can be ended by the human race.

98. The story of the human race has been very long and dramatic. We do not know of any other place in the universe where beings have the chance to make choices, to love one another, to experience thoughts and feelings and sensations. Will the story have an unhappy ending, or will the most important piece of progress the world has ever known take place? The human race has now reached a very dramatic crossroads at this time.

When the author refers to "the most important piece of progress the world has ever known," he is talking about

A. the type of progress that would end violence,
or
B. the type of progress that would make even more destructive weapons than we have now?

99. It's very helpful in learning anger control to think about this subject as the most important one for humanity as a whole. But even if you feel that the fate of humanity is totally out of your control, the course of your own life is not. Learning to be an expert at dealing with frustrations, conflicts, criticisms, and harmful acts will, without a doubt, improve the quality of your life. This goal is worth a great deal of time, effort, and study. If you make this goal a

priority and work very hard and long at it, you can change your life for the better, in many, many ways. I wish you the best in this most worthy of goals.

The point of this section, as well as of the whole chapter, is that:

A. It is very hard to change habits of dealing with provocations.
or
B. The subjects of anger control, conflict-resolution, and nonviolence are of great importance for the human race as a whole, and for every single member of it.

Chapter 2: The Skill of Fortitude

100. Fortitude means handling hardship well, putting up with not getting what you want, taking it when bad things happen. Fortitude is what you have when you "get tough" enough to withstand the bad things life has to offer without getting uselessly upset.

Fortitude means that when bad things happen, someone

A. is tough and handles it,
or
B. freaks out?

101. Can you imagine a two-year-old child falling onto the floor and kicking and screaming because he or she can't get a Popsicle? We think of the habit of having tantrums over little things as something that very young children do; we like to think that they get over this behavior as they grow older. But some people don't get over the habit. Rather than lying on the floor and arching their backs and kicking and screaming, they might yell obscenities at another person or punch the other person. From the other person's point of view, a two-year-old type tantrum would be preferable!

From this section, you can conclude that the author thinks that someone who goes to a bar and injures someone badly

in a fight because the person gave him a tiny criticism

A. is a real man and is to be admired,
or
B. resembles a two-year-old having a tantrum in some important ways, although the behavior is more harmful?

102. Some people think of fortitude as meaning that you get upset in proportion to how bad a situation really is. Certainly it's not fortitude to feel really bad over really little situations.

For example, a kid wants a certain type of food. The parent looks for it and says, "We're out of it." The kid screams and cries and yells at the parent, "I hate you! Why didn't you get some!"

The child by this action is demonstrating

A. very poor fortitude skills, because the response is out of proportion to how bad the situation is,
or
B. a bad response that is appropriate because the situation is so very bad?

103. Sometimes, though, it's not very useful to feel really bad for a very long time, even when the situation is very bad. For example: a person finds out that she has incurable cancer. She has

only a few weeks to live. She thinks to herself, "Which do I want to do: have fun and enjoy life for the time I have left, or feel very upset and scared and angry that I'm going to die?" She decides to try to have all the enjoyment she can in the time that is left. She decides that spending lots of time being upset and feeling bad would not be useful to her.

This is an example of fortitude because the person

A. refused to spend lots of time getting upset, because the situation was "no big deal,"
or
B. refused to spend lots of time getting upset, even though the situation was a "big deal," because it was not useful to get upset?

104. So a better definition of the skill of fortitude is not to feel worse or get more upset or have more of a tantrum than is useful for the situation. If it's useful to get upset and angry and scared and worried, then let's do it; if it's not, then let's try not to! This is not to say we will always succeed! Sometimes we feel lots of painful feeling, even though we would rather not. But if we get straight in our minds that we would prefer to feel only the anger or upset feelings that are useful to feel, then at least we have a clear idea of the goal of fortitude we are striving toward.

This section tells us that:

A. When it's not useful to feel bad, it's very easy just not to feel bad.
or
B. It's helpful to have a goal of not feeling worse and acting more upset than is useful, despite the fact that this goal is often difficult to achieve.

105. When can it be "useful" to feel angry or upset? Sometimes those feelings energize us to do something about a bad situation. Perhaps if we went happily along, we wouldn't feel so motivated to make wrong situations right.

Here's an example. Two fathers hear good evidence that their sons have been badly bullying other kids.

The first father thinks, "Boys will be boys," and My son is just having his fun." The father doesn't get upset and goes happily on his way.

The second father thinks, "My son is getting into some really bad habits. This is a serious problem. I hate the idea of someone in my family making victims of weaker people!" The second father is worried about his son's welfare, and angry about his son's bad behavior. He is energized to make a strong plan to put an end to the bullying. He takes his son around to all the kids he has bullied and has him apologize. He has his son practice kindness instead of bullying with hundreds of fantasy rehearsals. He makes sure to find out about any future bullying. His son stops being a bully.

The second father is an example of someone who

A. had bad feelings that were useless and bad fortitude skills,
or
B. had bad feelings that served a useful purpose, because they energized him to make a bad situation better?

106. A woman finds out that her husband, without telling her, has sprayed very poisonous chemicals on their lawn to try to kill weeds. The lawn is the place where their two-year-old daughter likes to play. The chemicals could be dangerous to the child's brain development. The woman is very angry. She is energized by her anger to look up all she can about the chemicals, and insist in no uncertain terms that her husband stop using them on the lawn. It turns out that, when her husband is informed of the danger, he feels bad and is more than willing to stop using the chemicals. As a result of the woman's spending her energy in the way she did, her child is protected from danger.

The anger the woman felt in this example was useful because it

A. energized the woman to accomplish a useful result,
or

B. made the woman feel so depressed that she couldn't do anything?

107. Suppose that the woman had become so angry that she physically attacked and severely injured her husband. Or suppose that she had become so angry that she divorced him right away, not giving him a chance to change his behavior and be more careful the next time. Or suppose that the woman just continued feeling angry over a long period of time in a way that was painful for her but accomplished nothing.

These would be examples of

A. feeling anger and upset feelings that were very useful,
or
B. feeling anger and upset feelings that were not useful, but even harmful?

108. Sometimes people learn that they get their way by having tantrums. Suppose that there is a child who wants to be noticed by his parent. He is ignored when he politely asks his parent to play or to give him attention. But when he screams obnoxiously or kicks or hits, he gets noticed and gets the attention he craves. He is getting rewarded for screaming and hitting, isn't he? Or another kid asks his brother politely to give back something the brother borrowed. The brother ignores him. Only when he hits his brother does he get his things returned.

Sometimes kids who experience this fall so much into the habit of being aggressive that they can't stop it, even when it is no longer useful. For example, the kid grows up and gets married. He screams at his wife and hits her to get back something she borrowed, when she would have been more than happy to give it back if he had asked politely. He breaks up his marriage because he can't tell the difference between useful and useless anger.

A summary of the lesson of this section is that:

A. If you find that anger and aggression really are useful, watch out that you don't get into a habit so strong you can't break it later.
or
B. If anger and aggression are useful early in your life, they will probably keep on being just as useful.

109. Let's get an image in our minds of the way a person of fortitude acts. The person of fortitude sizes up situations to see how bad they really are. He or she decides which situations are worth doing something about and which ones should just be tolerated. When doing something about bad situations, the person chooses the best way to respond. If the best response involves getting angry or showing signs of distress, then the person can do it; if the situation can

be handled best with calm and cool and calculating means, the person prefers this. But the person does not "lose it" and go into a big angry display when such behavior does no good or sets back the cause.

The person of fortitude

A. never feels anger or distress,
or
B. chooses to act angry or distressed only when it is useful to do so?

110. We've said that the person of fortitude sizes up situations, to figure out how much of a "big deal" each situation is. How do you do this? How do you tell the difference between important bad things and trivial bad things?

A situation is bad to the degree that it keeps you from obtaining your really important needs and wishes. What are those needs and wishes? To protect your body – to keep safe and healthy. To have enough money to get what you really need in life. To have some good relationships with people. To be successful in some kind of work. To do something to help the world. To do activities you enjoy at least some of the time.

How much has some event interfered with your abilities to do these things? How much has this incident reduced your total fortunes in life, the things you really need to be happy? That's what determines how bad the situation is.

What's a summary of this section?

A. A situation is bad to the degree that it makes you feel bad.
or
B. A situation is bad to the degree that it reduces your total fortunes in life.

111. Let's think more about measuring the degree of misfortune in events. Here are some useful questions to ask: 1. How much has this event reduced my total fortunes in life? 2. If the bad things this event caused need to be reversed, can they be? 3. If the bad results can be reversed, how much money, time, and effort will that take?

Suppose that one kid accidentally breaks a second kid's wooden pencil. The second kid thinks, 1. "How much has this reduced my chance to write and draw? None at all really, because I already have more pencils than I need." 2. "How reversible is this? If I need to get a new pencil, I can always do so." 3. "How much time, money, and effort would it take to get a new pencil? Very little."

After thinking these things, the second kid would probably conclude that the accident the friend had was

A. a very big deal,
or

B. very small stuff?

112. Many people in the world get themselves very upset over very small stuff. When they can't play a video game that they really had their hearts set on playing, for example, they feel that something 10 on a scale of 10 bad has happened

When this happens, it's useful to think about some situations that actually DO come close to 10 on a scale of 10 bad. The benefit of doing so is that you realize how unimportant some of the situations are that people get themselves thoroughly upset over. If you don't want to think about real human tragedy right now, skip to the end of this chapter.

The author feels that the point of thinking about *really* bad situations is that:

A. It is entertaining, and this is why horror movies make so much money.
or
B. It helps us get perspective on how unimportant some of the things are that we let ourselves get upset over.

113. Here's the "gaining perspective" exercise. Please practice rating how big a deal each event is, how awful it is, on a scale 0 to 10. 10 is the most awful, the worst situation. 0 is not a problem at all.

You are a parent, and you discover that, in a moment of insanity or drunken anger, you have caused the painful deaths of your own children. Awfulness Rating:_____

As a parent, it is hard to imagine anything worse than this. Did you rate that a 10? How could it get worse than this? Let's try:

You are the president of the United States, and you discover that, in a moment of insanity or drunken anger, you have launched nuclear weapons that will destroy not only your own children, but yourself and all life on earth. Awfulness rating:_____

The good thing about the last situation is that it's over quickly. How about some that last longer:

You realize that you have released a chemical into the environment that will cause everyone, including yourself and your family, to become brain damaged to the point that they feel really bad and frustrated, and so confused all the time that they can't accomplish anything. Yet it will take a few years for humanity to die out, during which time you know that you have caused this to happen. Awfulness rating:_____

You get a condition where you feel severe pain 100% of the time. You find out that this pain will not end. Awfulness rating:_____

You are in a very poor country where a famine develops, and there is no way to get food, and you face the almost certain prospect that you and your family will slowly starve to death. Awfulness rating:_____

You discover that you have incurable cancer and are very likely to die in a few weeks. Awfulness rating:_____

You permanently lose the use of both arms and both legs, but can still speak and think as well as ever. Awfulness rating:_____

You are in a country that is at war, and you and your family comes home to find that your house and everything in it has been destroyed by a bomb. Awfulness rating:_____

You have invested your money in some things that become worthless. You lose all your money that you had saved up over a very long time. But you still have your family and your ability to work and learn. Awfulness rating:_____

The author is expecting you to give the events on this list, especially the first few,

A. high awfulness ratings,
or
B. low awfulness ratings?

114. Except for the incidents about all people's being destroyed, most of the events above, unfortunately, happen to good numbers of people somewhere on earth very often. They are not horror movie fantasies.

Did you find that, in comparison to destroying your children or destroying all life on earth, merely having your house blown up or losing your life savings seemed not very awful?

The author is expecting that you would rate getting your house blown up or losing all your money as

A. 10 on a scale of 10 awful,
or
B. less than 10 on a scale of 10 awful?

115. Now please try to keep in mind the same rating scale that you used for the events listed above. Please continue rating some more events. Bear in mind that these are events that have stimulated people to have major tantrums or to be very aggressive.

You want to play a video game, but someone makes you do some work first. Awfulness rating:_____

You are standing in line for an amusement park ride, but someone cuts in front of you. Awfulness rating:_____

You are playing a board game with someone, and you lose. Awfulness rating:_____

Someone you hardly know insults you. Awfulness rating:_____

Your family is going to a restaurant, and you want to go to a certain one, but the family decides to go to one you don't like as much. Awfulness rating:_____

You have eaten supper, and you have to wash the dishes. Awfulness rating:_____

You are driving a car, and the person in front of you is going too slowly to suit you. Awfulness rating:_____

There is some work you must do, but it is boring. Awfulness rating:_____

The author's point with all this is that:

A. We should not get ourselves too upset over small stuff.
or
B. More people should experience truly awful things, so they won't be such spoiled brats.

116. In a future chapter we will deal more fully with how you think about situations, and one of the important types of thoughts is "not awfulizing." There are two ways of not awfulizing. One is to think, "This situation is not

such a big deal." The other is to think, "This situation *is* a big deal, but I can take it. I can cope with it." Hopefully, keeping in perspective the bad events that human beings often experience will help you to "not awfulize" when it is useful to you not to upset yourself too much.

When something really is a "big deal,"

A. it's impossible to "not awfulize,"
or
B. it is possible to "not awfulize," by thinking, "Although this is a very bad situation, I can handle it"?

Chapter 3: A Plan for Learning Conflict-Resolution, Anger Control, and Fortitude

117. If you want to get better at conflict-resolution, anger control, and fortitude, how do you do it? This chapter will outline a plan that you can use. We will list several steps you can take. Some people have succeeded in learning these skills without taking all these steps. But I believe that you are more likely to succeed, the more of these steps you take.

In learning anger control,

A. you must do every one of these steps if you hope to succeed,
or
B. you will be more likely to succeed, the more of these steps you do?

118. Here are the steps:

    1. Goal-setting
    2. Internal sales pitch
    3. List of choice points
    4. Learning the terms for:
        Steps in fantasy
           rehearsal
        provocations
        goals or motives
        types of thoughts
        behaviors
        responses to criticism
        conflict-resolution steps

    5. The Four-thought Exercise
    6. Learning relaxation and
        emotional control
    7. Decisions
    8. Fantasy rehearsals and
        role-plays
    9. Self-monitoring
    10. Celebrations exercise
    11. External rewards
    12. Reading and reminding

These are the names of

A. various goals, other than anger control, that are also worthwhile,
or
B. tasks you can do that help you achieve the goal of anger control?

119. Now let's go over these in a little more detail. When you do goal-setting, you state your goal in a very specific and concrete way, and write it down. To say, "I want to get better at anger control," is not specific and concrete.

The following is concrete and specific: "I want to go for at least six months without hitting, kicking, or otherwise physically hurting anyone. I also want to have no more than two episodes of raising my voice in anger during that time."

Here's another concrete and specific goal: "I want to handle at least 90% of the choice points during the next two weeks in a way very similar to the way I have decided will be the best response."

Here's another concrete and specific goal: "I want to do what I can rate as a 'good' job of conflict resolution for at least 95% of the conflicts I have over the next week."

Here's another: "I want to try to raise the weekly rating of my family's emotional climate from 'so-so' to 'good' for at least four weeks."

A characteristic of concrete and specific goal-setting is that:

A. It's possible to tell whether you've met the goal or not.
or
B. You go to some professional and take a test.

120. When you set your goal, it's good to write it down, and to read what you have written often. That way you constantly remind yourself of your goal.

The second thing to write down and frequently read is called the "internal sales pitch." A sales pitch is a list of reasons why someone should do something. An internal sales pitch is a list of reasons you make up, meant to remind yourself of the worthiness of

your goal. The internal sales pitch is the answer to the question, "*Why* do I want to get better at anger control, conflict-resolution, nonviolence, or kindness?"

It's much easier to keep yourself motivated to work at a goal if you know and can remember in a flash *why* you want to succeed at it.

The point of the internal sales pitch is to

A. convince someone else to use anger control,
or
B. help yourself stay motivated to work at anger control?

121. Max writes the following:
Reasons for mastering anger control:
1. I won't get fired for blowing up at bosses.
2. I won't lose friends by losing my temper at them too much.
3. I won't be likely to hurt anybody or get hurt myself by getting into a fight.
4. I will feel good about making the world a little kinder and less violent, rather than the other way around.

This is called

A. the list of choice points,
or
B. the internal sales pitch?

122. Jane writes the following:
Reasons for getting skilled at conflict-resolution:

1. I wouldn't spend so much time feeling silently mad at my family members.
2. I would help my family members not be so spoiled, because I would stick up for myself more.
3. I would probably like my family members more.
4. I would be able to tell people outside the family what I want in more polite ways that don't risk losing friendships.

It sounds as if Jane

A. has had lots of trouble with being violent,
or
B. has had trouble with not feeling she can do anything about problems that make her mad?

123. Jay writes:
Reasons for mastering anger control, conflict-resolution, and nonviolence:
1. All people face situations where someone wants something different than what they want, and if I can handle these really well, my life will be happier.
2. If I get really good at handling provocations and conflicts, I can help other people get good at this too. This will make the world a better place.
3. I find the subject of conflict-resolution really fascinating.
4. I'm very interested in world peace, and these subjects seem to be a good way to help make a peaceful world.

The list that Jay has made is called the

A. internal sales pitch,
or
B. Twelve-thought Exercise?

124. The next step in the plan for anger control is called the *list of choice points.* This could be a list of the sorts of situations that have caused you to lose your temper in the past. It could also be a list of situations that you think could be hard for you in the future. Finally, it could also be a generic list of provocations, such as the list included in this book. Here are some examples of choice points:
1. My brother borrows something of mine without asking, and doesn't put it back.
2. My teacher says to me, "Hey, straighten up," in a mean-sounding voice.
3. I'm going to get in line, and someone runs and gets in line right in front of me.

A choice point is a

A. situation that could make you mad,
or
B. reason why you want to learn anger control?

125. What is the reason for getting together a list of choice points? So you can practice with them. One of the main strategies of anger control is to figure

out really good ways of handling provocations, and to practice over and over handling them in those good ways. (Usually you practice through fantasy rehearsal or role-playing.) The choice points are the situations you practice handling well.

Ted has had a big problem with losing his temper. His anger control trainer has him make a long list of the situations in which Ted has lost his temper in the past. What is the trainer probably trying to do?

A. make Ted feel embarrassed over these situations,
or
B. give Ted practice with many situations he has faced in the past?

126. The next step in the process is called *learning the terms*. This means that you learn words for the types of responses you can make to provocations. Learning the terms helps you to think of good options. There are terms describing the *thoughts*, *emotions*, and *behaviors* that you can choose from when you respond to provocations. Another special type of thoughts and feelings is called *motives*. The more familiar you become with all these terms, the easier it is for you to think carefully about what to do.

This section said that you learn words for the different types of responses to provocations so that:

A. You will be able to speak to other people about the options.
or
B. You will be able to think more clearly about what to do.

127. Here's an example of some of the "terms" we are talking about:

Behaviors in Response to Provocations

1. *Ignoring* the provocation.
2. *Differential Reinforcement:* not only ignoring the unwanted things, but also later reinforcing (or rewarding) the good things the other person does.
3. *Assertion*: firmly sticking up for what you want, without being aggressive.
4. *Conflict-Resolution and Negotiation*: trying to do some rational joint decision-making together, using the seven steps we will talk about later.
5. *Criticism Response*: using one of the ways of responding to criticism that we will study later.
6. *Relaxation*: relaxing on purpose, in order to handle the situation more calmly.
7. *Rule of Law*: appealing to authority or a set of rules.
8. *Apologizing*: a sincere apology for what you did that upset the other person can make things better for all concerned.

9. *Away from the Situation:* postponing communication; leaving the situation or putting off dealing with it till you cool down; leaving politely if possible or permanently avoiding a provoking person.

10. *Friendliness and Kindness*: doing good and speaking kindly to those who provoke you is sometimes the best choice.

11. *Force – of a Nonviolent Nature*: When necessary, using force, for example, to prevent someone from being violent, without trying to hurt the person. For example, if a person is knocking things over and hitting people, in a fit of rage, other people put him in a room and lock the door for a while so he can cool down.

12. *Tones of Voice*: If people don't want to anger themselves and others, they will do well to speak with tones that are lower in pitch, lower in volume, and slower in tempo. In other words, they speak in a deep, soft, and slow voice.

These terms are names for

A. ways you might feel after a provocation,
or
B. ways of acting in response to provocations?

128. We often somehow get programmed to respond to provocations in certain ways. Many people are programmed to respond by yelling or hitting. Many others get the urge to yell or hit, keep themselves from doing it, and stay angry without thinking of anything else to do. But if you can program yourself to go very quickly through a list of options and pick which one will work best in this situation, you are much better equipped to deal with provocations. You can use your thinking brain to figure out what to do. The tools the thinking brain uses are *words*. When you have words for options, you can think of them much more effectively.

The point of this section is that:

A. Learning words for options helps you to quickly figure out what's best to do.
or
B. once you get programmed to hit or yell, it's difficult to change that behavior.

129. What you read above is a list of possible *behaviors* to use in response to provocations. We will learn words for *thoughts, feelings, and motives* as well. When you have all these words in your vocabulary, you will be much more able to think about what you do.

If you have read any of the other books in this series, you are familiar with words for twelve types of thoughts that people say to themselves. These twelve thoughts are:

1. Awfulizing.
2. Getting down on yourself.
3. Blaming someone else.
4. Not awfulizing.
5. Not getting down on yourself.
6. Not blaming someone else.
7. Goal-setting.
8. Listing options and choosing.
9. Learning from the experience.
10. Celebrating luck.
11. Celebrating someone else's choice.
12. Celebrating your own choice.

Blaming someone else and goal-setting and so forth are types of

A. behaviors,
or
B. thoughts?

130. Suppose that someone doesn't get a part in a play she tried out for. If she awfulizes and blames someone else, she might think, "This is terrible! That play director should never be able to get away with this! What a terrible person!" On the other hand, if she does goal-setting and celebrating her own choice, she might think, "My goal is to handle this frustration without getting too upset over it. I'm really glad that I tried out for the part; that took courage."

It's a pretty safe bet that she will feel less angry while doing

A. awfulizing and blaming someone else,
or

B. goal-setting and celebrating her own choice?

131. Four of the twelve thoughts are particularly useful in practicing dealing with provocations. These are:

> not awfulizing
> goal-setting
> listing options and choosing
> celebrating your own choice

When you practice making up each of these four thoughts in response to a choice point situation, you are doing the Four-thought Exercise. (If you make up an example of all twelve of the types of thoughts, you are doing the Twelve-thought Exercise.)

The four thoughts for the Four-thought Exercise are

A. getting down on yourself, blaming someone else, awfulizing, and imagining,
or
B. not awfulizing, goal-setting, listing options and choosing, and celebrating your own choice?

132. Suppose that a kid is a vegetarian. The kid is eating with other kids who are eating meat. The other kids are saying, in taunting tones of voice, "Oh, this meat is so wonderful. Oh, I just love it!"

This is a situation that any of us, vegetarian or not, can use to do the Four-thought Exercise. Here's how it sounds:

(Not awfulizing) I don't like it that they are trying to taunt me like this, but I can handle it. It's not such a big deal.

(Goal-setting) My goal is not to play into what they're doing by getting very upset. I don't want to reinforce them for trying to make me angry.

(Listing options and choosing) I could just say nothing. I could say, "You like those dead animals, huh?" I could say, in a fairly friendly tone, "I think my being here is helping you enjoy your lunch!" I like that last one, because it doesn't put us in competition with one another.

(Celebrating my own choice) I'm glad I picked that one. And I'm glad I thought about it and stayed cool.

What you have just read is an example of

A. the Four-thought Exercise,
or
B. the internal sales pitch?

133. Anyone who wants to get better at anger control should practice the Four-thought Exercise many, many times with many different choice points. One of the purposes of this book is to help you learn to do this exercise well. Part of doing it well means choosing good goals, listing good options, making good choices, and celebrating joyously. If you can do this exercise well enough and often enough, I believe you will make very important progress.

The author believes that if you do the Four-thought Exercise very often and very well,

A. you will improve in your ability to handle provocations,
or
B. you will be able to understand some other ideas that may someday help you handle provocations better?

134. Whenever someone becomes an expert at something, that person learns many new words to think with. When someone becomes an expert at mathematics, the person has words for variables and functions and equations and tangents and derivatives. When someone becomes a doctor, the person learns words for the various parts of the body and for what goes on normally, and for all sorts of diseases and treatments. Expert chess players learn words for different ways of winning pieces, such as a fork and a pin. It's hard to think of a field where you can become an expert without learning many new words. It's the same way with anger control and conflict resolution and nonviolence.

The step called "learning the terms" is necessary

A. only when becoming expert at anger control,
or
B. when becoming expert at almost anything?

135. When you have learned manywords to name thoughts, feelings, and behaviors, you are almost ready to be able to decide what to do in any provocation situation. But there is another skill that is very useful: learning to turn down your level of arousal. By the word *arousal* I mean how excited you are, how emotional you are, versus how much you are cool and calm and relaxed. A person who is so angry that he can't control himself is in a state of high arousal.

A person who is just about to drift off to sleep is in a state of

A. low arousal,
or
B. high arousal?

136. You can lower your level of arousal when you want to. How do you do it? Here's one main secret: relax your muscles. It's hard to feel very much emotional arousal when your muscles are loose and limp and relaxed. The muscles of the face are especially important. Imagine someone who is very angry. Do you imagine the person's neck muscles straining, and the person's jaw clenching, and the person's face contorting into a tense expression? If you relax your head and face and neck muscles, you can usually turn down your level of arousal.

If you want to handle a provocation with less tension and arousal, you should

A. grit your teeth and bear it,
or
B. relax your jaw muscles and the rest of your head and neck muscles?

137. There are other ways to help turn down your level of arousal. You can imagine things that are relaxing and pleasant. You can say things to yourself that are calming. There are other ways as well.

But turning down your level of arousal is not a skill that comes overnight. It takes lots of practice. You practice relaxing, over and over, in a situation where you are *not* mad. This helps you get ready for the much more difficult job of relaxing when you *are* mad.

If you want to be able to calm yourself in a provocation, you should

A. just make up your mind to do it when you face the next provocation,
or
B. do lots of practicing with relaxing before you face a provocation?

138. Here's another tip about learning to relax. A certain type of thermometer will allow you to measure the temperature of your fingertips. If you are in a room where the temperature is in the low 70s (Fahrenheit), your fingertip temperature gives a pretty good measure of how relaxed you are! As you get more relaxed, your fingertips tend to get warmer. If you get really relaxed, your fingertip temperature goes over 95 degrees. There have been times when I have warmed my fingertips by over ten degrees by relaxing. If you play with such a thermometer a lot and figure out what to do with your mind and body to make your fingertip temperature go up, you will learn a lot about how to relax.

If you want to learn to relax, you should practice

A. raising your fingertip temperature, or
B. lowering your fingertip temperature?

139. When you are practicing relaxation, an important meditation technique is called the *good will meditation*. In using this technique, you sit and relax and close your eyes. You imagine yourself and think about the course of your life. You wish for yourself:

May I become the best I can become.

May I give and receive compassion and kindness.
May I live happily and productively.

After wishing these things for yourself, you let your mind go to various people in your life, and wish the same things for them. You do this in a relaxed, meditative state.

This is called the good will meditation because

A. you are wishing that you and other people will have good things happen, or
B. you are wishing that everyone will get what he or she deserves, which may be a very painful punishment lasting a long time?

140. Now suppose you have learned lots of words for thoughts, feelings, and behaviors, and you've also developed some skill in turning down your level of arousal. The next step is to take your list of choice points and decide, "What thoughts, feelings, and behaviors would work best in this particular situation?" This step is called *decisions*. For example, when the other person turns up the music so loud that it bothers me a lot, what do I want to think, feel, and do?

The step we are talking about now

A. is practicing over and over doing something that works well in the situation,

or

B. figuring out what would work well in the situation?

141. Once you have decided what you want to do in a situation, the next step is to practice. It does not work simply to think, "OK, I've decided what to do, now it will be easy to do it. Whenever anybody says anything mean to me, I'll stay cool." The problem is that we have habits of responding in certain ways, for example by yelling or hitting. When a provocation comes up, things seem to happen very fast. Often people start screaming or hitting before they even realize what they're doing. But if you practice over and over first, then you can build up a new habit. You can be ready when the provocation comes, so that it won't catch you off guard.

The main idea of this section is that:

A. Once you decide what to do in a certain situation, you just do it, and it's as simple as that.

or

B. Once you decide what to do in a certain situation, you have to rehearse many times if you want to be able to act that way in real life.

142. How do you practice? In the first chapter we mentioned *fantasy rehearsal*. When you do a fantasy rehearsal, you imagine yourself in the situation, and you imagine yourself handling the situation in exactly what you have decided is the best possible way. It's often best to speak aloud, putting into words the thoughts, feelings, and behaviors that you want to do in the imagined situation.

When you do a fantasy rehearsal, you

A. practice the way you *want* to handle the situation in real life,

or

B. portray the way you *really would* handle the situation in real life?

143. Here is an example of a fantasy rehearsal by a man who works as a foreman for a construction company.

"I've shown one of my workers exactly where to build a certain wall. I go and supervise some other people, and when I come back, I find that he has started building the wall in the wrong place. Now we will have to spend time tearing it down and doing it all over again. This is a real frustration for me.

"But it's also an opportunity for me to practice anger control. Let me stop and think before I speak to him. I'll take a few seconds to cool off. I know this worker didn't do this on purpose. And it's not the end of the world – just a little time and a few materials wasted. What's my goal? My main goal is to stay cool. I want to be fair to him, and I want to be kind. I want to solve the problem of his not understanding or remembering what my directions were. What are my options? I could warn him that he may be fired. But this is the first mistake he's made like this. He hasn't been working here long. I think my best option is to talk with him about how to prevent this from happening in the future.

"I'm feeling proud of my decision. Now I'm saying to him, 'This wall isn't in the right place. We're going to have to tear it down and put it up in the right place. But first, let's talk about how you and I can get it straight what the directions are, so that this doesn't happen again.'

"He looks embarrassed, and I'm very glad I didn't yell at him. We think some about what to do in the future. We decide that he will say back to me what the directions are and show me exactly what he's going to do, so I'll know he understands. This will be a good practice for other workers to follow, too.

"I feel really good that I was able to stay cool and not be mean to him and come up with a good solution to the problem."

The point of the man's making up this fantasy rehearsal is to

A. practice staying cool in his imagination, so that he will be able to do it better in real life,
or
B. make up a story that is entertaining and exciting?

144. When you want to practice ways that people can talk tone another, a good way to do it is by role-playing. Role-playing is the same as being an actor, and acting out what people say to each other. In learning anger control and conflict resolution, it's particularly useful to role-play people's "joint decision" conversations – where they talk with each other to try to find a good solution to the problem they have.

But it's very important to remember that the best conversation may not be the most entertaining one. It can be funny when people insult each other in witty ways or put pies in each other's faces and so forth; this is called slapstick comedy. Your goal, on the other hand, is to reach agreement on the very best option you can come up with, and have the two people be as polite and thoughtful as you can. Making up these role-plays is hard work.

The type of role-plays this book focuses on is

A. social conversation, where two people are getting to know each other, or

B. joint decision, where two people are trying to resolve a conflict or solve a problem they have?

145. Here's an example of a joint decision role-play. The conversation is between two family members.

First: Can we talk for a moment about the music you're playing? It's keeping me from falling asleep.

Second: So it's too loud for you?

First: Yes.

Second: I knew you had gone to bed, but I didn't know that it would keep you awake. It's my way of relaxing after doing all my work.

First: So your music helps you relax after you're done with your evening's work.

Second: Yes.

First: What options do we have? You could use headphones, or turn it down.

Second: Or I could turn it off, or take it downstairs to listen to it.

First: These sound like good options. Want to think about which ones would be best?

Second: I think my going down to the basement would suit me best. I feel sure it would not be too loud for you then, and I would rather be there than here, now that I think of it.

First: Sounds great. Thanks a lot.

Second: You're welcome.

The person acting out this joint decision role-play is supposed to

A. get a very accurate picture of how people usually act in real life,
or
B. get good practice at rational and polite conflict-resolution, in order to come closer to that ideal in real life?

146. The person who really wants to improve in anger control will do many, many fantasy rehearsals and role-plays. It's not enough just to think, "When a provocation comes up, I'll stay cool and come up with something really wise to do and say." When provocations arise in real life, most people act before they have time to even remember what their goals were. They act quickly, in whatever way is the strongest habit. If you want to act in the best way, you have to practice over and over to build up a new habit. You practice when you're not in the "heat of the moment." You practice when it's easy to stay cool. You practice so many times that, when the real-life provocation comes, you'll be ready for it with a habit of staying cool and acting reasonably.

Why do people need to do lots of fantasy rehearsal and role-playing instead of just practicing in real life?

A. Real-life practice doesn't work.
or
B. You need to build up the habit of acting reasonably, so that when the real-life situation comes you'll be ready for it.

147. Suppose a basketball player thinks of a new move that he feels will be useful. He says, "That's a good move. I'll just remember that, and use it in the next game."

A second basketball player also wants to use the new move. But he practices it over and over, all by himself slowly at first, then with another player to guard him. He goes through it hundreds of times. By the time the game comes up, the move has become automatic to him.

Which player do you think will be more likely to use the new move successfully in the game?

A. the one who planned to remember it,
or
B. the one who practiced it until it became automatic?

148. In anger control, as with any sport, the more you practice your "new moves" until they become automatic, the more likely you are to use them

successfully when the "real thing" comes along.

But, as in sports, you don't just practice. You watch very closely to see how you do in the real situation. For anger control, this means keeping careful track of how you act toward the real people in your life. Are you able to stay cool in provocations? Are you able to make the emotional climate better so that you face fewer provocations? Do you raise your voice in anger less frequently? Do you hit people less frequently? Keeping track of these behaviors is called *self-monitoring*.

Self-monitoring means that you

A. make yourself do well,
or
B. keep track of how you are doing, especially by counting different types of things you do?

149. When you self-monitor, you can tell when you are on the right track or the wrong track. You can think to yourself, "I need to do more of what I've been doing lately," or "I'm slipping – I need to get back on track," or "This last week set a new record! I'm doing great!"

Self-monitoring gives you feedback about whether what you're doing is working or not. For example: Ted does lots of fantasy rehearsals of staying cool when criticized. He now finds that he is hardly ever hitting or yelling. Then he stops doing fantasy rehearsals, and he finds that his rate of hitting and yelling starts creeping back up. He decides that he'd better get back into training with fantasy rehearsals.

The purpose of self-monitoring is so that you can

A. prove to someone else that you've done what you should do,
or
B. know whether what you're doing is working or not in keeping yourself successful?

150. Another way of keeping track of what you are doing is called the *celebrations exercise*. This means remembering the little stories of how you did a good job of anger control, conflict resolution, or nonviolence. You tell that story to someone, or write it down, or just go over it in your mind. This is very much like a fantasy rehearsal, only you are remembering what you did, rather than imagining what you would like to do.

Fantasy rehearsals work because mentally rehearsing doing something good builds up the habit. Do you think that recalling something you actually did should work the same way?

A. yes,
or
B. no?

151. Ted writes in his celebrations diary:

"4-3-2005. Today my boss said, 'What's the matter with you? You didn't produce very much last week. Are you goofing off?'

"I thought, 'Hey, I'm getting criticized; this is a chance to practice staying cool. I want to speak in a calm voice. I don't want to rub it in that he made a mistake. I want to defend myself in a very gentle and polite way.' And I relaxed my muscles for a second. Then I said to him, very politely, 'Are you remembering that there was the holiday that week, and we were only here three days that week?' Then he said 'Oh,' and that he was sorry, and he moved on. I feel good that I didn't get super-angry and yell at him as I probably would have done six months ago."

The "celebration" of this event took place

A. at a party,
or
B. inside Ted's own mind?

152. When you celebrate, you congratulate yourself and feel proud. You are rewarding yourself for what you do, by what you say to yourself. These types of rewards are very important. They are "internal" rewards – they take place inside your own head.

But sometimes it's good to rig up a different kind of reward for your accomplishments. These are "external" rewards: they are things that other people can see or hear. Let's say that Ted very much wants to buy something – a book, for example. He orders it, but has it shipped to his friend. He tells his friend, "Please give this to me only when I can tell you that I haven't hit anybody or yelled at anybody for a whole month straight."

Ted counts the days. When a month has passed, he stops by his friend's house and picks up his prize, along with the congratulations of his friend.

The book and the congratulations are

A. internal rewards (inside Ted's head only),
or
B. external rewards (something someone else could see or hear)?

153. There's one more very important step in the process. Even after you've succeeded in your goal, you can't just forget about it. You need to keep reminding yourself of what you've learned. One way to do this is to keep reading about the topic. You can read a little bit of this book every day. You can teach anger control to someone else, which keeps the ideas in your mind. You can read about the lives of nonviolent heroes, or books on how to promote nonviolence in the world. You can get together with other people who are interested in nonviolence; this continually reminds you of the nonviolence principles that you have learned.

This last step may be logically called

A. goal-setting,
or
B. reading and reminding?

154. Reading and reminding was the last of the twelve steps toward learning anger control. Do all these steps sound simple and easy? If they sound like a very large amount of hard work, unfortunately, that's correct. Many people who say they want to learn anger control and conflict resolution and nonviolence do not succeed. The job is just too much work for them. But those people who do succeed at this are a very distinguished group. They deserve to feel very proud of their accomplishment, because it is one that very few people master.

The author feels that learning anger control, conflict-resolution, and nonviolence

A. is an easy task if you buy this book,
or
B. requires so much work that if you succeed, you have done something very admirable indeed?

Chapter 4: How To Do Fantasy Rehearsals

155. Here's perhaps the most important advice on learning better anger control: do many fantasy rehearsals of handling provocations in positive, appropriate ways.

Fantasy rehearsal means using your imagination to practice handling a situation. In your imagination, you respond to the provocation with just the thoughts, emotions, and behaviors that you have decided will work out best. Then in your imagination, you celebrate handling the situation so well.

Fantasy rehearsal means that you

A. imagine the bad ways of handling the situation, so that you get them out of your system,
or
B. imagine the best possible way of handling the situation, so that you can practice handling it in that way?

156. Why is fantasy rehearsal so important? Why can't you simply decide on the ways you want to handle provocations, and then wait until these provocations come up in real life, and then handle them the way you've decided to? One important reason is that in real life we usually have to respond to situations very quickly. When someone says something that provokes us, we can't sit and think for a minute or two before responding. Thus often we respond by reflex or habit. It takes many repetitive practices to change a habit.

Another reason for doing fantasy rehearsals is that we can decide upon the best response to a situation when we are not in the "heat of the moment." We can choose and practice a response when we are cool and calm and rational.

A couple of reasons for doing fantasy rehearsals are that:

A. You're outside the heat of the moment, and you can do enough repetitions to change your habit.
or
B. Practice does not change habits.

157. There has been a great deal of research on fantasy rehearsal. Some of this research has taken place with sports performances. More than twenty-five years ago Richard Suinn studied ski racers. He asked half of them to do fantasy rehearsals of their upcoming race. He asked the other half to do a different activity. The racers who had practiced skiing in their imaginations had faster times than the ones who had

not. Since that time, there have been many other studies on fantasy rehearsal and athletic performance. The conclusion is that the practice you do in imagination builds up habit strength, just as the practice you do in real life does. As of 2005, I have read that almost all Olympic athletes use fantasy rehearsal.

As an as an example of fantasy rehearsal, an Olympic high jumper might imagine himself

A. jumping over the bar and clearing it with the exact motions that he hopes to use in the contest,
or
B. sprouting wings and flying over the bar?

158. Fantasy rehearsal has been studied in many situations other than sports. One study found that people could train themselves not to be afraid of snakes by imagining themselves handling them. Another study found that people could train themselves to be more appropriately assertive with other people by practicing in their imaginations.

The studies mentioned in this section show that fantasy rehearsal can help with

A. getting rid of fears and acting appropriately to other people,
or

B. making money and reading faster?

159. Other studies have used modern machines to create pictures of what is going on in our brains. Some researchers have asked some people to carry out a certain movement in real life, and other people to imagine themselves making the movement. These scientists found that the brain's activity patterns are very similar when we are imagining a movement and when we are actually carrying it out. These studies are another piece of evidence that practice in imagination has effects like those of practice in real life.

These studies with brain scanning machines have shown that:

A. What goes on in the brain with fantasy rehearsal is not at all like what goes on with real-life rehearsal.
or
B. What happens in the brain with fantasy rehearsal is very similar to what happens with real-life rehearsal.

160. What are the parts of a fantasy rehearsal? We can remember the "steps" of fantasy rehearsal by the mnemonic "STEBC," which stands for:

Situation
Thoughts
Emotions
Behaviors
Celebration

In the situation part, we describe the setting and the series of events that we are responding to. In the thoughts part, we say aloud what we would like to think to ourselves in the situation. In the emotions part, we say how we would like to be feeling in the situation: determined, curious, sympathetic, or whatever. In the behaviors part, we say what we would like to do or say in the situation. In the celebration part, we imagine that we have handled the situation just as we would like to, and we practice congratulating ourselves for such an expert handling of the situation.

When doing a fantasy rehearsal, we are supposed to imagine

A. what we would realistically do in real life, even though that might not be a good idea,
or
B. what we would most like to do in real life, even if that isn't our present habit?

161. When we do fantasy rehearsals, we speak in the present or present progressive tense. We say, "I *am walking* here, and the person *says* to me this, and I *am thinking* this, and I *am feeling and doing* this." You say it this way because you want to imagine that it's all happening right now. It would be harder to imagine that if you said, "I *walked* here, and the person *said* it this

to me, and I *thought and felt and did* this."

Which should you say when you are doing a fantasy rehearsal?

A. "I am feeling determined not to lose my cool."
or
B. "I didn't want to lose my cool."

162. When you do fantasy rehearsals, it's a good idea to speak them out loud. In that way you and possibly someone else can hear exactly how the rehearsal goes. Another option is to write out the fantasy rehearsal. A third option is to speak the fantasy rehearsal into a tape recorder. In all these options, you get to compose very specifically the words that you would use in thinking about the situation.

An option not mentioned above is to

A. write out the fantasy rehearsal,
or
B. just picture yourself handling the situation well, without using any words?

163. The most important part of doing fantasy rehearsals well is to make good and wise choices about the thoughts, emotions, and behaviors that you want to rehearse. If you make an unwise choice, you may be doing yourself more harm than good, by getting yourself into bad habits rather than good ones.

The most important thing to do in fantasy rehearsal is to

A. speak as if it's happening right now, or
B. make a wise choice about what thoughts, emotions, and behaviors you want to rehearse?

164. No book can tell you exactly what to do, think, and feel in each situation. (Even if one could, you probably wouldn't like to be bossed around like that!) But this book can help you to organize your thoughts when you make your own choices. Much of the rest of this book will classify different types of thoughts, emotions, and behaviors so that you can think more efficiently about which ones will be best for you, in any given situation.

It's also good to keep in mind that nonviolent behaviors are almost always better than violent behaviors, that intense rage is not very often a useful emotion, and that calculated thoughts about what's best to do almost always work better than repetitive thoughts about how terrible and evil another person is.

What's a good summary of the section you just read?

A. Don't believe anyone who tells you that any thought, emotion, or behavior is better than any other.

or
B. While you have to decide what's best in each situation, certain rules usually hold, for example, that nonviolence usually works better than violence.

165. In the rest of this chapter, we will look at examples of fantasy rehearsals for handling provocations. Here's the first one:

(Situation) A friend borrowed my book, and promised to return it today. But now it's almost bedtime, and the book still hasn't been returned.

(Thoughts) This isn't so terrible. It's not that I desperately need the book. And if my friend isn't totally dependable, so what else is new? I'm not, either. I'll just call my friend and remind her, in a polite way. That's a good option.

(Emotions) I'm feeling some humility about all this, because there have been plenty of times I've forgotten to return things on time, too. But I'm also proud that I'm handling the situation well so far.

(Behaviors) I call up my friend and chat for a while in a friendly way. Then I say that I'm going to be needing the book back, and would she like to come over to my house to return it, or would she rather that I stop by her house?

(Celebration) Hooray for me! I handled the situation really well!

When the person says, "I call up my friend and chat for a while," is the person describing

A. behaviors,

or

B. thoughts?

166. Here's a second example:

(Situation) I'm playing basketball, and a person charges into me. It should be a foul, but the referee doesn't call it.

(Thoughts) I know it doesn't do any good to try to point out missed fouls to a referee. Plus, the game is going on; I don't have time to worry about this. My goal is to keep playing as well as I can.

(Emotions) I'm feeling determined to play as well as I can and not to let myself get too bothered by this.

(Behaviors) Another one of their players has the ball and he is in my zone. I'm guarding him closely. I'm concentrating on what I'm doing.

(Celebration) Hooray! I didn't lose my cool. I didn't play worse because of anger. I kept concentrating on doing my best.

When the person says, "I'm feeling determined . . . " is that

A. an emotion,

or

B. a situation?

167. Here's a third example, where a man thinks about talking with his wife:

(Situation) I suggest to my wife that we do some dancing together. My wife tells me that she doesn't like to dance.

(Thoughts) It's disappointing to hear that, but it's certainly not the end of the world. I can handle it. This is an opportunity to practice self-discipline, and to find the best solution to this problem that we can. I think the first steps are to use calm and friendly tones of voice and to find out more from her. Being a good listener is a good option to start with.

(Emotions) I'm feeling curious about exactly what she likes and doesn't like.

(Behaviors) I'm saying to her, "Can you tell me more about that? For example, are there circumstances where you might enjoy it, like maybe if people weren't watching us, or the music weren't so loud?"

(Celebration) Hooray! I'm handling this well so far!

When the person says, "This is an opportunity to practice self-discipline," is that

A. a thought,
or
B. an emotion?

168. In the next examples, we will leave out the labels for the different parts of the fantasy rehearsal. The next example stars a person who has recently seen a doctor:

The doctor gave me advice on what to do. But I'm reading some articles on the Internet stating that the doctor was wrong and that the doctor's advice was bad.

It's not unusual that people disagree. I can handle that. My goal is to stay cool, and to figure out what's best for my health. I can search for still more articles, from trustworthy sources. If the same idea keeps reappearing, I can talk it over with my doctor, without getting mad at the doctor. I can always get another opinion from another doctor. My choice for right now is to keep searching and reading. I think that's a good choice for now.

I'm feeling cool, calculating, and determined to do what's best for me.

I'm relaxing my muscles, and I'm figuring out ways of looking for the most trustworthy sources of information about my illness.

Hooray for me! I think I'm handling the situation well.

When the person thinks, "I'm handling the situation well," that is called the

A. celebration,
or
B. situation?

169. Here's the next example of a fantasy rehearsal:

I'm in a crowd of people. Someone bumps me and steps on my foot. The person says, "Excuse me," but in a way that doesn't sound very sorry.

I'm glad I'm not hurt badly. I'm glad I chose to wear fairly stiff shoes. My goal is to stay cool and do something appropriate. I could say, "That's OK," but the person has already moved on away. I think the best option is just to forget about this.

I'm feeling proud of myself that I don't need to punish the other person.

I'm turning my attention back to the people I'm with, and I'm starting to talk with my friends again.

Hooray for me! I used good anger control.

When the person says, "I'm starting to talk with my friends again," the person is imagining

A. a behavior,

or

B. a thought?

170. The next example stars a kid who is not at all fat:

A kid who likes to joke a lot sees me and says, "Hey fatty, how are you doing?" He has a big grin on his face.

I don't think he's trying to make me feel bad. Otherwise, he would have picked some name to call me that had to do with one of my weaknesses or faults. He just wants to have some fun and not be bored. That's fine with me. I'll do some of the same stuff with him.

I'm feeling lighthearted as I try to think up something good to say back.

I smile back at him and say, "Pretty good, Grumpy, how are you doing?"

I'm really glad that I responded in a friendly way rather than getting angry at him.

When the person says, "I'm feeling lighthearted," the person is imagining

A. a thought,
or
B. an emotion?

171. You will notice that good fantasy rehearsals do not necessarily make entertaining drama. If I am writing a play and I want to entertain an

audience, I may want to make my characters misunderstand one another and get into very interesting and exciting conflicts with one another. Just keep in mind that, as you write the story of your own life, you do not have to entertain an audience. You want to avoid painful conflicts and big blowups. You want to make the stories about your responses to provocations be quiet and dull. There is plenty of opportunity for excitement and entertainment in the stories of your having fun with other people.

The point of this section is that you should make your fantasy rehearsals of responses to provocations

A. very exciting and entertaining to someone else who would read or hear them,
or
B. the best response you can think of, which usually is a fairly unexciting one?

Chapter 5: Listing Your Choice Points

172. Have you already written your goals for anger control or for better handling of provocations? Have you written your internal sales pitch, or list of reasons for wanting to achieve this goal? Do you look at these written documents often? If so, you've made a great start. If not, you may want to do this before moving to the next step, which is described in this chapter.

The recommendation for the goals and the internal sales pitch is to

A. think about them one time,
or
B. write them down and refer to them often?

173. The next step is listing choice points. To do this, you search through your memory. You recall any situations that provoked you. You recall anything that made you lose your temper. You recall anything that made you stay angry for a long time without losing your temper. As you think of these situations, you write them down. You are also free to make up situations. You can answer the question, "What are situations like those that make me angry?" or "What things that people could do would make me feel very uncomfortable?" You generate as long a

list as you can possibly think of. This activity is called listing choice points.

When listing choice points, you make a list of

A. the things you could do in a situation that makes you angry,
or
B. situations that might make you angry?

174. In listing choice points, you may wish to think about the categories of conflicts, criticisms, frustrations, and harmful acts.

Mr. Smith makes a list of choice points. Here's the way his list begins:

1. My wife would like to spend money on redoing the kitchen, whereas I would like to save the money for our retirement.

2. My daughter wants to stay up late, but I want her to go to bed early.

3. My boss wants me to work overtime and wants me to be available at the last minute, but I would like to be able to plan my working hours ahead of time.

4. My neighbor likes to shoot off fireworks late at night on holidays, but I want to be in bed and asleep without the noise.

These choice points fall into the category of

A. conflicts,
or
B. criticisms?

175. Sam makes a list of choice points. Here is the way his list begins:

1. Another kid at school bumps into me.

2. My sister spills milk on my homework papers.

3. I'm playing basketball, and someone grabs my wrist as I'm shooting for the basket.

4. A neighbor's dog runs around without a leash, and growls at and scares my dog.

These choice points fall into the category of

A. criticisms,
or
B. harmful acts?

176. Jane makes a list of choice points. her list starts out in this way:

1. I say something to someone at lunch, and the person says back, "Well, duh!"

2. I answer a question in class, and the kid next to me whispers, "That was a retarded answer."

3. I'm eating lunch with a friend at the house, and my mother says to me, "Jane, don't be a slob. Eat like a civilized person."

4. I play a song on the piano that was perfect except for one note, and my sister says, "You got that note wrong!"

These choice points fall into the category of

A. criticisms and disapproval,
or
B. miscellaneous choice points?

177. Tong makes a list of choice points. Here is the way that his list starts out:

1. I have gotten my hopes up to do something with someone. I am going to meet that person somewhere. I show up at the right time and place, but the other person doesn't show.

2. I have been working for a while on my computer, and then it shuts down and I lose my work.

3. I have just gotten involved in a fun and interesting activity at school, but

then the teacher commands me to put it away and go somewhere else.

4. I put some coins in a vending machine to get some food. The machine takes the coins but nothing comes out.

These choice points fall into the category of

A. frustrations,
or
B. facilitations?

178. There is a great deal of overlap among these four categories of choice points. For example, suppose Mark is at school and he reaches for his book. Another kid grabs the book first, hits Mark, and says, "That's my book, you little thief." This one situation contains conflict, a harmful act, criticism, and frustration. It's the same way with many anger control choice points. But the four categories of choice points are still useful in helping us think of situations, even though many situations will be examples of two or more of them.

To experience a situation that is an example of both a conflict and a frustration

A. happens very frequently,
or
B. is impossible?

179. What is the reason for listing your choice points? It isn't just an academic exercise. You will use this list when you practice handling provocations. You will take each of the provocations on your list, and decide what is the best response to it. You will figure out what thoughts, emotions, and behaviors you would like to do in that situation. Then you will practice over and over in your imagination, doing those desired responses: you will use fantasy rehearsal. But without choice points, you can't do fantasy rehearsals. You need a list of provocations if you are going to learn to handle provocations better.

The purpose of listing your choice points is

A. to get to know yourself better,
or
B. to have several situations that you use to practice with?

180. If you run out of provocation situations or choice points to practice with, you can find a very long list of them near the back of this book. There is a list of conflicts, and a list of other types of provocations. It is very useful to practice with situations that other people have encountered, as well as the ones that you have encountered.

You will be practicing with provocations that are:

A. situations that have happened to you, and you alone,

or

B. a wide variety of situations that have happened to other people as well as you?

181. Why is it useful to practice with situations that you never have experienced, and that you are not likely to ever experience? It's useful because almost any situation you practice with is sure to have at least a little in common with something you will experience in real life. For example, Mack is a 10-year-old boy. He practices with a choice point in which the main character is an 80-year-old woman. The woman can't hear well, and asks someone to repeat something several times, and the person yells at her impatiently. Mack finds that the next day, someone is impatient with him because he doesn't catch on to how to do a math problem right away. He finds that the way to deal with this criticism and impatience is very similar to the way he practiced when playing the role of the 80-year-old woman.

The point of this section is that you should

A. not bother practicing with choice points that don't apply directly to you,

or

B. make up, list, find, and use all the different sorts of situations that you can?

182. When you practice dealing with choice points, you will want to imagine them as vividly as possible. Therefore, you want to describe the choice points as concretely and specifically as you can. Give the details. Tell where you are, what you are doing, and what someone else said or did.

For example: Fred gets the urge to write, "My sister says something ignorant to me." But he realizes that this doesn't give a concrete image of what is exactly going on. So, for a more specific example, he writes, "I have brought a lot of school books home, and I put them down. My sister sees me do this, and she says, 'If you had done more work in school, you wouldn't have had to bring home so many books.'"

Which of the following choice points is described more concretely?

A. My sister irritates me.

or

B. I'm on the couch at home trying to study, and my sister, who's sitting beside me, starts twirling my hair around her finger. I've asked her not to do that.

183. Some of the provocations and choice points listed near the end of this book are fairly general. Before you start to work with the situation, for example, by doing the Four-thought Exercise with it, or doing a fantasy rehearsal of

handling it, or doing a role-play of a conflict-resolution conversation about it, you can imagine details that make the situation more specific.

For example, suppose you are given the following situation. "One spouse wants to spend money on something nice; the other wants to save the money for the future." From this general situation, you can generate any number of specific situations. For example: "A man wants to spend $20,000 on a new car. But his wife thinks that, because the car they already own has been driven for only 60,000 miles, it can last a lot longer. She thinks the money should be saved to someday pay for their children's education."

What is another specific situation that could be created from the same general situation that we have just thought about?

A. "A woman wants to buy a new dress, but her husband thinks that she already has enough clothes, and should keep the money in the bank."
or
B. "A husband and wife disagree on what to do about something important."

Chapter 6: Thoughts, the Twelve-thought Exercise, and the Four-thought Exercise

184. One of the great discoveries of the 20th century was cognitive therapy. The idea behind cognitive therapy is really quite simple, and it has been known for many centuries. The idea is that how you feel and how you act are very much influenced by what you say to yourself and what pictures you imagine. In other words, your emotions and behaviors are very much influenced by your thoughts. By consciously choosing your thoughts, you can influence your emotions and behaviors in very useful and important ways.

Which of these sentences is a summary of the basic idea of cognitive therapy?

A. If you want to feel or act differently, learn to think differently.
or
B. Actions, not thoughts, are the only important thing.

185. Here's an example of someone's using this idea. Suppose that Mrs. Jones finds herself getting much too angry at her two-year-old child. She finds herself screaming at her child or even hitting him in her anger. As a way of changing this, she examines what she is saying to herself. She notices that, when her little boy tries to climb up from a couch on to a table top, even though she does not at that moment say anything mean to her child, she says to herself, "What do you think you're doing, you little brat?" In lots of other situations, she notices herself saying similar sorts of blaming sentences. She realizes that these things she is saying to herself are making herself angry at her child.

The mother in this example felt angry because she

A. had a lot of blaming thoughts,
or
B. listed lots of options?

186. To continue this story, the mother learns to speak to herself in a different way. When she sees her son starting to climb, she decides to say to herself, "He's only two-years old. He doesn't have the judgment to protect himself. I want to protect him. How can I make this situation more safe?" When she practices over and over speaking to herself in these words and with a very calm tone of voice, her anger toward her son decreases.

In this example, the new sentences that she started saying to herself made her feel

A. gentler and kinder,

or

B. more angry?

187. Do you believe that changing the words we say and the words we think to ourselves can reduce violence and save lives? I am very sure that this is true.

Once I saw two men who had had a minor traffic accident. One of their cars had dented the other's car. As a police officer arrived on the scene, the two men were screaming profanities at each other, looking very much as if they were about to get into a fight. The police officer said, in a very low voice, "The next one of you who says a cuss word is going to jail. If you don't believe me, just try it out." The effect upon the mood of the two men was amazing. They both instantly became quiet and cooperative. When they stopped stimulating themselves by yelling curse words, they became calm.

In this example, changing the language that the men used

A. had no effect on their emotions and behavior,
or
B. had a dramatic effect on their emotions and behavior?

188. If you are working on anger control, one of the most important things that you can do is to try to get curse words and swear words out of your working vocabulary. These words

stand for blaming thoughts that tend to make us angrier.

The advice for anyone interested in anger control is to

A. think curse words, but don't say them out loud,
or
B. try to substitute other thoughts for those involving curse words?

189. Whenever there is too much anger, there are almost always blaming thoughts. "What does he think he's doing?" "You little snit!" "Why can't you see that . . . " "You're so stupid!" "You idiot!" "You're evil!" These are the sorts of thoughts that manufacture anger.

When there is overly great anger, there are almost always

A. blaming thoughts,
or
B. thoughts of getting down on oneself?

190. Not surprisingly, one of the thoughts most useful in anger control is that of "not blaming someone else." This type of thought is not just the absence of blaming thoughts. It is a conscious decision not to keep running blaming thoughts through the mind. Here are some examples of thoughts that fall into the "not blaming someone else" category: "He's only a two-year-old child; I don't want to blame him; he

doesn't know any better." "She spilled water on me, but I don't want to blame her, because it was just an accident." "The lady at the store is telling me I can't get my money back without a receipt. I don't like that policy, but this lady didn't make that policy; it doesn't do any good to blame her."

You have just read examples of a thought called

A. not awfulizing,
or
B. not blaming someone else?

191. In the examples of not blaming someone else that you have read so far, in some sense the unwanted event was not the person's "fault." Is it possible to "not blame someone else" in a rational way when the harmful act really is the other person's fault? The answer is yes. Even when the other person is totally blameworthy, it is not usually useful for us to keep thinking about how blameworthy the person is. When thoughts of blaming the other person are not useful to us, we can always make a conscious decision not to waste our energy on blaming. Such decisions can be really useful examples of "not blaming someone else."

To "not blame someone else" when the other person is at fault and has done something bad on purpose

A. can be a really good idea,

or
B. is always a really bad idea?

192. Here's an example. Suppose that another kid is bullying Mike in school. Mike finds himself saying to himself, over and over, "He is so mean. I hate him. My unhappiness is all his fault. He is bad through and through." After a while, Mike figures out that these blaming thoughts are not getting him anywhere. They aren't solving the problem. Mike thinks to himself, "I don't want to waste so much energy blaming him. I want to put my energy elsewhere." Mike then starts figuring out what his goal is and what his options are for reaching that goal. He decides to talk with his parents, his teacher, and his principal. He decides to stick up for his right not to be harassed at school. He decides to insist that the principal have a meeting with the parents of the boy who is bullying him. These thoughts help him to put an end to the bullying.

In this example, Mike decided to "not blame someone else" because

A. it wasn't the other person's fault,
or
B. blaming thoughts weren't as useful to Mike as other ways of using his energy?

193. Here's another example. Harriet is 55-years old. When she was a child, her father abused her. He beat her

mercilessly when she made everyday mistakes, and sometimes when she had done nothing wrong at all. Harriet finds that, every day of her life, thoughts like this go through her mind: "Why did he do that? Why did I have to get such an evil parent? He was such a bad person!"

Harriet finds that these thoughts simply make her feel bad and make her more irritable with other people she comes into contact with. She begins to practice "not blaming someone else" by thoughts along these lines: "Of course I don't like what he did. But I don't want to spend my life's energy blaming him. It's not because he doesn't deserve it. It's because I've got better things to do."

In the example above, Harriet decided to quit blaming so much because

A. she figured out that blaming wasn't useful to her,
or
B. she figured out that it wasn't really her father's fault?

194. So far we've been talking about two types of thoughts that are the most obviously connected with anger control: blaming someone else, and not blaming someone else. Now we will begin to think about some of the others of the twelve thoughts. Let's list the twelve thoughts with an example of each one. If you become very familiar with these categories, you will find it easier to choose what thoughts work best for you at any given time.

1. Awfulizing: This is bad; this is terrible; I can't stand this.
2. Getting down on yourself: I made a mistake; I did something wrong; I'm a bad person.
3. Blaming someone else: He made a mistake; he did something bad; he's a bad person.
4. Not awfulizing: This isn't the end of the world; I can take it.
5. Not getting down on yourself: I may have made a mistake, but I don't want to punish myself too much.
6. Not blaming someone else: I may not like what that person did, but I don't want to spend my energy blaming him.
7. Goal-setting: Here is what I would like to accomplish in this situation: . . .
8. Listing options and choosing: I could do this or that or this other thing . . . I think this is the best one.
9. Learning from the experience: I learned something from this; next time I'll know to do things differently in this way: . . .
10. Celebrating luck: I'm glad about this part of the situation, which is lucky for me.
11. Celebrating someone else's choice: I'm glad this person did this thing.
12. Celebrating your own choice: Hooray for me! I'm glad I made a good choice, and carried it out.

It is useful to become familiar with these categories because

A. doing so helps you choose what thoughts you want to think,

or

B. you can tell other people when they are thinking the wrong things?

195. Here's a very important idea: all of these types of thoughts are sometimes very useful, even awfulizing, getting down on yourself, and blaming someone else. *The goal is to be able to choose your thoughts according to what is most useful for the situation you are in.* Many people get stuck in certain patterns, (most often awfulizing, getting down on themselves, or blaming other people) and continue to use these patterns, even when they are clearly not useful. They use these patterns by reflex and habit, not because they have consciously decided that these thoughts will work best. When you find yourself moving from one thought to a second, because you think the second will be more useful, you have something big to celebrate. When this happens often, you have been liberated in a very important way. You are free from rigid habits of thought, and you are free to choose what sort of thought serves you best.

What's the very important idea of this section?

A. You should never awfulize, get down on yourself, or blame others.

or

B. You can free yourself to choose the thoughts that will serve you best in each situation.

196. When you are training yourself to choose your thoughts according to what works best, one of the main goals is flexibility of thinking. By flexibility, I mean the ability to think in any of several different ways. The opposite of flexibility is rigidity. Rigidity occurs when you can only see one way of thinking about the situation you're in, and you can't change it, even if it isn't working well.

Suppose that someone is driving a car, and another driver changes lanes in front of him, forcing him to slow down. He honks, screams, and gestures at the other driver in a fit of rage, and starts tailgating him. He is thinking, "You idiot!"

Later, he talks with someone about this incident. The person says, "Would you like to be able to think in a different way?"

The man replies, "Well, I just can't! He IS an idiot! They should not let such idiotic drivers on the road!" The man continues to believe that, because the other driver is an idiot, there is no possible other way to think about him.

The man in this little story is giving an example of

A. flexibility of thoughts,
or
B. rigidity of thoughts?

197. The Twelve-thought Exercise helps you make available to yourself all twelve thought patterns. To do this exercise, you pick any situation. (It can be a provocation, or it can be anything else.) Then you practice making up an example of each of the twelve types of thoughts, about that situation.

Here's how the Twelve-thought Exercise would sound, as done by our angry driver:

1. (Awfulizing) This is really bad that he cut me off like that!

2. (Getting down on yourself) I'm having to slam on the brakes; I must have been going too fast. I wasn't driving well; I was irresponsible.

3. (Blaming someone else) He shouldn't have pulled in front of me like that! He's driving very badly!

4. (Not awfulizing) OK, so I have to slow down, and I will have to pass him. No big deal. I can handle that.

5. (Not getting down on yourself) Even though I may not have been watching for him closely enough, I don't want to spend my energy punishing myself for that.

6. (Not blaming someone else) I don't like what he just did, but everyone makes mistakes. I don't want to keep dwelling on the mistake he made.

7. (Goal-setting) My goals are to keep cool, to relax, and to pass him when it's safe to do so.

8. (Listing options and choosing) I could tap gently on the horn, or I could just keep quiet. I can relax my muscles a bit to help me stay cool. I can pass him right away, or I can slow down my driving a little. I'm choosing not to honk, but to relax my muscles, drive more slowly for a while, and pass him when it's safe.

9. (Learning from the experience) I learned to watch for drivers who pull in front of me and to be prepared to slow down.

10. (Celebrating luck) I'm glad that this is the worst situation I've run into so far driving today – I could have had something much worse happen.

11. (Celebrating someone else's choice) I'm glad the person got as far in front of me as he did before changing lanes. I'm glad the thousands of other drivers I've shared the road with have not done anything that bothered me.

12. (Celebrating your own choice) I'm glad that I was able to stay cool about this situation and make a good choice of

what to do. I'm really glad I didn't get into a rage.

The Twelve-thought Exercise makes clear that:

A. There is only one correct way of thinking about a situation.
or
B. There are several different ways to think about any situation, and you can use the thoughts that will help you handle the situation best.

198. I recommend doing the Twelve-thought Exercise many, many times with the conflicts, provocations, and criticisms listed in the appendices at the end of this book. The more you can increase your flexibility of thinking, then the more you can make good choices about how you want to think about a certain situation.

Going through all twelve thoughts is a very important exercise. But we need a shorter exercise in addition, one we can do more quickly. When a real-life situation arises, you usually won't have time to think in all twelve ways. But with practice, you can learn to go through four of these thoughts very quickly. Such practice is done by the Four-thought Exercise. In this exercise ,you use not awfulizing, goal-setting, listing options and choosing, and celebrating your own choice. When a provocation comes up in real life, you usually can flash all four of these types of thoughts across your mind, especially if you cultivate the habit of thinking about them quickly.

What are the four thoughts that we use in the Four-thought Exercise?

A. not awfulizing, goal-setting, listing options in choosing, and celebrating your own choice,
or
B. not blaming someone else, learning from the experience, getting down on yourself, and celebrating luck?

199. Let's go over why these thoughts are so useful in response to provocations. Let's think about not awfulizing. Anger and violence are responses to threats and danger. The more we think that something horrible has happened or is about to happen, the more intensely we feel anger or fear. On the other hand, if we believe and recognize that the situation we are dealing with is not a very big deal, we are less likely to be intensely angry.

Do you remember my mentioning a murder that took place during a conflict over who would get to use a phone next? People manage to work themselves up into thinking that things are very important when they are not very important at all. Suppose that both of those people fighting over the phone had been able to say to themselves, "This is no big deal. This is not all that important. I can handle it if I don't get my way on this. If I don't get to use the phone right away, it's not going to ruin my life." These are "not awfulizing" statements. If both of the men had thought these "not awfulizing" statements, it is hard to imagine that a killing would have taken place.

Why is not awfulizing so useful in anger control?

A. We naturally don't get as angry over situations that we realize aren't very bad threats to us.
or
B. It's impossible to be angry after uttering the sentence, "It's not awful."

200. It's sometimes a good idea to not awfulize about situations that are truly awful, just as it is sometimes a good idea to not blame someone else in situations where the other person is truly blameworthy. Imagine that someone has done something truly awful to me. Suppose the consequences are truly terrible. Even then, repeatedly telling myself how bad things are may not be my best use of energy. If someone is threatening to kill me, for example, is it most useful for me to think: "This is terrible! I can't stand it! This is a REALLY bad situation!" or, "I don't want to waste time on awfulizing: let me figure out what to do, quick! . . . "

The point of this section is that:

A. When things are awful, you should awfulize!
or
B. Often deciding not to waste your time awfulizing is a good thing to do, even when things are awful.

201. Buddhist writings describe an exercise called "The Parable of the Saw." In this exercise, you imagine that someone has sawed off both your arms and legs! The Buddhist students practice thinking this about their attackers: "We will remain with a friendly heart, devoid of hatred, and, beginning with these people, we will develop the thought of loving-kindness."

I'm not sure how useful it would be, in real life, to feel loving-kindness toward the people who did such a deed. I am sure that at times it is very useful to vigorously oppose people who have treated you unkindly, rather than treating them in a friendly manner. I am sure that the choice of how to act is more complicated than simply acting kind and loving and friendly to everyone at all times. But the exercise with the Parable of the Saw illustrates a great truth: if you practice in imagination thinking and feeling in un-angry ways, even in the situations most likely to make you angry, you increase your mental flexibility. You increase your ability to control your own thoughts and feelings. You get closer and closer to the point where anger is something you control and choose, based on its usefulness, rather than something that takes control of you.

The reason that the author recommends practicing "not awfulizing" and feeling loving-kindness, in imagination, with situations where people have done horrible things to you is that:

A. You should always act kind and friendly to anyone who hurts you.
or
B. Practicing being un-angry even in situations where anger would be most justified, gives you more control over your thoughts and feelings?

202. Let's think about goal-setting. Very often, when people get angry, the goal that they appear to be working toward is to punish and get revenge on the other person, even if this goal also harms themselves. They choose this goal by impulse, even though calm reflection would tell them that it's a stupid goal. A large part of anger control is learning to aim toward different goals: making sure that no one is harmed, finding a just solution to the problem, and doing the right thing. Goal-setting thoughts allow you to fix your attention on what you really want to make happen in the situation.

Suppose you face a provocation and you think to yourself, "my first priority is to stay cool and keep my head. I also want nobody to get hurt." The type of thought you are thinking is

A. goal-setting,
or
B. getting down on yourself ?
203. The third thought of the Four-thought Exercise is listing options and choosing. Why is this thought pattern so important? This is the type of thinking where you figure out what you want to do in the situation. If you can think of several options, ponder their advantages and disadvantages, and then choose the one that you think makes things come out best, you are using rational decision-making.

Listing options and choosing is aimed at helping you to

A. relax,
or
B. make a good decision?

204. When listing options and choosing, I recommend listing only ethical, nonviolent options. Although thinking of an outlandish or funny option may sometimes free up your creativity to think of a good option you wouldn't have landed on otherwise, thinking of violent and hostile options usually just wastes your energy.

Which of the following types of option lists does the author prefer?

A. Let's see: I could hit him or scream at him, or I could speak softly to him.
or
B. Hmm, I could just ignore what he said, or I could say, "You can think whatever you want," or I could say, "OK, I hear your complaint."

205. The fourth thought in the Four-thought Exercise is celebrating your own choice. Why is this so important? When you say to yourself, "Hooray, I did a good job!" you are rewarding yourself for making a good choice. You are making yourself feel good. One of the central ideas of psychology is that people tend to repeat behaviors that make them feel good. They tend not to repeat behaviors that bring no rewards. It's your job to reward yourself for making good decisions.

The point of celebrating your own choice is to

A. make it more likely that you will make a good choice again,
or
B. show other people what a good choice you made?

206. Let's look at some examples of the Four-thought Exercise. Let's use the following situation: A kid has done much work to prepare a homework assignment. Another kid accidentally makes a large ink mark across the homework paper.

Not awfulizing: This isn't the end of the world. No one has been hurt or killed. It's only a homework paper.

Goal-setting: I want to be kind to the other kid, because I do think it was just an accident. I also want to get credit for my homework.

Listing options and choosing: I could say nothing to the other kid, or when he apologizes I could say, sort of jokingly, "Don't worry about it too much. Just worry about it a little bit." I think I like that one. With the homework, I could try to copy it over, or just turn it in as it is, or turn it in with a little note explaining what happened. I think I'll just turn it in as it is, and explain it to the teacher if I get asked about it. Celebrating your own choice: I'm glad I stayed cool about this situation. And I think my decisions were good!

This example is to demonstrate how to do the

A. Four-thought Exercise,
or
B. the celebrations exercise?

207. Here's another example: A man is working in his office. A construction worker is remodeling the office next to him. The worker's radio is turned up enough that the noise bothers the man.

Not awfulizing: This is annoying, but it isn't terrible. I think it's a situation that will be easily solved.

Goal-setting: My goal is not to be distracted from my work anymore, and to achieve that in the gentlest possible way.

Listing options and choosing: I could complain to the building manager. Or, I could directly ask the construction worker to turn down the radio. I could ask him in a friendly and polite tone, or I could ask him in a little firmer or harsher tone. My guess is that it will work fine if I directly ask the worker, and do it in a friendly tone. I'll try that first and go to other options if that doesn't work.

Celebrating your own choice: Hooray, I think I made a very reasonable choice!

The choice that the person made in the listing options and choosing part of this exercise was to

A. politely ask the other person to change his behavior,
or
B. put up with the annoying situation, without doing anything?

208. Here's another example of the Four-thought Exercise. You are telling a story to some people, and one of them says, "Come on; get to the point! You don't have to keep going over and over the same thing!"

Not awfulizing: If I was getting a little long-winded, that's not the most terrible thing in the world. And if this person was getting impatient without a very good reason, that's not terrible either.

Goal-setting: I want to keep cool and not get too angry at the person who criticized me. I don't want to have to feel that this person can boss me around however he wants to. But I do want to tell the story without making people impatient. I want to figure out if I should be more concise as a general habit.

Listing options and choosing: I can just get to the point of my story more quickly and finish it up. Or, I can ask other people if they're getting impatient too. Or, I can just stop talking now, and say, "I'll give someone else a chance to talk." Later on, I can ask some of my friends if they feel impatient when I'm telling stories. I think I'll stop talking now, and ask my friends later.

Celebrating your own choice: Hooray, I made a good decision, and I've kept really cool so far.

One of the goals the person had for this situation was to

A. decide how much to work on changing the behavior he's been criticized for,
or
B. show the person who criticized him that the criticism was wrong?

209. Here's another example of the Four-thought Exercise. In this example, we will leave out the labels of the four thoughts.

In this situation, imagine that you are a parent. Your child has asked to invite a friend to spend the night. You say no, because your child has something to do early tomorrow morning. Also, the house is a mess and the family needs to clean it up instead of entertaining friends. When you say no, your child screams at you and calls you obscene names. Here are the four thoughts:

My child is not very good at tolerating frustration. This is a serious problem. But it's not the end of the world. My child can learn to change.

My short-term goal is not to reinforce this bad behavior of my child. I want to help him learn that bad behavior does not get him what he wants. My long-term goal is to help him learn fortitude and anger control.

For the present, I could just ignore what he said, or I could tell him that, because he responded in that way, he won't be able to have a friend sleep over for at least two weeks. I think the second option would be better for him. For the long term, I can talk with my wife about getting a system of consequences in place. I can also start teaching him anger control myself. Or I can try to find someone else to do so. I will make some plans with my wife and also see how it goes when I try to start teaching anger control to my son myself.

Even though I feel bad about his behavior, I feel good about the choices I have made.

When the man in this example said, "I want to help him learn that bad behavior does not get him what he wants," this is an example of

A. listing options,
or
B. goal-setting?

210. In the next situation, imagine that you are a student in school. The teacher looks at your hands and says, in a grouchy, irritable tone of voice, "Go wash your hands!"

Here are the four thoughts:

I'm being told to do something in a way that sounds bossy and impolite. This isn't the first time this has happened, and it won't be the last. I can handle it.

My main goal is to stay out of trouble. I also don't want to cause a disturbance in the class, for the sake of the other students. It would be nice if I could change the way the teacher talks, but I'm not sure this goal is realistic.

The best option for right now, I'm pretty sure, is just to get up and go and wash my hands without giving any dirty looks and without saying anything. I could also say, "OK," in a cheerful tone of voice. I think I'll do that. Maybe sometime in the future, I could write a very polite note to the teacher requesting that she tell us what to do in a more cheerful way, and maybe even say please sometimes. I will think about that later on.

Hooray for me, I made some good choices!

The main goal the student chose was to

A. teach his teacher a lesson,
or
B. stay out of trouble?

211. Here's another example: Someone sees a couple of other people smiling and talking to each other. As she passes them, they look at her and are silent. As soon as she has passed them, they look at each other and laugh.

She thinks: They could have been talking about me, and laughing at me. Or they could have been talking about something silly, not having to do with me, and feeling self-conscious when I

walked by. Whatever it was, I can handle it. It's not a problem for me.

My goal is not to get upset over this, but to relax and go on about my business and enjoy myself.

I could ask one of them later what they were laughing at. Or I could just forget about it. Or I could turn my attention to someone who wants to chat with me, and maybe talk about this situation. Or I could just get on with my work. I think I'll choose to forget about it and get to work.

Hooray, I made a reasonable choice. I feel good that I didn't let it bother me.

When the person in this example thought, "I feel good that I didn't let it bother me," that was an example of

A. listing options,
or
B. celebrating her own choice?

212. I recommend that you practice the Four-thought Exercise many times with real-life provocations or anger control choice points you have listed. Also, if you take each of the provocations, conflicts, and criticisms in the appendices to this book, and practice with them until you can do the Four-thought Exercise quickly and automatically, you will go a long way toward achieving a great habit of anger control.

Even those situations that don't apply to your life are good for practice, for two reasons. First, they let you practice taking someone else's point of view, seeing things from someone else's perspective. This is a skill that is helpful for anger control in and of itself. Second, any provocation situation has things in common with other provocations, and your practice with one will generalize to others.

The author recommends

A. practicing the Four-thought Exercise only with the situations most relevant to your life,
or
B. practicing the Four-thought Exercise with any and all provocations, whether or not they have anything to do with your experience?

Chapter 7: Choosing Your Goals or Motives

213. In the last chapter, we spoke about one of the most important types of thoughts to have: goal-setting. This chapter takes a more thorough look at different types of goals. Another word for goal is *motive*.

Suppose someone bumps into you by accident. What is your immediate goal? What do you want to happen? Do you want to get the person back for what he did to you? This is called the goal of revenge. Do you want to do something just unpleasant enough to teach the other person not to do that again? This is the motive to use punishment to teach the other person. Do you mainly want to show the other person who is boss, or to make sure he knows that he can't push you around? Do you want to make sure that you, and not the other person, wins the competition? This is called the goal of dominance – dominance means being more powerful than the other person. Do you want to protect yourself by harming or threatening to harm the other person, so that he won't do something worse to you? This is the goal of defense, or self-protection. Do you want to make a big loud scene, just for the excitement of it? This goal is called stimulus-seeking.

Wishes for things like protecting yourself, punishing the other person's behavior, or excitement are called

A. stimulus-seeking,
or
B. goals, or motives?

214. Let's think more about the same situation, where someone bumps into you. Is your goal to stay out of a situation where you, or anyone else, will be hurt, physically or emotionally? We can call that motive avoiding harm. Is your goal to prove to yourself that you can stay cool, and build up your habit of staying cool? This motive is self-discipline. Is your goal perhaps to try to understand what the other person is feeling? Understanding what others are feeling is called empathy. If the other person is feeling embarrassed, do you wish to say something so the other person won't feel so bad, out of the wish to be kind or build a good relationship? This is the motive of friendship-building or kindness. How about this: would you like to figure out a plan that will help people not to bump into each other so much in the future – for example, an agreement that people will stay toward the right side of the hall? This is the motive for problem-solving.

This example illustrates that:

A. People can respond to a certain situation (such as being bumped into) with only one goal.
or
B. There are lots of possible goals that people can have when responding to the same situation (such as being bumped into).

215. Here is a list of goals or motives:

revenge
sadism

dominance
defense
punishment
stimulus-seeking

avoiding harm
self-discipline
problem-solving
empathy and understanding
kindness or friendship These motives are best described as

A. things that people can want or aim toward, when in situations with other people,
or
B. different types of people you will meet?

216. I divided these goals or motives into three groups. Revenge and sadism are not rational motives, and should be

avoided. Dominance, defense, punishment, and stimulus-seeking are motives to be careful about. They are sometimes necessary and sometimes useful, but often lead to aggression and greater conflict if overused. The last group, avoiding harm, self-discipline, problem-solving, empathy, and kindness, tend to lead toward peace and conflict-resolution.

The three groups of motives are arranged in order of

A. how long they take,
or
B. how much they tend to promote peace and nonviolence?

217. Let's practice telling the difference between these motives. Suppose that someone is very angry at a family member, because the family member borrows his things without returning them. He yells at the family member, not with any hope that this will change things, but just out of the wish to get back at the family member.

This is the motive for

A. revenge,
or
B. empathy?

218. Suppose that someone else is in the same situation. This time the person thinks, "Each time this happens, I will say something to him that will make

him feel just bad enough to stop this behavior."

The motive is

A. dominance,
or
B. punishment?

219. Someone else is in the same situation. The person thinks, "I will have a conversation with him. I will try to find a way that both of us can be happy. I will try to search for a plan that will work."

The goal is

A. revenge,
or
B. problem-solving?

220. Suppose the person thinks, "An important goal is that neither of us gets hurt. I don]t want to hurt his body or his feelings, and I don't want him to hurt me. I'll pick a time and a way of dealing with this, so that the chances of harm are as little as possible."

The goal here is

A. avoiding harm,
or
B. dominance?

221. A person is driving, and although he has done nothing wrong, another driver honks at him and gives him "the finger." The person thinks to himself, "This is an opportunity to practice staying cool. This is a chance for me to prove to myself that I can choose my own emotions." The person's goal is

A. self-discipline,
or
B. punishment?

222. A girl is singing. Her younger sister says, "Please don't do that." The older sister wants to find a solution that will make them both happy, so she asks, "Tell me more, please. Is it too loud, or are you trying to concentrate, or do you just not like my singing?"

The motive is

A. problem-solving,
or
B. stimulus-seeking?

223. Someone is in a parking lot. A man says to him, "What do you think you're doing, parking so close to my car?"

He replies, "Nobody talks to me like that, buddy. If I don't hear an apology coming from you in about two seconds, you're going to find that your car is the least of your worries."

The motive is

A. problem-solving,
or
B. dominance?

224. Someone else is in the same situation. He thinks, "He's really mad. But this is my chance to practice staying cool. Anger control has been a problem for me, but if I stay cool in this situation, I will really have made a triumph over my problem."

The man's motive is

A. kindness and friendship,
or
B. self-discipline?

225. Someone else has the same thing happen. He thinks, "I want to understand what this guy's problem is." So he says, "I guess you're worried that I'll scratch your car when I open the door. Is that the problem?"

The motive is

A. empathy,
or
B. punishment?

226. Suppose that the other man then says, "Yes, it's a new car and I don't want it scratched." So the second man says, "It's easy enough for me to move. That will solve that." He takes a few seconds and moves his car.

The motive is

A. revenge,
or

B. problem-solving?

227. A woman breaks a cup. She says, "Oh, curse it," and hits her fist against a table and starts crying.

Her husband thinks, "I want to discourage her from acting that way in the future." So he says, "You're acting like a baby."

His motive is

A. stimulus-seeking,
or
B. punishment?

228. Suppose the same thing happens. Another man thinks, "She looks like she's having a hard time. I want to be nice to her." So he says, "Here, I'll help you clean that up."

His motive is

A. punishment,
or
B. kindness?

229. Suppose that the same man thinks, "I want to understand what she's going through." He says, "It looks like you've been having a rough time. Would you like to talk about it?"

His motive is

A. defense,
or

B. empathy and understanding?

230. It's winter, and two kids are on a playground. The first is bored. He wants to get some excitement going. So he grabs the other's hat and runs.

The goal is

A. stimulus-seeking,
or
B. punishment?

231. After the first kid grabs the second's hat, the second kid thinks, "I've got to do something to protect myself from people who pick on me." So he runs after the first kid, hoping to tackle him.

His motive is

A. defense,
or
B. empathy?

232. Another kid also has a kid grab his hat and run. But this kid thinks, "Hey, he wants to play with me. This is like tag. He wants to have fun. That's what people do when they become friends." So he laughs and has fun chasing after the first kid. He grabs the first kid's hat and laughs while that kid chases him. After a while they trade hats. Then the second kid points to a playground climbing toy and says, "Come on, let's climb up that thing!"

The motive is

A. problem-solving,
or
B. friendship?

233. Two people play a board game. One of them thinks, "I want to have a good time with this person so that we will like each other better."

The motive is

A. friendship,
or
B. punishment?

234. Two people play a board game. One of them thinks, "I can't let the other person beat me. I've got to prove that I'm on top. If I lose, he will be more powerful than I am. But I want to be the one with more power."

The motive is

A. friendship,
or
B. dominance?

235. A man has committed a crime against a person's sister. The person thinks, "That bad person! I want him to pay for what he did! He needs to suffer, like he made my sister suffer!"

The motive is

A. revenge,

or

B. defense?

236. Someone else is in the same situation, where someone committed a crime against a family member. This person thinks, "I hope that criminal gets a stiff sentence. That might teach him not to do such things."

The motive is

A. empathy,
or
B. punishment?

237. Someone else is in the same situation. This person thinks, "We need to protect ourselves from this person's doing anything like this again. The best way to do that is to keep him in jail."

The motive is

A. defense,
or
B. friendship?

238. It's good to have different motives at different times. If someone is trying to hurt you, it's good to want to protect yourself, or to have the motive of defense. If someone is trying to make friends with you and treat you kindly, it's good to have motives of kindness and friendship.

The point of this is that:

A. Your main motives should always be kindness and friendship.
or
B. Your motives should be appropriate for the situation you're in.

239. Some people seem to be biased toward one motive or another. Some people tend to think that other people are threatening them or trying to hurt them. They tend to be suspicious and mistrusting of other people. Other people require more evidence before they conclude that someone is trying to hurt them.

What you've read is that:

A. When it comes to motives, people are all the same.
or
B. Some people are much more disposed to certain motives than others.

240. Some psychologists once did an experiment. They studied aggressive people and non-aggressive people. They showed each of them pictures of people, and asked them what the person was trying to do. For example, one of the pictures might have been of someone coming toward you with an outstretched hand. The experimenters asked the people to say what they would think someone was trying to do if the person looked like that. The aggressive people tended to think things like, "He's going to try to hit me." The nonaggressive

people tended to think things like, "He's coming to shake my hand." The conclusion was that aggressive people tend to see other people as more threatening and dangerous than nonaggressive people do.

In the experiment you just read about,

A. all the people who observed the same situation had the same motive in responding to it,
or
B. different people saw the same situation in very different ways, which would lead them to have very different motives?

241. In the pictures the experimenters used, it was impossible to tell exactly what the person had in mind. This is the way it is so often in life. When a teacher corrects you, is she trying to humiliate you, or to help you learn? When a friend calls you by a nickname, is this his way of being friendly, or a way of making fun of you? When a parent enforces a rule about bedtime, is that parent trying to push you around, or to help you do better tomorrow? When a coach makes you run, is he enjoying making you feel tired and out of breath, or is he enjoying seeing you get into better shape and gain self-discipline? Sometimes you can never know for sure.

The point of this is that:

A. You can always tell why someone does something.
or
B. You can often not tell why someone does something.

242. Here's something that makes things even more complicated. Sometimes, if you *think* people are acting mean to you, you act angry at them, and this makes them *really* act mean to you! For example, someone notices that Larry is tall and skinny, and in a friendly way says, "Hey, String Bean!"

Suppose Larry gets very offended by this, and gets a very indignant look on his face. He says, "My name is not String Bean! You shut up!"

The other kid now feels attacked, and he attacks back by doing the opposite of what Larry wants. Now he taunts and teases and tries to get other kids to do the same.

On the other hand, if Larry had simply responded to the nickname with a smile and a friendly reply, the other kid would be much more likely to be friendly back.

This is an example where

A. thinking that someone was trying to be mean resulted in that person's actually trying to be mean,
or

B. a kid was mean to Larry from the very beginning, calling him bad names?

243. Sometimes when you think someone is mean, you act in a way that leads the other person to be mean. And likewise, sometimes when you think someone is being friendly, you act in a way that actually leads the person to be friendly. These are examples of *self-fulfilling prophecies*. A prophecy is what you think will happen. When your expectation makes itself come true, we have a self-fulfilling prophecy.

When what you expect about another person makes you act in a way that makes those expectations come true, it's called a

A. causal prediction,
or
B. self-fulfilling prophecy?

244. Here's another example of a self-fulfilling prophecy. Rick comes toward Clint with his hand stretched out, wanting to shake Clint's hand. But Clint thinks that Rick is going to hit him. So Clint gets a very angry look on his face and hits Rick. Now Rick feels really angry at being attacked so unjustly. So Rick hits Clint back, hard.

In this example,

A. thinking that someone was friendly led the person to act friendly,
or

B. thinking that someone was mean led the person to act mean?

245. Here's another example of a self-fulfilling prophecy. Joe has just played a song on the guitar. Mason, who can play better, doesn't feel friendly to Joe, but just wants to prove that he is better than Joe is. Mason says, "Your strings buzz so much because you don't put your fingers where they're supposed to go."

Suppose Joe is not sure whether Mason is trying to be helpful or not. He decides he will act as if Mason is trying to be helpful. He says, in a friendly voice, "Oh, I'm glad to hear there's a way for me to make them sound better. Where should I put my fingers, Mason?"

Mason says, "You put them right behind the frets, like this."

Joe tries it. He says, "Hey, that works! Great! Mason, you really helped me! Wow, I owe you one!"

Now Mason feels friendly toward Joe, and acts friendly.

The prophecy Joe made that fulfilled itself was that:

A. Mason would be friendly to him.
or
B. Mason felt unfriendly to him.

246. On the other hand, suppose Joe had thought, "He's just trying to prove how much better than me he is - he's not being friendly." Then Joe might have said, "When I want your opinion, I'll ask for it." Mason might have said, "That's why you're such a lousy guitar player."

What's the order in which things happen in a "self-fulfilling prophecy"?

A. You make a prophecy. Someone tries not to make it come true. But it comes true, anyway.
or
B. You believe something is a certain way. Your belief affects how you act. Your actions make your belief come true.

247. Why have we been talking about self-fulfilling prophecies? Self-fulfilling prophecies are one reason why, when you're not sure, it's good to pick friendly and kind motives. It's good, when you're not sure, to act as if people are trying to be nice to you, because sometimes that will cause them to be nice. And for the same reason, sometimes it's good to act as if someone is trying to be friendly, even when you're sure that the person *isn't* feeling friendly!

Self-fulfilling prophecies are a good reason why it's often a good idea to

A. act as if the other person is trying to harm you, just to be safe,
or
B. act as if the other person would like to be friendly to you?

248. A very important word in the title of this chapter is the word *choosing*. One of the major purposes of studying this book is that you can choose what motives you want to have in the situations of your life. You can *choose* whether you want to work toward friendship or revenge, kindness or punishment, dominance or empathy.

Sometimes it does not feel as if you can choose. Sometimes things happen so fast that it feels as if you have no choice but to have whatever motive you're most in the habit of using.

For example: John is doing schoolwork, and a classmate looks over his shoulder. The classmate says, "You missed that one." John is so strongly in the habit of revenge and defense that, before he even has time to think, he lashes out with "Shut up!" and pushes the classmate away.

In this example, do you think that John feels as though he is *choosing* the motives of revenge and defense?

A. Yes, because he is pondering what to do.
or

B. No, because he acts before he has a chance to think or consciously choose.

249. Suppose, however, that John decides, "The next time something like that happens, I want to understand what the other person is saying, to solve whatever problem there is with my work, and to be friends with the other person. I'm going to practice, over and over, acting in a way that seeks these goals." Then he practices many times. The next time someone corrects him on his work, he acts in the ways that he has practiced.

Is it clear to him now that he had the power to choose his motives?

A. Yes, because the choice he made resulted in his changing his behavior.
or
B. No, because he couldn't put this choice into effect without doing a lot of work.

250. This is the way it is with lots of choices. It's often very difficult to choose what you want to do, and do it, right on the spot. But if you choose to do something, and then you work and practice for a long time with imaginary situations, so that you can learn new habits, you can change your habits.

Here's an example that has nothing to do with anger control. Jane makes a choice: "I choose that I will play *Canon in D* on the piano." At the time that she

chooses, she doesn't know how to play this song.

If she were to sit down right after she makes her choice, and try to perform the song, would it sound like this was something she had any choice over?

A. Yes, because she knows how to play it already.
or
B. No, because she hasn't practiced and learned and worked enough to play it yet.

251. Then Jane spends hours working on this song, practicing it over and over. Finally she gets to the point where she can play it well. She plays it for some people.

At this point, is it clear that Jane was able to choose whether she would play the song or not?

A. Yes, because now she is able to do what she chose to do.
or
B. No, because she couldn't do what she did without working.

252. In the same way, you can decide what kinds of motives you want to pursue, in any given situation. You can make the sorts of "goal-setting" statements to yourself that you think will make things work out best. In a certain type of situation, you can replace motives of revenge, aggressive

defense, punishment, dominance, and stimulus-seeking with motives of avoiding harm, kindness, friendship, empathy, and problem-solving *if you choose to do so*. However, it takes lots of work and practice to put this choice into effect.

The point is that:

A. You have no choice: you must use the motives of kindness, empathy, friendship, and problem-solving.
or
B. You can choose your motives and put them into effect, if you are willing to work and practice at them.

Chapter 8: Choosing Emotions

253. For years some mental health professionals have told people that "all emotions are good." This statement is usually followed by the statement, "It's what you do with them that counts." However, growing numbers of therapists have realized that this advice may be misguided. In any given situation, some emotions are definitely better to have than others. Emotions spur us or predispose us to certain types of behaviors. If we could choose, we would definitely want to feel the emotions that would spur us toward appropriate behaviors. And it is becoming clearer and clearer that people can choose what emotions they want to feel in a given situation, and gradually cultivate the ability to feel the emotions they choose.

One of the main points of this section is that:

A. All emotions are good.
or
B. In any given situation, some emotions are better than others.

254. Here's an example to illustrate this point. Suppose you arrange a party for a new friend of yours. In the middle of the party, the honored person is crying and sulking. Someone asks what's wrong, and she says, "I like chocolate cake best, and that's white cake. I am just furious about that!" Which assessment of this reflects reality better: that "all emotions are good," including the fury and rage the person feels over the cake, or that the person's furious feelings are just as bratty and undesirable and worth avoiding as her behaviors?

The author uses this situation to illustrate that:

A. There's no such thing as an undesirable emotion.
or
B. Emotions can be undesirable when they get in the way of handling the situation well.

255. Imagine two children playing in the street. A car comes toward them, fast. One is scared and runs out of the street. The other feels delighted, and dances around laughing until someone drags him out of the street at great peril to her own life.

In this story, was the emotion felt by the first child more desirable than the one felt by the second? Of course it was! When escape and avoidance are necessary and can save your life, fear is more appropriate than mirth.

The point being made is that:

A. Often one emotion is more useful and appropriate to the situation than another.
or
B. All feelings are equally good in all situations.

256. Suppose that two people carelessly spill hot coffee on someone else. The first person feels sorry and remorseful, and those feelings lead him to resolve to be more careful. The second person feels greatly entertained, and perceives that burning the other person was great fun.

Would it be appropriate to tell the second person, "You shouldn't feel that way?" Of course it would be. Despite the fact that the words "You shouldn't feel that way" are heresy to many psychotherapists, it's obvious that some feelings are clearly better and more desirable than others, just as some actions are. Feelings spur us to certain sorts of actions, and the sorts of feelings that spur us to bad or destructive actions should be avoided.

The author feels that the mental health professionals who say that all feelings are always good are

A. very wrong,
or
B. absolutely right?

257. Provocation situations are those where people might tend to feel angry.

But do we have to feel angry whenever a provocation takes place? No. Plenty of people have experienced provocations without feeling angry at all.

Here's an example. Ralph is on a debate team. He's debating in a very important tournament. Ralph finishes a speech and sits down to listen to his opponent. Ralph's opponent was greatly angered by something that Ralph said. Ralph's opponent starts screaming at Ralph and calling him obscene names. Instead of feeling angry, Ralph feels overjoyed. Can you guess why?

Ralph has just realized that his team has won the debate. The judges could not possibly choose as a winner a debater who screams curse words. Instead of thinking, "That bad person; I've got to get him back," Ralph is thinking, "Hooray, the debate prize is going to be ours!"

This situation illustrates that:

A. All people feel angry whenever a provocation takes place.
or
B. People do not always feel angry when a provocation takes place.

258. Here are some emotions that you might choose to feel in response to provocations:

determination
curiosity

coolness and calculation
sympathy
humility
pride

Often these emotional states will serve you much better than high anger will.

How do you "choose to feel" a certain emotion? You do it by thinking the thoughts and acting out the behaviors that go along with the emotion.

This section lists six other emotional states that

A. you can choose to feel in response to provocations, by thinking the thoughts and acting out the behaviors that go with them,
or
B. you can't control, because no one can control emotions?

259. Let's go over the thoughts that go along with the six alternate emotions. Determination is the strong wish to achieve a goal. So when we think thoughts such as "I must accomplish my goal! I want it very badly," we feel determined.

Curiosity is the wish to know the answer to a question. So when we think thoughts such as, "Humh, I wonder what the answer to this is?" we feel curious.

Cool and calculating are words that describe the emotional state that goes along with thinking hard about what to do. So when we think, "Let's see, if I do this, this is likely to happen; if I do this other choice, this will probably occur . . . " then I'm probably feeling cool and calculating.

Someone is in a foreign country. A child riding in a car going by sticks her tongue out at the person. The person's main thought is, "I wonder why she did this. I wonder if this gesture means the same thing as it does in my country."

The person is probably feeling

A. curious,
or
B. very angry?

260. Sympathy, or compassion, means feeling sorry about someone else's having problems, and wanting things to come out better for that person. So when we think, "I wish that person didn't have to feel so bad," we tend to feel sympathetic.

Humility means realizing that we ourselves are not perfect. It's how we feel when we think thoughts such as, "This other person made a mistake. But I've made even bigger mistakes."

Pride means feeling good when we've done something good. When I think, "Hooray for me, I've done a good job of anger control so far," I probably am feeling proud of myself.

Rich is on the baseball team. A teammate drops a fly ball. Rich thinks, "My teammate has dropped almost as many fly balls as I have – but not quite!"

Rich is probably feeling

A. humility,
or
B. great anger?

261. A man is at an outdoor concert, and a four-year-old child he's never seen before wanders up to him and slaps him very hard on the leg. The man thinks to himself, "I had some trouble with anger control before, but I very much want to do a good job of anger control right now." How do you think the man is feeling?

A. determined,
or
B. exhausted?

262. Suppose the same man thinks to himself, "I think this child must have some sort of behavior problem, or he wouldn't have done this. I feel sorry for his parents. And I feel sorry for him, too."

The man at this moment is probably feeling

A. sympathetic,
or
B. embarrassed?

263. Suppose then that the same man thinks, "Let's see; this child appears to have wandered away from his parents. I think I'll stand up and look around to see if I see anyone who might be the child's parent. Maybe I'll quietly ask the people around me if they know where the child came from."

At this moment, the man is more likely to feel

A. cool and calculating,
or
B. very angry?

264. Suppose that while trying to deal with this situation, the man thinks to himself, "I'm doing a very good job of anger control with this situation. Hooray for me!"

At this moment, the man is likely to feel

A. proud,
or
B. scared?

265. A man's son backs into another car in a parking lot. The man's first impulse is to feel very angry. But then the man thinks, "How big is this mistake, compared to some of the ones that I've made in my life? Not very big." What the man thinks probably makes him feel

A. even more anger,

or

B. humility?

266. A woman sits in a college classroom. She hears some other students a couple of rows back, whom she hardly even knows, making insulting comments about how she looks. She turns around and studies them for a few minutes, thinking, "This is very strange. I wonder what is causing them to act this way? Perhaps I can learn from this situation. Maybe, at some point, one of the students would be willing to answer some questions about this."

This student is probably feeling

A. curious,

or

B. happy?

267. A boy is doing some work at school. The teacher asks the students to put their work away and to start something new. But the aide says to the boy, "You're very close to finishing. Please go ahead and finish."

The teacher, who didn't hear the aide, sees the boy and in a very rough tone of voice says, "I said put that away! What's the matter with you, can't you hear me?"
The boy thinks, "It will be better if the aide tells my teacher what went on

rather than if I do. Let me look around a second and see if the aide heard that and see if I can give her an opportunity to explain. If she explains, things will work out better than if I explain it."

With thoughts like this, the boy is probably feeling

A. cool and calculating,

or

B. sleepy?

268. The boy also thinks to himself, "Hooray for me for handling this well so far. At some time in the past, I would've already yelled back at the teacher."

With thoughts like these, the boy is probably feeling

A. proud,

or

B. compassionate?

269. The aide does hear what the teacher has said, and explains to the teacher, "I asked him to go ahead and finish." The teacher says to the boy, "I'm sorry; that was our mistake." The boy says, "That's OK; I've made lots bigger mistakes than that."

With that thought, the boy is probably feeling

A. humility,

or

B. confusion?

270. The six emotions we have focused on in this chapter are certainly not the only alternatives to anger in provocations. In certain circumstances you may want to respond to provocations by feeling amused, relieved, disappointed, or any of a variety of other emotions. However, the six emotions listed in this chapter are usually quite useful, and are often very good substitutes for anger. Here's an exercise to do: take any provocation situation (such as the ones listed near the back of this book). Make up thoughts that would be conducive to each of the six emotions we've talked about in this chapter. In this way, you can practice the thought patterns that lead you to these very useful emotions.

The exercise suggested is to

A. take any provocation, and figure out thoughts that would lead to each of the six emotions discussed in this chapter,
or,
B. take any thought and figure out six different emotions that it could lead to?

271. One of the main ideas of this chapter is that, if there is an emotion more useful to feel than anger, you can help yourself feel that emotion by thinking the thoughts that go along with it. However, choosing your thoughts is not the only way to choose your emotions. If you want to feel a certain way, you can also use the

facial expressions,
bodily gestures,
and tones of voice

that go along with that emotion. In other words, you "act as if" you are feeling that emotion.

One consequence of this idea is that, if you do not want to feel angry, you should not use the facial expressions, bodily gestures, and tones of voice that go along with anger.

So if someone wishes not to feel angry, should that person

A. clench his fists, bite down hard with his jaw muscles, frown, and speak loudly and fast,
or
B. do the opposite of these?

272. Some psychologists did a very interesting experiment. They asked people to change their facial expressions, but their requests to people did not contain any words for emotions. They would say things such as, "Move your eyebrows down," or "Pull the corners of your mouth back." Some people received instructions for a happy face, and others for sad or angry faces. Then the psychologists asked the people to rate their feelings. The people with happy faces actually felt happier

than the people with sad or angry faces. This experiment showed that what we do with our facial expressions can actually affect how we feel.

The scientists found that changing your facial expression

A. can't change your emotions because they're on the inside,
or
B. can change your emotions, because emotions are connected with what your body is doing?

273. Another way of putting the lesson from this experiment and others like it is that. if you want to feel a certain way, act the part.

Speaking of acting, here's a method that some actors use. Suppose that at a certain point in a movie or play, you want to portray a certain emotion; let's use determination as our example. You bring to mind an incident from your own past life in which you felt very determined. This helps you act out determination on the stage. So, if I'm acting the part of a parent who is determined to help his handicapped child learn to walk, I might remember the feeling of determination I had when I took my last chemistry test.

You can use the same method in trying to feel ways other than angry. Recall the times in your life when you have felt determined, curious, cool and

calculating, sympathetic, humble, or proud. You can refer to these incidents when you are practicing handling provocations.

The advice in this section is to

A. remember times in your past life when you felt a certain way, if you want to feel that way now,
or
B. always stay focused only on the present?

Chapter 9: Relaxation

274. When people do things in anger that they later regret, they are usually very excited, or aroused. Their bodies are often releasing a lot of the hormone adrenaline. Pumping lots of adrenaline often makes us less inclined to think carefully. You are usually very excited or "adrenalinized" if your heart is pounding, your hands are sweating, you are breathing faster, you feel a trembling feeling, your muscles are tense and jumpy, and you find yourself wanting to move and talk very fast. If you want to do well in a physical fight, it is probably useful to get yourself into this state. But if you want to make a careful, well reasoned decision, it's usually much easier if you get yourself calm and cool and relaxed.

This section says that the state of high excitement or being "adrenalinized"

A. is never useful,
or
B. is useful for a physical fight but probably not for a careful decision?

275. Scientists have studied how well people perform in various tasks, depending upon how excited or aroused they are. If they graph the results, the curve usually looks like an upside-down U. If you are so relaxed that you're about to fall asleep, your performance in most tasks is not very good. As you get more excited, your performance improves. Then you reach the top of the curve, the place where your performance is best and the excitement is ideal for the task. After that, getting more excited interferes with your performance. The more aroused you get, the worse you do. This upside-down U shaped curve is called the Yerkes-Dodson curve. It's named after some of the researchers who studied it.

This section is about the fact that:

A. As we get more excited, our performance just gets better and better.
or
B. As we get more excited, our performance first improves, and then gets worse.

276. The goal of this chapter is not to help you eliminate excitement, but to help you find the right level of excitement for whatever you are trying to do. If you are trying to win a 100-yard dash, you will probably want to be very excited and to pump lots of adrenaline. If you are trying to use good anger control in a provocation, you will probably want to turn the level of excitement about as far down as you can get it.

Your goal for regulation of your excitement level is to

A. lower your excitement as much as you can at all times,

or

B. try for the best level of excitement for whatever task you are facing?

277. Because a lower level of excitement is so useful in anger control, the rest of this chapter will be about ways of relaxing and turning your level of excitement down.

One of the most important ways of getting relaxed is to make your muscles loose and limp. Have you ever tensed your muscles to "flex" like a bodybuilder? Do you ever clench your fist, or clench your jaws? Muscle tension like this makes your muscles hard. When we get scared or angry, we naturally tend to make our muscles more tense. On the other hand, if we make our muscles soft and loose and relaxed, our brains tend to notice this. Our brains tend to think, "If my muscles are relaxed, that must mean that everything's OK." Relaxing the muscles tends to make us less scared and angry.

The point of this section is that relaxing your muscles

A. is a behavior which has nothing to do with your emotion,

or

B. tends to make you feel less scared or angry?

278. Which muscles of the body are most closely tied to your emotions? For most people, the answer is the muscles of the face. If you want to know how someone is feeling, you naturally look to see what that person is doing with the muscles of his face. Is he smiling, frowning, opening the mouth with surprise, or looking scared? Many people have found that, if they can relax their facial muscles, they can turn down their level of excitement.

This section says that, if you are interested in emotional control, very important muscles are those of the

A. face,

or

B. legs?

279. How do you become an expert at relaxing your muscles? You do not simply say to yourself, "The next time I experience a provocation, I'll try to relax my muscles." Why doesn't this work? Because there's not enough time to remember to do this in the provocation itself. Plus, it takes lots of time to get skilled at the art of muscular relaxation. To become an expert, it's best to practice often. You sit or lie down, and notice how much tension there is in your muscles. You see if you can reduce that tension. Sometimes it's useful to tense the muscle on purpose. Then, as you relax it, you try to keep going as far as you can in the direction of relaxation. You let your attention

roam around your body to various muscle groups and try to relax them one by one.

Learning muscle relaxation is accomplished by

A. just one firm decision,
or
B. lots of practice?

280. There's a useful machine that helps when you are learning muscle relaxation. It is a biofeedback machine that tells you your muscle tension. The word *biofeedback* means that you measure something happening with your body, and you use those measurements to help you control your body better. In the case of muscle tension, you tape little sensors onto your skin over the muscle, and connect the sensors to the machine. The machine tells you how much tension there is in your muscles. You play around with different ways of relaxing the muscles until the reading on the machine is very low. In this way, you get to find out how relaxed your muscles really are.

The biofeedback machine that we are talking about

A. actually relaxes your muscles,
or
B. lets you know how much you've relaxed your muscles?

281. The only problem with machines that measure muscle tension is that they cost a lot. But there is another biofeedback machine that you can buy for only a few dollars that will also give a pretty good measure of how relaxed you are. This machine is a digital thermometer, the type that has a wire on it and a sensor at the end of the wire. Some of these are sold specifically for biofeedback; others are sold for use as indoor and outdoor weather thermometers. In my experience, both types work about equally well.

If you hold the sensor between your fingertips, the thermometer tells you your fingertip temperature. As you become more relaxed, your fingertip temperature tends to go up. This is because, when you relax, the little blood vessels in your hands get bigger, and there's more blood flow to your hands. The heat from the rest of your body can go into your hands more easily. When you are very relaxed, your fingertip temperature can reach as high as 95°F or 35°C. Anytime you are able to raise your fingertip temperature by relaxing, you are practicing taking control of your own degree of arousal.

When you are measuring your relaxation with a thermometer,

A. warmer fingertips mean greater relaxation,
or

B. colder fingertips mean greater relaxation?

282. For some people muscle relaxation is the best way to become less aroused. For others, the best method is imagery. Imagery means your fantasy, or the things you imagine. If you are holding in your mind a picture that you are about to get eaten by a monster or beaten up by a mean person, it is very hard to be relaxed, no matter how much you try to make your muscles limp.

The methods of relaxation we are talking about now involve taking control of the

A. size of your muscles,
or
B. pictures you hold in your mind?

283. Some people find it relaxing to travel, in their fantasy, to relaxing places or events. Which of the following images is most relaxing to you?

a warm beach,

a cabin in the woods, with snow falling around you,

a waterfall,

your own bed, when you wake up in the morning without any responsibilities to take care of,

a cool pool of water in a mountain stream,

drinking water when you are very thirsty,

hearing musicians play a relaxing concert,

watching autumn leaves drift to the ground?

These are images that

A. some people have found useful when practicing relaxation,
or
B. you should always call to mind when you are in a provocation?

284. A very useful image for relaxation, but one that very few people are taught to use, is the image of kind acts between people. When you practice relaxing, at some time please experiment with imagining examples of the following types of kind acts. Imagine someone . . .

helping someone else,

teaching something to someone else in a kind way,

speaking in very kind or friendly tones of voice to someone else,

being a good listener for someone else,

being joyous with someone else,

touching someone else with kindness, respect, and affection.

The images this section recommends are

A. kind acts between people,
or
B. images from nature?

285. Another relaxing image to cultivate is that of a self-nurturing part of yourself. The phrase "self-nurturing" means taking care of yourself, being kind to yourself. Your self-nurturer may say things to you such as, "I want the best for you. I'm on your side. Let's see if we can figure out what will work best. I think it's going to come out OK in the end. You can do it. I'm rooting for you."

Another thing that the self-nurturing part of yourself might say is:

A. "Why did you mess up like that?"
or
B. "It's OK; you will be able to make things better quickly."

286. Another very important part of relaxation imagery is the tones of voice with which you speak to yourself. If you wish to relax yourself, speak to yourself in tones that are

low,
slow,

and soft.

In other words, don't use a fast, loud, and high-pitched voice. Use the opposite.

If you've ever heard a relaxation recording, with instructions on how to relax, it is very likely that the speaker used low, slow, and soft tones. If you speak to yourself in that same way, you help yourself relax.

This section discussed which of the following aspects of your voice?

A. the pitch, tempo, and volume,
or
B. the length, width, and height?

287. Speaking of relaxation recordings, it is often very useful to practice listening to one of these while sitting in a comfortable chair and getting into a dreamy and comfortable state. Some people have found it useful to listen to relaxation recordings while drifting off to sleep at night. Some of the other books in this series include a relaxation script that you can record in your own voice. You can also obtain this from me as an audiotape, recorded in my voice.

This section has to do with the technique of

A. paying attention to your breathing,
or

B. listening to recorded relaxation instructions?

288. Another relaxation technique is becoming aware of the rhythm of your breathing. When we are excited, we tend to breathe faster. When you are relaxing, it will often be useful to get into a slow rhythm of breathing. Slow breathing is also an indicator that you are feeling relaxed; it's sort of like a built-in biofeedback device that you don't have to buy. To use this technique, you simply notice how slowly you breathe when you are feeling very relaxed; at other times when you are relaxing, you try for the state of mind in which you feel like breathing that slowly.

This section has to do with

A. using slow breathing as an aid to relaxation,
or
B. breathing very fast to help yourself relax?

289. Another important technique is called the good will meditation. First you sit and relax yourself, using the techniques we've mentioned so far. Then you think about yourself. You wish for good things to happen for yourself, as follows:

May I become the best I can become.
May I give and receive compassion and kindness.

May I live happily and productively.

As you say each sentence to yourself, you may vividly imagine some image that illustrates that outcome. For example, when you think, "May I give and receive compassion and kindness," you may imagine yourself being a good listener for someone who needs some support, and letting the same person listen to you.

You start the good will meditation by having positive wishes for

A. yourself,
or
B. your worst enemy?

290. After you have wished these things for yourself, you start to imagine other people in your life, one at a time, and you wish the same things:

May she become the best she can become.
May she give and receive compassion and kindness.
May she live happily and productively.

Again, you visualize the outcome. For example, you come around to imagining a person you know who is always cranky and irritated. When you wish, "May he live happily and productively," you may visualize him working cheerfully, whistling to himself.

The next step in this meditation is to wish well for other people,

A. all at the same time,
or
B. one by one?

291. You try to include all the important people in your life sooner or later, including the people you don't like. If there is someone you don't like, you imagine that the person becomes the best he can become, so that you now can like him. You imagine him giving kindness and compassion rather than being mean. You imagine him making a good contribution to people rather than making life miserable.

Maybe these outcomes will never take place. But stranger things have happened in the history of the world! Enemies have been known to become friends. And, even if this never happens, having good wishes for your enemies increases your mental flexibility and your ability to control your own thoughts and emotions.

In the good will meditation, you wish for good to happen to

A. your friends, and bad to happen to your enemies,
or
B. all the people in your life?

292. When you do the good will meditation, you are not trying to magically change other people. You cultivate good wishes for the effect on yourself. Hoping for good outcomes for others, as well as yourself, is a more pleasant way to go through this life than if you are constantly wishing for bad things to happen to all the people who have been mean to you. It is much easier to work out good solutions to problems with other people if you have a basic wish for things to turn out OK for the other person, than if you are wishing for the other person to suffer.

You do the good will meditation

A. because your wishes magically make good things happen for other people,
or
B. because wishing for good outcomes affects your own mind in a good way?

293. Doing the good will meditation about someone does not mean that you can't protect yourself from that person. For example, a woman has been physically abused by a boyfriend. She decides to break off the relationship and never see him again, for self-protection. In her good will meditation, she hopes that he will learn from this experience and become a better person for it. She doesn't count on that outcome enough to risk her own safety! She stays away from him, while wishing the best for him. She realizes that his learning to give and receive compassion and kindness may take a long time or may never occur.

The point of this section is that, when you do the good will meditation about someone,

A. you still protect yourself from that person if you need to,
or
B. you act as if the person has been changed, and the person will change as if by magic?

294. When you become expert at relaxing during practice sessions lasting five to twenty minutes, then you are ready to try very brief relaxation sessions. In these, you take about five seconds out of whatever activity you are doing, and practice relaxing very quickly. Then you go on about your business.

This technique helps you to transfer your relaxation skills to the activities of real life.

This section spoke of "brief relaxation sessions" that take about

A. five seconds,
or
B. fifty minutes?

295. The final step in using relaxation to help you in anger control is to incorporate relaxation into your fantasy rehearsals. At some point during your fantasy rehearsal, you say, "I am relaxing." As you say that, you actually practice relaxing. While doing a fantasy rehearsal of handling a provocation, you relax your muscles and lower your level of arousal. This practice will help you to stay cool in real-life provocations.

This section advises you to

A. practice relaxation for twenty minutes a day,
or
B. do relaxation during fantasy rehearsals of anger control?

Chapter 10: Behaviors To Use in Provocations

296. How well can you think of effective, nonviolent options for dealing with provocations? People who can think, quickly, of a variety of nonviolent options for provocations have been found to function much better in the world than those who cannot. It's up to you to decide what option will work the best in any given situation. But the more familiar you are with different types of nonviolent options, the more likely you are to find one that will work. Gaining such familiarity is the goal of this chapter.

The goal of this chapter is to

A. become familiar with several types of nonviolent options for provocations, or
B. prevent violent options from coming into your mind?

297. Here are the types of behaviors we will consider in this chapter:

Menu of BEHAVIORS:

- Ignoring the person who is provoking you.
- Differential reinforcement.
- Assertion: calmly saying what you want.
- Conflict-resolution: trying to do a "joint decision" conversation.
- Criticism responses: practicing one of several types of responses to criticism.
- Relaxation: using a relaxation technique to calm yourself.
- Rule of law: appealing to an authority to enforce rules. The authority may be a teacher, parent, judge, the United Nations, etc.
- Away from the situation: getting away from the person who is making you angry or angry at you, temporarily or permanently.
- Apologizing or empathizing.
- Friendliness: kindness, cheerfulness, humor.
- Force – of a nonviolent nature.
- Tones of voice: low volume, tempo, and pitch, positive if possible.

A mnemonic using the first letters of these phrases is Ida Craft. The underlined letters are used twice.

The list above is a set of

A. thoughts you can use in provocations, or
B. behaviors you can use in provocations?

122

298. Jim is getting onto a school bus. As he walks down the aisle, a kid he doesn't know giggles and says to him, "Hey, stink bug!" Jim continues to go toward his seat, without giving any sign that he has heard what the other kid has said. When he sits down, he doesn't fret about what the kid said.

The strategy that Jim uses in this situation is

A. nonviolent force,
or
B. ignoring?

299. There are two senses in which ignoring might "work" for Jim. First, if the other kid is trying to get some attention and excitement by provoking Jim, he isn't getting it. Thus Jim is not reinforcing the other kid for his provocation. If the kid is not reinforced in any other way, the kid may not do such provocations anymore. Thus Jim's ignoring might lead the other kid to stop calling Jim names.

There's a second sense in which ignoring might "work." If Jim can really pay no attention to the other kid, then Jim is not bothered by the name-calling - even if it never stops! By ignoring the other kid's behavior, Jim makes it unimportant and not harmful to himself.

The two ways in which ignoring can "work" on provoking behavior are to make that behavior

A. stop, or not bother you, even if it continues,
or
B. get punished, or get listened to?

300. Ignoring makes provoking behavior gradually stop being repeated, if nothing else reinforces the behavior other than your attention.

Mr. Smith keeps a box of garbage bags outside his garage door. When his neighbor, Mr. Jones, needs a bag, he sometimes walks over and helps himself to one of Mr. Smith's bags. Mr. Jones's reinforcer for this behavior is the bag itself, not Mr. Smith's attention.

How likely is it that ignoring would lead Mr. Jones to stop taking the garbage bags?

A. very likely,
or
B. not at all likely?

301. Suppose that Mr. Smith is wealthy enough that losing a garbage bag every now and then is no problem for him. He ignores Mr. Jones's behavior, buys more bags when he needs them, and goes along quite happily. He feels that ignoring has worked quite well for him, even though Mr. Jones still takes a garbage bag every now and then.

In what sense has ignoring "worked" for Mr. Smith?

A. by making Mr. Jones stop his bad behavior,

or

B. by making Mr. Jones's bad behavior not bother Mr. Smith?

302. Mrs. Reynolds adopts a child who has been in a foster home. The foster parent tells Mrs. Reynolds, "I had a horrible time trying to keep this child from putting cinnamon on almost all her food."

Mrs. Reynolds decides to keep a cinnamon shaker on the table along with the salt and pepper. Other than refilling the cinnamon shaker when it gets empty, Mrs. Reynolds ignores the child's use of cinnamon.

Three months later, the child still puts cinnamon on almost all her food, just as much as she did before.

What conclusion do you think Mrs. Reynolds should draw from the fact that the child is still using cinnamon?

A. The child was using cinnamon to get attention.

or

B. The child really likes the taste of cinnamon.

303. Someone asks Mrs. Reynolds whether the strategy of ignoring the child's use of cinnamon has "worked."

Mrs. Reynolds replies, "Yes, it has worked well."

In what sense did the ignoring "work" for Mrs. Reynolds?

A. in the sense of making the ignored behavior gradually disappear,

or

B. in the sense that not concerning herself with this behavior allowed Mrs. Reynolds not to be bothered by it?

304. Differential reinforcement is better than simple ignoring if you want to change behavior. Differential reinforcement means that you ignore the behavior you don't like, but you also reward, or reinforce, the behavior that you do like.

Nancy has a little sister who is in the habit of coming up to her and whining that she is bored. This is annoying to Nancy. Nancy decides to ignore this provocation as much as she can. But Nancy decides also to watch very carefully for the times when her little sister finds a way to amuse herself, for example, by playing with toy people or reading a book or jumping rope. When her sister does things like this, Nancy goes up to her, watches her, speaks cheerfully with her, or plays with her.

Nancy finds that, over time, her sister gradually whines less often and finds fun things to do more often.

The technique that Nancy used to change her sister's behavior is called

A. differential reinforcement,
or
B. nonviolent force?

305. The next type of response to provocations is called assertion. Assertion means calmly asking someone to change their behavior, or calmly refusing to do what someone else asks. Assertion almost always works better than silent anger or loud hostility.

Linda and Tom are married. They go to visit Linda's mother, Alice, who is very bossy. Alice issues nonstop requests and commands from the time they arrive. "Take off your shoes; leave them here; no, not right there - over there. Come in this room. Sit down. Not in that chair." As this continues, Tom grows angrier and angrier. He says nothing.

The way Tom has responded to this provocation so far might be called

A. assertion,
or
B. silent anger?

306. After a while, Tom has had all he can take. He "loses it" and screams at Alice, "Just shut up! You (expletive)!" As a result of this one behavior, his wife (who had also been annoyed by her mother's bossiness) begins to seriously consider divorcing him.

When Tom "lost it," the way he acted might be called

A. assertion,
or
B. loud hostility?

307. Suppose that instead of using silent anger and loud hostility, Tom had used polite assertion. Suppose that he had said to Alice, "Alice, could I ask you a favor please? Could you please try to tell me what to do less often? It would really make me enjoy my visit much more if you could try that."

It's very possible that Alice would be greatly offended by this polite request. There is no guarantee that she would stop being so bossy. But at least there's a chance that the honest request could help her change her behavior in a good way. And even if it doesn't, Tom has maintained his reputation as a reasonable person in the eyes of his wife.

The direct request for a change in behavior modeled in this section is called

A. assertion,
or
B. ignoring?

308. Jane is offered a cigarette at a party. She decides that she would like to respond with assertion.

Which of the following is an example of an assertive response?

A. "Do you think I'm an idiot like you are?"
Or
B. "No, and I'd like to request that, if you smoke, you do it far from me, please, because I don't like breathing smoke."

309. Ted it is trying to sleep because he has to go to work tomorrow morning. His neighbors in the apartment building are playing music so loudly that it is impossible for him to sleep.

What is an example of using assertion in this situation?

A. for him to keep quiet and just clench his teeth and try to sleep anyway,
or
B. to say to them, "I have to get you to turn the music down. I need to work in the morning, and the music is keeping me awake."

310. Suppose that Ted goes back to bed, but within five minutes the music is as loud as it was before.

What is an example of using assertion now?

A. for him to say, "You (expletive)! If you don't turn that down, I'm going to kick your teeth in!"
or
B. to say, "I'm sorry, but the music is still just as loud. If it's not turned way down, I'll be forced to call the building manager or the police."

311. Ron is selling his car, and is asking $5,000 for it. Someone comes to look at it, and says to Ron, "I'll give you $500 for it."

Which of the following is an example of an assertive response?

A. "Get the (expletive) out of here, you (expletive)!"
or
B. "No, that's not anywhere close to a price I would accept."

312. Bill has had a serious drinking problem. He is trying to stop drinking alcohol. His wife, Lisa, asks him to go to a party where lots of alcohol will be served. He explains that he cannot go to places where drinking is going on. She says to him, "Oh, come on; don't spoil my fun; go with me."

Which of the following is an example of an assertive response?

A. "Oh, OK, just this time."
or
B. "No, that would be a really bad decision for me. Could I ask you a

favor? Please don't even ask me to go to parties where everyone is drinking alcohol."

313. Michelle is playing with another girl in the neighborhood named Miriam. Miriam very frequently makes comments such as, "I'm in a more advanced class than you are," or "My dog knows how to do lots more things than yours does," or "I have a much better toy than the one you have." Suppose that Michelle wants to respond to this in an assertive way.

Which of the following is an example of assertion?

A. "Miriam, when you keep saying that you are better than I am or that something of yours is better than mine, it bothers me. Could you please try not to do that so often?"
or
B. to say nothing?

314. Emma has a friend who is nice to her when they play with each other one-on-one. But when they are with a certain other girl named Briana, Emma's friend and Briana ignore Emma and do not include her. Emma is now alone with her friend again. She considers talking with her about this problem.

If Emma wishes to use assertion, which of the following is an example of this?

A. to say nothing, for fear of making her friend mad,
or
B. to say, "I'd like to mention something you do that makes me feel bad. When you and I are with Briana, you ignore me and pay attention only to her. Have you ever noticed this?"

315. Jessica makes comments at a club meeting. Another girl often rolls her eyes and says, in an exasperated tone, "Oh, Jessica!"

What is an example of an assertive response on Jessica's part?

A. "Don't you 'Oh Jessica' me, you little (expletive)!"
or
B. "I don't appreciate the rolling eyes and the tone of voice you use. If you disagree, please just say why."

316. The next option for responding to provocations is called conflict resolution, or joint decision. This means that you try to do several things to solve the problem between you. You try to understand the other person's goals and motives. You try to make your motives and goals known to the other person. You think of various options for solving the problem, together. You weigh the advantages and disadvantages of the various options. You try to find an option that you can both agree on.

There is a lot to learn about this process. Therefore, it will get its own chapter, and we will not deal with it more now.

The process of having a conversation where you define the problem, list options, and choose an option together with another person is called

A. conflict resolution, or joint decision-making,
or
B. relaxation?

317. The next set of responses to provocations has to do with responding to criticism. Criticism is being disapproved of, being insulted, being put down, or even getting some helpful corrective feedback. These are provocations that can best be responded to when you identify them as criticisms and go to your mental list of options for criticism.

Each type of criticism gives you the message, "You are an imperfect person." One of the biggest aids to good response to criticism is accepting from the very beginning that indeed you are an imperfect person. Everyone else is also an imperfect person. The more you can become comfortable with this fact, the more you can rationally decide how to respond to criticism.

Do you want to debate with the critic? Do you want to agree that you are a very imperfect person? Do you want to give the critic silent eye contact? Do you want to make a plan to think more about the problem the critic is raising or implying? We will discuss these and other options more in a separate chapter on responding to criticism.

One of the points made in this section is that:

A. Handling criticism is easier if you accept the fact that we're all imperfect.
or
B. You should never let anyone call you imperfect and get away with it.

318. The next response to a provocation is relaxation. Some people advise counting to ten in provocation situations. If you want to take a few seconds to do something other than think about the problem, I would advise relaxing the muscles and using other relaxation techniques to calm yourself, while going through the four thoughts of the Four-thought Exercise. As we discussed in the previous chapter, getting to the ideal level of arousal for dealing with provocations usually involves turning the level of arousal down. When you fantasy rehearse handling provocations, it's good to practice relaxing while doing so.

In provocations, it's usually useful for you to

A. turn up your level of excitement,
or

B. turn down your level of excitement?

319. The next type of response to provocations is an appeal to the rule of law. The rule of law is one of the greatest inventions of the human race. It was created because people simply cannot solve all the conflicts that they have just by working with one another. Sometimes they have to go to a higher authority to settle the issue.

The rule of law means that we try to decide ahead of time what is just and fair and right, and write down these decisions as rules or laws. Then we try to enforce these decisions, without regard to whether the people involved are pretty or ugly, rich or poor. When people are treated fairly according to such principles, we say that there is *justice*.

Suppose that. when a pretty girl, whom the teacher likes, asks to go to the bathroom, the answer is always yes. On the other hand, when a certain boy, whom the teacher doesn't like, asks to go to the bathroom, the answer is usually no.

In this situation, is the rule of law being used with justice?

A. yes,
or
B. no?

320. Our laws can't possibly cover every situation. Sometimes the best we can do to try to achieve justice is to define someone as an authority whose decision we will accept. For example, Ed's company is dumping something into a river that Frank would like to drink out of downstream. Ed says that the substance is harmless, but Frank thinks it's harmful. They can't agree. The most they can agree on is that they will go to court and abide by whatever the judge decides. But if they agree upon just this much, they will never need to fight each other to settle the question. They have accepted the rule of law.

In the situation we just described, who was the authority?

A. Frank and Ed,
or
B. the judge?

321. Suppose that a kid is being bullied in school. He is being physically pushed around and hit frequently. Assertive responses to the bully do no good. The bully is not at all interested in conflict resolution. This is a prime example of a situation where the rule of law needs to be in effect. Laws and rules exist partly to give power to people in ways that can overcome the power of violence and force.

Which response on the part of the kid getting bullied would be an appeal to the rule of law?

A. to let the bully know exactly how he felt,
or
B. to discuss with parents, teachers, and principal what the school rules are and how they should be enforced?

322. It is usually necessary to "appeal" to the rule of law rather than just sitting back and letting the rule of law intervene. This means that you have to go to the authority figures whose job it is to enforce the rules and insist that they do their job. This also means that you often have to do a lot of work to organize the evidence supporting your case.

This section says that making justice take place is

A. a lot of work,
or
B. something that happens automatically?

323. The next nonviolent response to provocations on our list is moving "away from the situation." This response also takes into account the fact that people are imperfect. If people could always stay cool and calculating and rational, they could simply discuss each conflict until they had solved it. But sometimes the more they talk, the angrier at each other they become. Sometimes the very sight of the other person is enough to make one of them feel huge anger. When any one person feels so angry that he or she is about to get violent, or even so angry that productive conversation is impossible, both people will do well to get away from each other. It's better to take time to cool off than to continue to inflame each other.

Two people are having an argument. One of them is so angry that he knows he doesn't even want to solve the problem with the other. He only wants to punish or hurt the other. What does this section say about the option of his excusing himself and stopping the conversation?

A. This is a cowardly thing to do.
or
B. This is probably a very good idea.

324. When two people are in a relationship, it is good for them to discuss ahead of time the plans for ending a conversation and postponing talk about a subject. Sometimes one person wants to end the conversation, but this only makes the other person more angry. When the first person walks away, the second person follows and keeps talking. This situation sometimes leads to violence. How can we prevent the ill effects of angry arguments? If people can agree ahead of time, before they get angry, that if one

person wants to postpone the conversation, then the other person will respect that decision, much suffering can be prevented.

The point of this section is that:

A. People should agree ahead of time to postpone conversations when either one of them is too angry to talk productively.
or
B. People should agree ahead of time to keep talking until the issue is settled.

325. So far we've been talking about the strategy of getting away from the situation temporarily when either or both of two people become too angry at each other. However, another important part of the "away from the situation" strategy is avoiding a violent or hostile person permanently.

Tina accepts a new job. When she makes a small mistake, her boss grabs her by the shoulders, screams at her, and shoves her. Afterwards, Tina talks with coworkers who tell her that the boss has done worse things than that to other people. Tina leaves in her boss's mailbox a letter quitting the job, and she departs, never to return.

The strategy that Tina has used is called

A. assertion,
or

B. away from the situation, permanently?

326. Sam goes to play with a boy in his neighborhood whom he doesn't know well. They are playing a game together, and when Sam starts to win, the other boy becomes very angry. The boy picks up a small but heavy television set and throws it hard at Sam's head, narrowly missing him. Sam knows right away how badly he could have been hurt if the television had hit his head. Sam heads straight for the front door and walks home, never to return to that boy's house.

The strategy that Sam has used is called

A. away from the situation, permanently,
or
B. relaxation?

327. Many other kids are bullying a seventh grade boy at his school. His teacher seems not to like him, and his principal seems not to take his side. After his parents try without success to negotiate with school staff and parents of other children, they pull him out of the school altogether; he starts getting his education at home by computer courses and gets together only with kids who are nice to him.

The strategy that is used here is called

A. away from the situation, permanently,

or

B. nonviolent force?

328. The next response on the list is apologizing or empathizing. This response may make you curious. We are talking about ways of responding when someone else provokes you. Why should you ever apologize to them, rather than the other way around?

The answer is that many, if not most, of the provocations you will encounter during your life will be from people who are feeling provoked by you. Do you remember in the first chapter when we spoke about a vicious cycle, in which each person punished the other, for punishing him?

Here's an example. Lisa has three friends visiting. Lisa's mother yells to her, "Lisa! Pick up the clothes you left on the bathroom floor, right now!"

For Lisa, getting this command, in a critical tone of voice, while she is with her friends, is a provocation.

What was the provocation for Lisa's mother?

A. Lisa's leaving the clothes on the bathroom floor,

or

B. speaking angrily to Lisa?

329. Suppose that Lisa says to her friends, "Please excuse me for a second." She runs and gets her clothes and puts them in her hamper. She says cheerfully to her mom, "Sorry about the clothes on the floor."

When Lisa says "Sorry about the clothes on the floor," to her mom, this is an example of

A. apologizing,

or

B. assertion?

330. Later, when Lisa's friends are gone, Lisa says to her mom, "Mom, I'm sorry I left my clothes on the bathroom floor. Could I ask you something? When a group of my friends is here, could you please try not to criticize me in front of them all, and at least not in such a harsh tone of voice?"

What Lisa is doing after she says, "Could I ask you something," is called

A. apologizing,

or

B. assertion?

331. This example illustrates that when you apologize, you don't give up your right to be assertive. You aren't saying that you are a thoroughly bad person. You aren't saying that everything is your fault and none of it is the other person's fault. You can still ask the other person to change in some way.

The main point of this section is that:

A. You shouldn't apologize unless you want the other person to get the upper hand.
or
B. Apologizing doesn't take away your ability to stick up for yourself and be assertive.

332. Suppose that Lisa's mother says to her, "I'm sorry I embarrassed you in front of your friends. Next time, I'll try to say things like that to you privately."

What Lisa's mother is doing now is called

A. apologizing,
or
B. assertion?

333. Suppose that Lisa's mother continues, "But I would like to ask that you pick things up and put them away, especially when guests are coming over to the house. I very much dislike it when guests see things lying around on the floor."

What Lisa's mother is doing now is called

A. apologizing,
or
B. assertion?

334. Lisa says, "I understand. It especially bothers you when guests see things lying around where they shouldn't be."

What Lisa is doing now is not apologizing, but she is accomplishing much of the same purpose. She is letting her mother know that she understands, or empathizes with her. She is giving her mother the message that she doesn't want to fight about this.

Do you think that if Lisa's mother feels that her own wishes are understood and taken seriously, she will be

A. more likely to do what Lisa has asked her,
or
B. less likely to do what Lisa has asked her?

335. Mrs. Brown has asked Mr. Brown to go to a concert with her, and Mr. Brown has said that he would rather not. Mrs. Brown whimpers, in a very hurt and angry tone of voice, "You never do what I want. You only want to do what YOU want!"

Mr. Brown says, "I'm sorry that my not wanting to go to this concert makes you feel very bad."

What Mr. Brown just said is an example of

A. apologizing or empathizing,

or
B. the rule of law?

336. Mr. Brown says, "Can we think of some more options? You could get someone else to go with you. Or, if you want to do something with me that night, we could look for things that both of us will enjoy."

Do you think that the apologizing or empathizing Mr. Brown did earlier will let Mrs. Brown be

A. more open to options such as the ones he's just named,
or
B. less open to options such as the ones he's just named?

337. Another option for responding to provocations is friendliness, kindness, or humor. This option is to "do good to those who provoke you."

A person goes to see a therapist because of some problems. On the first visit, the person says to the therapist, "I don't think you can help me. I'm not even convinced that any of you therapists know what you're doing. Sometimes I think you're all a bunch of quacks."

The therapist replies, "I imagine it's hard for you to come and work with me, when you can't trust that it's going to do any good. It's true that although many people are helped, there are some that we can't get better. I very much

hope you're one of the ones who will be much happier as a result of this."

The person was insulting to the therapist; the therapist responded by

A. debating with the person who was insulting,
or
B. being kind to the person who was insulting?

338. Emma and Mary are playing together. Mary says, "I'll bet I can jump rope many more times than you!"

Emma gets the urge to say, "So what? That doesn't make you better than me."

But then Emma says, "Oh, have you been practicing jumping rope? If you have, I'll bet you've been getting into really good shape, because jumping is great exercise!"

Which was an example of responding to a provocation by being friendly or kind?

A. the thing that Emma got the urge to say,
or
B. the thing that Emma actually said?

339. Lee is playing with a puzzle that Pat owns. When Lee tries to solve the puzzle, and fails, Lee says, "This is a stupid puzzle!"

Pat gets the urge to say, "There's nothing wrong with that puzzle, and I wish you wouldn't insult my things."

But then Pat thinks about the fact that Lee is probably feeling embarrassed that he couldn't get the puzzle. Pat feels a little sorry for Lee. Pat says, "I couldn't solve that puzzle either, without someone showing me how. It's a really hard one."

Lee says, "Would you show me how?"

Pat says, "Sure!"

Why was it kind of Pat to say that the puzzle was hard?

A. It helped Lee not to feel so embarrassed about not being able to solve it.
or
B. It gave Lee the clue he needed about how to solve it.

340. A woman is at a party. A four-year-old child says to her, "Wow, you look like a really OLD lady!" The woman is at first offended, and gets the urge to say, "Who asked you?" in a mean tone of voice. But instead the woman decides to have fun with the child, and says, in a very dramatic tone of voice, "Yeah! But do you know what's going to happen tomorrow? I'm going to be EVEN OLDER! Can you believe it?" One of her friends who is listening to this thinks this is funny, and the two of them laugh together.

The woman responded to the child's provocation with

A. humor,
or
B. assertion?

341. The next option for responding to provocations is the use of force. But the type of force that I am referring to here is not that which is aimed at hurting the other person, but rather moving the other person or keeping the other person from moving.

Suppose that a person is very drunk and also has a very bad anger control problem. Suppose that this person is throwing things and hitting out at people and is dangerous. An example of violent force would be to hit the person in the head and knock him unconscious. An example of nonviolent force would occur if several people get a bed mattress and force the person up against a wall with the mattress. Then the people get the person's arms and legs and bind them together with handcuffs. Then the people take the man to a place where he can be locked up for a while and where his drug intoxication can be treated if necessary.

The meaning of nonviolent force is to

A. hurt the other person, but only in self-defense,

or

B. simply move the other person's body, without trying to hurt the other person?

342. A six-year-old boy goes into a rage and starts hitting his younger sister. His parent takes his arms, crosses them in front of his chest, and holds him in the corner so that he can't move. (The parent is very careful not to put too much pressure on the child's chest, so as not to interfere with his breathing.) When he calms down, he is released.

This is another example of

A. assertion,

or

B. nonviolent force?

343. The last option we'll list for responding to provocations has to do with tones of voice. When people become very angry at each other, they tend to speak faster, louder, and with higher pitch. Conversely, if you want to keep yourself and the other person calm, try to speak slowly, softly, and with a low pitch. These are the tones of voice that tell yourself and the other person, "Stay cool. Be rational. Don't get too upset."

The type of speech that is being recommended is

A. slow, quiet, and low in pitch,

or

B. fast, loud, and high in pitch?

344. One man parks close to another man's car in a parking lot. The man who was there first says to the second man, "I don't know what the (expletive) you think you're doing, you (expletive)!"

The other man considers two ways of reacting. In the first, he screams at the other man, in a high-pitched voice, "Don't you talk to me like that!"

The second option is to stand and look at the two cars for a few seconds, and then to say slowly, quietly, and in a low tone of voice, "I sure don't like it when people talk to me like that."

Which response will make it less likely that the two men will get into a fight and hurt each other?

A. the first,

or

B. the second?

345. In addition to using tones of voice that are low and slow and soft, often a tremendous difference is made if those tones can be positive and enthusiastic.

A mom has given her kids a meal. The kids get up to play without cleaning up first. The mom gets the urge to say, in a harsh tone of voice, "Where do you

think you're going! Get back in here
and wash these dishes!" Instead she
says, in a pleasant and enthusiastic tone
of voice, "Hey kids, I need your help
with something before you go to play.
It's some dish work!"

Which way of speaking do you think
will make fewer provocations come up
in the future between family members?

A. what she got the urge to say,
or
B. what she actually said?

Chapter 11: Guidelines for Conflict-Resolution Conversations

346. A conflict situation is one in which people have wants or wishes that appear to be incompatible. If two or more people can each get what they want, their wishes are *compatible*. If one person's getting what he wants means that the second can't get what she wants, their wishes are *incompatible*.

For example, one person wants to play music loudly; the other person wants to sleep. If these two people live far away from each other, these wants are compatible. But if they live in apartments next door to each other that don't have good sound insulation, their wants seem incompatible.

As another example, one person wants to spend money on pretty things, whereas the other person wants to give money to charities that help prevent war. If these two people don't even know each other, they each do what they want and there's no conflict. However, if they are in the same family and are sharing their money, buying an expensive rug may mean that they can give less money to the War Prevention Charity.

Conflict exists whenever two people

A. want different things,
or
B. have seemingly incompatible wants?

347. You will notice that we are talking about wants that *seem* to be incompatible, not wants that are definitely and eternally incompatible. There is a story about two people who both wanted the only orange left in the house. It appeared that their wishes were incompatible. However, when they spoke with each other, they found out that the first person wanted to eat the orange and throw the peel away. The second person turned out only to be interested in the peel: she needed grated orange peel to flavor a cake. The wishes that seemed to be incompatible turned out to be totally compatible.

In this situation,

A. the two people's wishes were incompatible,
or
B. the two people's wishes turned out to be compatible?

348. Here's another example. Two young children see a ball, and both of them want to play with it. At first it appears that their wishes are

138

incompatible. Each child thinks, "I want to have the ball in my hands, and I can't do that if the other kid has it." But they are lucky enough to be able to think about the situation more, and they realize that simply holding the ball is not much fun. They may realize that they can have a lot more fun throwing the ball back and forth to each other. By discovering that they want to throw the ball back and forth even more than they want to hold the ball, they have discovered compatible wants, or a way that they can both get what they want.

This story has a happy ending because the children discovered

A. a way that they could both get what they want,
or
B. that their wants were incompatible?

349. A husband and wife get a chance to spend an evening doing something fun together. She mentions a movie that he has no interest in. He prefers a different movie, that she would hate. It appears that their wants are incompatible. If they were to get into an angry argument about which movie to go to, it would appear to both of them that their wishes are incompatible. However, they are lucky enough to be able to think and talk about the situation without getting angry. One of them mentions going dancing. It turns out that both of them would rather go dancing than to see either movie. They

have discovered that their seemingly incompatible wishes were very compatible.

This story, as well as the two previous ones, illustrates that

A. wishes that seem incompatible are sometimes compatible,
or
B. disagreements never really get solved?

350. The process by which people turn seemingly incompatible wishes into compatible wishes is called conflict resolution. Through conflict resolution, you find ways that people can be happy without having to fight each other and defeat each other.

Finding ways to turn seemingly incompatible wishes into compatible wishes is called

A. compatibilization,
or
B. conflict resolution?

351. One type of option for conflict resolution is called a compromise. In a compromise, each person gives up some of what she wants so that they can make the deal work.

For example, one person would ideally like to sell a house for $100,000, and the other wants to buy the same house for $90,000. It turns out that they can both be reasonably happy with a sale price of $95,000. They compromise on that price.

For another example, two people go for a walk together. One wants to walk fast, and the other wants to walk slowly. They compromise on a walking speed that is somewhere in the middle. It's a little slower than one would prefer and a little faster than the other would prefer, but it's acceptable to them both.

When each person gives up some of what he or she wants in order to make a deal work, this is called a

A. compromise,
or
B. differential reinforcement?

352. Sometimes people can find even better options than compromises. Let's think about the two people who liked to go walking with each other but at different speeds. The one who likes to go faster is restless from having had to sit around all afternoon. She wants to get some exercise. The one who wants to go slow has already been getting lots of exercise from his work. He just wants to take in the evening breeze and see the sunset. They figure out an option that is even better than a compromise. She will go out running by herself, and get the exercise she needs. Then he will join her as she walks around the block to cool down. By this time she will be tired enough to want to walk more slowly.

This story illustrates that:

A. Sometimes people can find options that resolve conflict without having to compromise.
or
B. Whenever there is conflict, people should compromise.

353. When there is conflict, people tend to think in terms of who will win and who will lose. If the conflict ends up with one winner and one loser, we call that a "win-lose solution." But if the people can be creative enough to figure out a way in which both people end up happy, that is called a "win-win solution."

A woman is very concerned about animal rights and would the whole family to be vegetarian. Suppose that. when her husband thinks about vegetarian food, he thinks about lima beans and celery and okra and a few other vegetables that he doesn't like. Suppose he refuses to be vegetarian, and says, "You can't make me." In this case he wins, and she loses.

Suppose she were to say, "This is important enough to me that I'm going to leave you if you don't become vegetarian."

Suppose he were to say, "Oh, I can't believe this. Oh, OK, you win. I'll be vegetarian rather than get divorced over something so stupid." He would resent being on the losing end of the solution.

The solutions to this problem we have mentioned so far are all

A. win-win solutions,
or
B. win-lose solutions?

354. But suppose that. instead of using any of the win-lose solutions we have mentioned so far, this man and woman can think of several creative options. They try out the option that the woman will do some reading and research to figure out how to buy and make vegetarian food that tastes really good. Her husband decides to get into this venture also. Together, they find a many vegetarian foods that he likes even better than meat. She enjoys doing this research and she enjoys doing some extra work to prepare the food. He ends up happier than before, and so does she.

The solution that they came up with was a

A. win-win solution,
or
B. win-lose solution?

355. The skill of finding and agreeing upon good options for the resolution of conflict is one of the most important skills that people can have. Every day, people kill each other because of poor conflict-resolution skills. Every day, people make themselves miserable with their own family members because of poor conflict-resolution skills, when they could be having fun. The skill of conflict resolution may well determine whether the human race survives or extinguishes itself.

The author feels that the skill of conflict resolution

A. is of very high importance,
or
B. is not as important as the other skills discussed in this section?

356. In a chapter on motives, we mentioned the motive of problem-solving. The "problem" is to find the best solution to the conflict between people, the option that will make people happiest in the long run.

We also mentioned the motives of dominance and revenge. These are the motives to defeat the other person or to get back at the other person.

Which motive do you think leads to the best conflict resolution?

A. problem-solving,
or
B. dominance and revenge?

357. When two people start talking about a problem, they sometimes start out with the goal of problem-solving. But they get offended. They get angrier and angrier. At some point, they cross over a line and start trying to defeat the other person and punish the other person. If they are angry enough, they move into a zone where they don't even want to solve the problem. They would reject a solution to the problem, because now their overriding goal is defeating and hurting the other person. If this happens to both people, and if they are both accustomed to physical violence, these can be the conditions for a fight to the death. If they are not violent types, these feelings can lead to permanent separation.

The "line" that the author speaks of crossing over is

A. an actual line keeping the two people physically separated from one another,
or
B. an imaginary line that separates the goal of problem-solving from the goals of dominance and revenge?

358. How can people keep themselves oriented toward problem-solving, and not find themselves striving for dominance and revenge? How can they stay cool and calculating, and not find themselves overcome with anger?

Here is one way to achieve these goals: first, study carefully some guidelines on conflict resolution; second, practice repeatedly having conflict-resolution conversations, about all sorts of hypothetical conflicts, that follow these guidelines.

An activity the author is suggesting is to

A. practice good conflict-resolution conversations over and over,
or
B. be sure to express your anger whenever you have it?

359. Here are the seven guidelines for conflict-resolution conversations:

Guidelines for Conflict Resolution

1. Defining. Each person defines the problem from his or her point of view, without blaming, and without telling what the solution should be.
2. Reflecting. Each person reflects (or paraphrases the other's point of view) to let the other person know he understands.
3. Listing. They list at least four options.
4. Waiting. They don't criticize the other's options till they've finished listing.
5. Advantages. They think and talk about the advantages and disadvantages of the best options.
6. Agreeing. They pick an option (or set of options) to try.

7. Politeness. They don't raise their voices or put each other down or interrupt.

Mnemonic: Dr. L.W. Aap

The seven guidelines on this checklist are

A. types of conflict,
or
B. ways of talking when trying to resolve conflict?

360. Let's illustrate these guidelines with a conversation between two brothers, Michael and Ray.

Defining (by Ray):

Ray: Michael, can we talk about a problem? The problem is that I like to have privacy in my room, and you're in the habit of coming into my room without knocking.

Reflecting (by Michael):

Michael: So you are saying that there are times when you would like to be by yourself, and I break your privacy by walking into your room without knocking.

Ray: Yes.

Defining (by Michael):

Michael: When I want to tell you something or do something together, it hardly ever occurs to me that you would like to be alone. I just don't tend to think about that.

Reflecting: (by Ray)

Ray: So you're not in the habit of thinking about the issue of privacy.

Michael: That's right.

* * *

If Michael had said, "You're so rude barging into my room; you stay out of my room unless you're invited!" would that have followed the guideline on defining?

A. yes,
or
B. no?

361. The conversation continues.

Listing and Waiting:

Michael: One option is that we could get a lock so that you can lock the door of your room from the inside when you want to be alone.

Ray: Or, you could get into the habit of knocking before coming in when my door is closed.

Michael: Or, you could put a sign up on the door when you don't want to be disturbed.

Ray: Or, I could put a sign on the doorknob rather than on the door.

Michael: That sounds like enough options to me, does it to you?

Ray: Yes.

* * *

The guideline that refers to "waiting" is referring to

A. waiting until you're finished listing options before talking about how good the options are,
or
B. waiting until the reflections are done before starting to list options?

362. The conversation continues:

Advantages and Disadvantages:

Ray: The disadvantage of getting a lock is that it would take some money and some time to install it. The advantage is that it would solve the problem.

Michael: Another disadvantage is that you may not want to be locked inside your room if there's some emergency. But they make locks that you can get into by sticking any long thin thing into a hole in the doorknob. So that disadvantage could be overcome.

Ray: The advantage of my putting a "Do Not Disturb" sign on the doorknob is that it would be hard to miss it, and we wouldn't have to mess with a lock for the door.

Michael: My guess is that I would notice it and stay out whenever you want me to.

Agreeing:

Ray: Do you want to try the sign on the doorknob option, and see how it works, and maybe go to the door-locking option if it doesn't?

Michael: Sounds like a good plan to me. Let's go for it.

Politeness:

(They have been polite to each other throughout this conversation.)

* * *

It appears that politeness is

A. a step you do after you have finished with agreeing,
or
B. something you do throughout the whole conversation?

363. Let's think about why each of the seven guidelines is useful.

You define the problem without blaming the other person so that you can help the other person stay in the problem-solving orientation and not get into the dominance and revenge orientation. You define the problem without telling what the solution should be so that both people can think of several possible solutions.

Each person reflects, or says back, what he or she heard of the other person's point of view on the problem, so that each person can know that the other has listened to him or her. Also, if there are misunderstandings, these can be cleared up.

The people list several options so they can have a better chance of thinking of the option that will work out the best.

They wait until they are finished listing before criticizing options so they won't get sidetracked from thinking of as many good options as they can. If they get into arguing about one option, they can overlook other options that may solve the problem much more easily.

They talk about advantages and disadvantages of the options, rather than about the good and bad points of the other person. This keeps their attention focused on finding the best solution rather than attacking each other or defending themselves.

They agree on something, in order to stay in the cooperative frame of mind, and because finding an option they can both agree on is the whole point of the conversation. When they are not ready to agree on any substantive solution to the problem, at least they can agree to talk more about it at a certain later time, or to get more information about it, or to think about it some more.

They are polite to each other throughout the conversation in order to avoid the struggle for dominance and revenge and avoid triggering a degree of anger that would interfere with their goals.

The point of almost all the guidelines is to

A. help people think about solving the problem, without getting angry enough to seek dominance and revenge,
or
B. help people get all their feelings out so that no bad feelings are left inside them?

364. Let's look at another conversation that gives examples of these guidelines.

Boy: Dad, I wanted talk with you about something. I'm very interested in doing well in sports. But I get the feeling that you don't put much value on sports, and that you wish I would spend more time on school work.

Dad: So if I understand you, you are saying that you don't think I value your sports accomplishments as much as you would like me to, and I'm more interested in your doing well in school work?

Boy: That's right.

Dad: My point of view is that you understand my feelings on sports and schoolwork very well. I think that sports are largely a waste of time. I think that the energy and effort put into them would be better off going toward activities that make the world better. Schoolwork prepares you for jobs where you can make the world better.

Boy: So if I understand you right, you think sports are pretty much a waste of time and you wish people would do things that make the world better instead.

Dad: That's right.

* * *

Which guidelines have they followed so far?

A. They have both defined the problem and they have both reflected the other person's point of view.
or

B. They have listed options and they have agreed on something.

365. To continue the conversation:

Dad: Well, I guess one option is that you could do however much sports you want and not worry about what I think about it.

Boy: Another option is that we could talk more about the value of different activities and explore the question together.

Dad: An option along those lines is that we could try to read and do research and find out what activities really do make the world a better place.

Boy: We could also read and do research about the value of sports and about the advantages and disadvantages of them.

Dad: Sounds like some good options to me. Shall we discuss advantages and disadvantages?

Boy: Yes.

* * *

In this part of the conversation, they have

A. listed some options, while waiting to discuss the advantages and disadvantages of them,

or

B. done reflections to make sure they understood the other?

366. To continue the conversation:

Dad: I really like the idea of our working together on the question of what activities are most worthwhile. And I think the idea of reading and researching the question is a great idea.

Boy: I think so too. I don't think we should choose the first option. The disadvantage of that one is that we are sort of agreeing to disagree without either of us learning anything from it, whereas with the other three I can learn some things and maybe you can too.

Dad: That sounds good to me. Let's start reading and talking and exploring about the question of what activities are most worthwhile, and the advantages and disadvantages of sports, right away.

Boy: Sounds good to me!

* * *

In this part of the conversation, they

A. talked about advantages and disadvantages, and agreed on something,
or
B. listed options?

367. The last problem was an "abstract" one that dealt mainly with how people felt about each other and how they acted toward each other rather than with some very concrete solutions. They worked on the problem of whether they should talk with each other or leave each other alone about the question of sports activities, and not the more concrete question of which sports the boy should or shouldn't do.

Let's give an example of a much more concrete conversation between two young brothers, one where they can still follow the seven guidelines.

Tom: I think that's my shirt you're starting to put on.

Nick: You think this is yours?

Tom: Yes.

Nick: I thought it was mine. It was in my drawer.

Tom: It was in your drawer, so you thought it was yours, huh?

Nick: Yes. We could ask mom whose it is.

Tom: We could share it, and take turns wearing it. You could put it in my hamper when you're done.

Nick: I could just give it to you and wear another one.

Tom: Or I could let you have it if you like it a lot.

Nick: Want to think about what's best?

Tom: Yes. I like the idea of us both sharing it.

Nick: I like that too. That way we both get to wear it. Let's do that.

Tom: OK. Want to put it in my hamper when you're done with it?

Nick: Yep.

Tom: Sounds good.

* * *

When Tom said, "It was in your drawer, so you thought it was yours, huh?" that was an example of

A. listing an option,
or
B. a reflection?

368. There's a very important reason for studying these examples of conversations that use the seven guidelines: you prepare yourself for an exercise in which you make up conversations that meet these guidelines. For people who are serious about learning conflict resolution, I recommend that you do this exercise every day.

There are several ways to do the exercise. You can pick a pretend conflict and role-play it with someone else. You can pick a conflict and play both parts of it, speaking the words of each character out loud. You can pick a conflict and make up both parts of it, writing down what each character says. You can have both characters meet all seven guidelines. Or, you can have one character do an excellent job with the guidelines despite the fact that the other character, like most people in real life, does not follow the guidelines. There are lots of imaginary conflicts listed in the appendices to this book.

What do you imagine is the goal of this exercise?

A. to strengthen your habit of approaching conflict resolution in a calm and rational way,
or
B. to be very familiar with how people do a bad job of conflict resolution in real life?

369. People sometimes say, "People don't talk like this in real life." But the more you do the exercise of following the seven guidelines, the closer your real-life conversations will approach this ideal. The more of these guidelines you can actually carry out in real life, the more likely it will be that your conversations actually solve the

problem rather than make people angry
at each other.

The author believes that these seven
guidelines

A. are useful as an exercise, but not in
real life,
or
B. are very helpful in real-life
conversations as well as for practice
exercises?

Chapter 12: Responding to Criticism

370. "You're a dork." "Would you please try to sing on pitch?" "Your idea would never work." "If you keep on being so lazy, you'll never succeed." "You need to make your opening paragraph more interesting." "Your dive got a rating of 4 on a scale of 10." "You told me you would be home at 11:00 p.m., and you're arriving home past midnight." "You keep on talking, without listening!" "Mathematics isn't your strongest subject." "Fatty, fatty, two by four, can't get through the kitchen door."

These are all examples of criticism or disapproval. Dealing with criticism is a major challenge for most human beings.

All the critical messages listed above have in common that they are saying,

A. "There's something wrong with you or with what you did,"
or
B. "You are lazy."

371. People almost always wish to think of themselves as good, smart, competent, attractive, powerful, and likable. As a general rule, when people hear criticism, they tend to become angry. Most people do not like getting messages from anyone that they are imperfect in any way. Much of the time, people do not appreciate getting suggestions that they change their behavior in any way. It's human to prefer a fairly constant diet of admiration and praise from our fellow human beings.

The author feels that:

A. Everyone craves lots of constructive criticism so that they can improve themselves.
or
B. Almost everyone prefers to be admired than to be criticized.

372. As you go through your life, you will hear many criticisms. How do you want to respond to them? Many people are devastated by criticism. They go off by themselves and feel very depressed.

Other people, or the same people at other times, become very aggressive when they're criticized. They aim toward the goals of revenge, dominance, and punishment, and counterattack the other person as forcefully as possible.

But great depression and great anger are not usually useful ways of responding to criticism. Perhaps you're not surprised that this book advises a calm, rational approach to criticism. It advises that you think carefully about what option will be the response that makes things turn out best.

A way of summarizing what the author has just said is that:

A. When you are criticized, all emotions are good, including devastating depression and raging anger.
or
B. When you are criticized, carefully consider what response will make things come out best.

373. Before considering the *behaviors* you might use to respond to criticism, let's review the *thoughts*. People who feel devastated by criticism often respond by getting down on themselves.

For example: Timothy gives a book report at school in which he acts out a scene in a very dramatic way, playing both parts. Most people find his book report entertaining and enlightening. However, one classmate who is jealous of his ability says to him, "You made a fool of yourself up there."

Suppose Timothy were to think, "I acted like an idiot. I don't have enough sense to know when I should take a risk or play it safe. I'm not going to have any friends." Suppose that then he feels devastated and depressed. He would

feel this way because of the "getting down on himself" thoughts that filled his mind.

In this example, feeling devastated and depressed by criticism was the result of thoughts that we can call

A. learning from the experience,
or
B. getting down on yourself?

374. On the other hand, suppose that Timothy had thought to himself, "He has no right to speak to me like that! He is a terrible person!" Thoughts of this nature would probably lead Timothy to feel great anger rather than great depression.

Thoughts of this nature are called

A. blaming someone else,
or
B. listing options and choosing?

375. Another type of thought usually lies behind the response of great depression or great anger. Sometimes this thought doesn't get put into words. But if it were put into words, it would go something like this: "This is terrible that someone doesn't like what I did. This has set me back tremendously. I can't stand this!" We don't usually feel very bad unless we think that something very bad has happened or is likely to happen.

The type of thought we looked at in this section is called

A. awfulizing,
or
B. celebrating your own choice?

376. The opposite of awfulizing about criticism involves realizing that every human being, including ourselves, is imperfect. People are not going to like everything we do; let's get used to it!

Sometimes the criticism will be totally due to the other person's imperfection. The other person may criticize us out of jealousy, irritability, or mean-spiritedness. Sometimes the criticism will be totally due to our own imperfection. We will do something so obnoxious or incompetent that we invite criticism and disapproval. And sometimes the criticism results from a mixture of the other person's imperfection and our own.

But in any case, it's useful to think, "This isn't the first time anyone has been criticized, and it won't be the last. It's not the end of the world. I can handle it."

The thought you have just read is an example of

A. not awfulizing,
or
B. celebrating someone else's choice?

377. When criticism is constructive, we can often learn something useful from it. For example: Dawn's guitar instructor says to her, "Your left hand is not in the right position. You need to put your thumb on the back of the guitar neck, and not drape it over the fretboard. That way you'll be able to reach farther with your fingers."

Suppose Dawn thinks to herself, "I learned something from this. If my thumb goes here, I can reach farther."

What type of thought is Dawn thinking in response to the constructive criticism?

A. blaming someone else,
or
B. learning from the experience?

378. Even when criticism is totally nonconstructive, we can usually learn something from the experience, even if that learning simply takes the form of practicing handling nonconstructive criticism.

Suppose that Dawn gets onto the school bus, and a kid says to her, "Hey, poop-face!"

Dawn thinks to herself, "I have a chance to practice handling nonconstructive criticism. I'm practicing not letting it bother me. Each time I practice doing that well, I'm learning something important."

The type of thought that Dawn is saying to herself in this situation is

A. learning from the experience,
or
B. getting down on herself?

379. The thought pattern of goal-setting is particularly useful in dealing with criticism. Imagine that Jake is walking down the hall at school, and a kid he hardly knows insults him. He thinks of hitting the other kid, telling a teacher, getting friends to help intimidate the other kid, and so forth. But then he realizes that these are all options aimed at the goal of punishing the other kid, at improving the other kid's behavior. When Jake thinks more about his goal, he decides that it is not his job to improve the other kid's behavior. He decides that his goal is simply not to let the insult bother him. Now he thinks of different options: reminding himself that he wasn't harmed, thinking that the other kid has a problem, feeling sorry for the other kid for getting such bad social skills, reminding himself to be thankful for the friends he has, or concentrating on his next class and forgetting about the whole incident.

When Jake thought about this criticism more, he decided that his goal should have to do with

A. changing the other kid's behavior,
or

B. choosing his own reaction to the insult?

380. Once you have decided upon a goal, listing options and choosing among them is crucial in deciding how best you can reach that goal.

Rachel is wearing a belt that her father made for her. A friend of hers says, "That belt looks really weird."

Rachel thinks, "I could ignore that. Or I could say, 'What's weird about it?' Or I could say, 'Maybe so, but my dad made it for me, and I love it.'"

Rachel's thought pattern is called

A. listing options and choosing,
or
B. getting down on yourself?

381. Often it is useful to take your time in real life and to spend time listing options and choosing before you respond to a criticism. At other times in real life, you will not have time to list several options and to think carefully about the advantages and disadvantages of each of them before responding.

However, you do have time for such careful thought when you are planning fantasy rehearsals. You can take your time in deciding what response you like best. Then you can practice, through fantasy rehearsal, that type of response. When the real-life situation comes up, you will be more likely to land on one of the responses you've practiced in fantasy rehearsal.

The author is advising you to take advantage of the circumstance in which you have lots of time to list options and choose among them. This circumstance is

A. a real-life incident,
or
B. a session of fantasy rehearsal?

382. The rest of this chapter will explore some more behavioral options for response to criticism.

Almost every criticism is also a provocation. So, when we are thinking of ways to respond to criticism, the entire list of ways of responding to provocations is useful for us to remember. We can respond with ignoring, differential reinforcement, assertion, conflict resolution, rule of law, relaxation, going away from the situation, apologizing, friendliness and humor, force that is nonviolent, and tones of voice that are low, slow, and soft.

This chapter goes over several other options that are particularly relevant to criticism.

One of the points made by this section is that:

A. All the options we have studied before, for responding to provocations, are also relevant to criticism.
or
B. Criticism is a totally different type of provocation and none of the options we studied before are useful for it.

383. Let's consider the following ways of responding to criticism:

Ways of Responding to Criticism

1. "Thank you"
2. Planning to ponder or problem-solve
3. Agreeing with part of criticism
4. Asking for more specific criticism
5. Reflection
6. I-want statement
7. Silent eye contact
8. Explanation or debate, done rationally
9. Criticizing the critic

The options in this list are ways of

A. feeling, when you are criticized,
or
B. behaving, when you are criticized?

384. Why would I list the number one response as "Thank you?" I'm not referring to a sarcastic thank you, as in "Gee, thanks a lot; coming from you that's a compliment!" I'm referring to the fact that some criticism is actually constructive; someone gives it to help us! When someone is really trying to help, we need not to see that person as

an adversary to be countered somehow, but as someone on our side. It's appropriate to thank the person sincerely for the help.

The author suggests a "Thank you" in response to criticism because

A. it throws the critic off guard and reduces the power of his attack,
or
B. it is actually often the right and logical thing to do when the critic is trying to be helpful?

385. A teacher says to a student, "If you want to get a good grade on your essays, you are going to have to learn to spell better. You can write great ideas, but if you're misspelling easy words, the grader will mark you down. I think the best way to do this is to take a book of spelling words and start from the beginning and memorize them, and test yourself very often."

Which of the following is an example of the type of response to criticism we have just listed?

A. So, if I understand you right, I need to spend a good bit of time learning to spell better, huh?
or
B. Thanks for that good advice.

386. A track coach watches an athlete run a race. The coach says, "Man, you're not pacing yourself right. You're going for the glory of being out in front in the first half of the race. You want all the girls to be able to see you ahead of everybody else! But you can't keep up that pace, and you burn out at the end – my grandmother could have beaten you in those last 50 meters. You need to get that stopwatch and plan out the times for each part of the race, and stick to your plan!"

Now the athlete has a choice. Should he take offense at the insulting parts of this criticism, or feel grateful for the helpful parts? It is usually wisest to ignore the insulting parts and pay attention to whatever is helpful.

If the athlete wants to follow the advice in this section, he would say something like,

A. Excuse me, but I wasn't trying to show off for girls. How do you know what's going on in my head?
or
B. OK, thanks for that advice. I'll do it.

387. Here's an example of planning to ponder or problem-solve. David is rushing out the door for school. David's mother says to him, "David, you're leaving the kitchen and your own room in a mess again. This has to come to a stop."

David says, "OK, let me think about that one some. Maybe we can talk about some solutions tonight. Bye-bye, Mom."

Planning to ponder means saying, "This criticism is something I should think about, and I will." Planning to problem-solve means, "This problem is something we should talk about, and I'm willing to." But as the situation illustrates, often there isn't time right at the moment. Also, at the moment, people are sometimes too angry to do the best job of problem-solving. So sometimes making a plan to do some careful and unrushed thinking and talking is the response that best leads to a rational approach to the problem.

Which of the following is an example of planning to ponder or problem-solve?

A. "I would like to think about that criticism, and talk with you more about it later on,"
or
B. "You are only making that criticism because of your own jealousy."

388. Here's an example of agreeing with part of criticism. Randy says to Tony, "That's a junky-looking coat you're wearing."

Tony replies, in a cheerful, self-confident voice, "You're probably right. I guess to a lot of people it's probably junky looking."

In this example, Tony's cheerful way of agreeing with the criticism gives the message that:

A. I don't think it's horrible, or a very big deal, if the coat is indeed junky-looking.
or
B. No one criticizes anything of mine and gets away with it.

389. Here's another example of agreeing with part of criticism.

Lunk dares Pat to dive off a high bridge into a river of unknown depth.

Pat says, "No way."

Lunk says, "You're just scared."

Pat says, laughing, "You got that one right! Scared to do that, and proud of it!"

Pat's laughter and his words give the message that

A. being scared this situation is not something I'm ashamed of,
or
B. no, I'm not scared?

390. Sometimes people criticize because they enjoy the power of putting someone on the defensive. They enjoy making the other person try to prove that he or she is OK. If every time someone says to you, in some way or

another, "You have a fault," you have to defend yourself and prove to them that you don't have that fault, then you give that person a great deal of power over you. You let that person give you an assignment to defend yourself whenever the person feels like it. On the other hand, if your response sends the message, "Yes, I'm very imperfect, and I don't need to defend myself right now," you make the critic less powerful.

This section is saying that often a good way to make a critic less powerful is to

A. defend yourself and prove that the criticism is wrong,
or
B. agree that the criticism may be correct and not bother to defend yourself?

391. A girl is walking down the hall in high school. In front of a bunch of other kids, a boy says to her, "You are ugly!"

She replies, in a confident tone, "Well, you may be right. If so, that's too bad, isn't it?"

The confident tone in which she agrees that it is possible that she is ugly sends the message that:

A. She would feel good about herself even if that were true.
or

B. She is shocked and hurt that anyone would say something like that to her.

392. Agreeing with criticism is a much less complex response when the person's criticism of you is constructive. But, even when the criticism isn't constructive, it is still very useful. It lets the other person know that you have heard the criticism. It lets the other person know that your feelings aren't greatly hurt by the criticism. If the person is trying to be helpful, this information will be welcomed.

Mary's voice teacher says to her, "Feel how you're holding your Adams Apple, or your larynx, very high in your neck. That makes it sound like a bleating goat when you sing. Hold your larynx lower and try it."

Mary tries it, and says, cheerfully, "You're right, that does make it sound less like a bleating goat!"

Mary's response is called

A. asking for more specific criticism,
or
B. agreeing with part of the criticism?

393. Tom is staying up late working on a paper for school. His dad says to him, "You know, Tom, if you had not put this off so long, you wouldn't have to be staying up tonight."

Tom smiles and says, "You can say that again! That's for sure!"

Do you think that Tom's enthusiastic agreement with his dad makes his dad feel

A. less need to keep repeating the criticism,
or
B. more need to keep repeating the criticism?

394. One of the main advantages of agreeing with part of criticism is that it helps both you and the other person to stay out of the pattern of attacking and defending. This is true even when the other person makes totally nonconstructive, global negative statements about you.

For example: someone says to Ted, "You're a total idiot!"

Ted smiles, looks unfazed, and says, "Well, it's true that I'm not the world's greatest genius!"

There's a big difference between not being the world's greatest genius and being a total idiot. Thus Ted is agreeing with only part of the criticism.

By agreeing with part of the criticism and not all of it, Ted stays out of the defensive posture without having to agree with something that he clearly doesn't agree with.

This section illustrates the usefulness of

A. agreeing wholeheartedly with everything the critic says,
or
B. agreeing with only part of the critical message, sometimes?

395. What if you totally disagree with a criticism? One way to accomplish part of the purpose of agreeing with criticism is to acknowledge the person's right to think what he wants to. This is often accomplished simply by saying, "You can think whatever you want," or "You can say what you will."

A kid tries to get Tom to join in taunting Tom's friend. Tom refuses. The bullying kid says to Tom, "I know the reason you won't say anything bad against him. I think you're both gay, and you're in love with him."

Tom shrugs and says, "I guess you can think whatever you want, can't you?"

Suppose that the kid is into bullying out of motives of dominance and stimulus-seeking. Which possible response of Tom's would give this kid MORE of what he wanted?

A. "I guess you can think whatever you want."
or
B. "No! That's not true! You have no right to say that!"

396. The next response to criticism on our list is called asking for more specific criticism. Through this type of response, you ask the other person to tell you the specific behaviors that the person would like you to do less often or more often.

A kid says to Richard, in a singsong voice, "You're the teachers pet! You're the teacher's pet!"

Richard says to the other kid, "And do you have something you'd like me to do about that?"

The other kid just repeats, "Teacher's pet."

Richard says, "It sounds as if you don't like that, and it sounds as if you want me to do something different. What is that?"

The other kid turns to someone else who is more fun to tease.

In this example, the critic

A. could come up with some specific behaviors he wanted Richard to change, or
B. could not come up with some specific behaviors he wanted Richard to change?

397. Jock starts working for a construction company. One of his fellow workers says to him, "You are lifting that all wrong."

Jock gets the urge to say, "When I want your opinions on how I lift, I'll ask for them." But then he thinks again. He decides to use "asking for more specific criticism."

Jock says, "Tell me how you think I should be lifting it differently."

The coworker says, "You are lifting it with your back bent too much. If you keep doing that, you're going to hurt your back sooner or later. Straighten out your back and lift like this, and you won't hurt yourself."

Jock says, "Sounds like good advice. Thanks."

The result of asking for more specific criticism in this case was that:

A. The other person couldn't figure out anything to say.
or
B. The other person was guided to give useful information to Jock.

398. When you ask for more specific criticism, cultivate the attitude that, if there is any useful and constructive part of the criticism, you will use it, and if there isn't, at least you tried to find it.

Sally's mother says to her, "Sally, you are getting to be a slob."

Which of the following would be an example of asking for more specific criticism that Sally could use?

A. "What would you like me to do differently, Mom?"
or
B. "I don't like it when you call me names like that, Mom."

399. When the person comes up with one specific criticism, it is often useful to ask the person to keep going.

Sally's mom says to her, "For one thing, don't leave your socks and shoes all over the house, but take them back to your room and put them away."

What's an example of Sally's continuing to ask for more specific criticism?

A. "OK, socks and shoes back into my room. What else?"
or
B. "You are right. I do leave them around the house too much."

400. The next type of response to criticism on our list is the reflection. By using a reflection, you make sure that you hear the criticism accurately. You say back to the other person what the other person's point of view is, as you heard it. You remember that the reflection is an important part of the conflict-resolution procedure. By letting the other person know his or her complaint has been heard, and by making sure you hear it correctly, you have a chance to guide the discussion into constructive channels.

Here's an example of a reflection. Mrs. Black says to Mrs. Peterson, "You give too many orders to other people's children."

Mrs. Peterson says, "So you're saying that I'm overstepping my bounds, telling your children what to do when I should keep quiet, huh?"

When Mrs. Peterson says this, how do you think Mrs. Black is more likely to feel?

A. irritated that Mrs. Peterson is repeating her point,
or
B. happy that Mrs. Peterson has heard her point correctly and is willing to listen?

401. Rob says to Lynette, "You go on talking too long without stopping."

What would be an example of a reflection?

A. "So you feel I should stop much sooner and give other people a chance to talk, huh?"
or
B. "Can you give me some specific examples of when I've done that?"

402. Manny's tutor says, "You need to work on keeping going longer without getting so tired. You need more endurance."

What would be an example of a reflection?

A. "You're exactly right."
or
B. "So you feel I could really benefit by increasing my work capacity, huh?"

403. Reflections are also sometimes useful with nonconstructive criticism.

Tanya walks into a classroom, and someone behind her says, in a negative tone of voice, "Look at those shoes she has. Oh, my!"

What would be an example of a reflection that Tanya could say?

A. "Sounds as if you really dislike my shoes. Is that right?"
or
B. "What is your problem?"

404. Sometimes people use criticism to distract you from getting what you want, or to intimidate you into doing what they want. Many times this tactic works, because people spend time defending themselves rather than pursuing their goal. An "I want statement" consists of ignoring the criticism and assertively saying what you want.

A guy at a party is trying to get Fran to drink alcohol, and she has said no. He says to her, "You're scared, aren't you?"

Which of the following is an I want statement?

A. No, I'm not scared.
or
B. I'd like you to leave me alone, please.

405. Mrs. Brown is at a party with her son Jimmy. She says, "It's time to leave, Jimmy." He says to her, "You told me I could stay longer! You don't keep your promises!" Which of the following is an I want statement?

A. Mrs. Brown takes Jimmy's hand, starts walking toward the door, and says, "I want us to leave now, Jimmy."
or
B. Mrs. Brown says, "What? When did I ever say that?"

406. Jacintha makes an error in a basketball game, and Larissa, her teammate, says to her, "What were you thinking of?"

Which of the following possible replies by Jacintha is an I want statement?

A. "I don't want to hear that kind of stuff now."

or

B. "What have *you* been thinking of, Larissa; you've made as many mistakes as I have."

407. Next on the list of responses to criticism is silent eye contact. It is often a useful response to nonconstructive criticism. Silent eye contact means that you simply look at your critic, without saying anything. You don't glare at him. You don't look away as though you are trying to ignore him. You don't look scared. What often has the best effect is a "searching look." You might think about what is going on with the other person, what motives he is acting from, whether he is putting on the performance for someone else, whether she could possibly have some constructive criticism for you, and whether she seems angry or gloating or whatever else.

This silent eye contact gives you time to think about your next response. It lets the teaser or the critic know you are not intimidated. It lets the critic know that you heard. It does not reinforce any critics who are acting from stimulus-seeking or dominance motives. Sometimes some silent eye contact, followed by ignoring as you return to your own business, works well.

Michael is riding on a school bus. He hears a kid in the seat behind him say to his comrade, "Look at that little squirt on the seat in front of us." An example of the type of response talked about in this section would be for Michael to

A. look silently at the critic for a while, with curiosity, then turn away,

or

B. say, "Who are you calling a squirt?"

408. The next response to criticism is called explanation or debate, done rationally. This response is to argue with the critic, but to do so in a way that sheds light on the subject. What this means is to talk about facts, scientific findings, probabilities, advantages and disadvantages of options, and so forth, and not the bad points of the other person or the good points about yourself. This is particularly useful when there is some chance that either your critic or someone listening to you has a chance of being persuaded by logic and reasoning. If there is no such person, realize that you may be using this technique only as an exercise for yourself.

The author is advocating explanations and debates that appeal more to

A. reason, logic, and facts,

or

B. emotions, threats, and insulting the opponent?

409. Here's a situation that gives the opportunity for rational explanation. A

mother is leaving a grocery store with her husband and her three-year-old son. When the son can't get something that he wants, he starts screaming at the top of his lungs. The mother does not look at him or speak to him, but takes him by the hand and keeps walking out of the store. Her husband criticizes her by saying, "Why are you letting him get away with that? Why don't you tell them to quit doing that? You're too easy on him."

The mother replies, "I'm not paying attention to him because I've read that talking with him and paying attention to him at times like this only reward his screaming. I've also found that, since I started ignoring him when he does this, he's doing it a lot less often."

The mother is responding to the criticism by

A. rational explanation,
or
B. telling why it's her husband's fault and not hers?

410. Two doctors are talking about whether to give a certain medicine to a patient or not. One doctor criticizes the second by saying, "I think it's cruel of you not give this medicine to this person. I don't see how you can turn a deaf ear to the pain that this person is in."

What would be an example of a rational explanation, in response to this criticism?

A. "I don't turn a deaf ear to anyone's pain, and I resent your saying that."
or
B. "There are several studies showing that, when you try to withdraw this drug after giving it for a while, you get even worse problems than you had in the first place."

411. The last type of response to criticism on our list is called criticizing the critic. By this I am talking about a particular type of criticism that calls upon the critic to improve his way of communicating. I am not talking about the all-too-human tendency that people have to insult someone back whenever they feel insulted.

Here's an example. There is a political debate. One candidate says of the other, "My opponent is a socialist, a communist, and a liberal dodo-head. Any intelligent voter can see this."

The second candidate replies by criticizing the critic's techniques of communication, not the critic's general personality. The second candidate says, "Such name-calling does not shed any light on the issues. If you would like to speak in a more civilized way on the topics of the day, the way to do it is to mention specific issues, what you think should be done about them, and why."

The second candidate is criticizing the critic for

A. being a general fool,
or
B. speaking in a way that doesn't help matters?

412. On a school bus, the first kid, for no good reason, calls the second kid a bunch of obscene names. What would be an example of criticizing the critic for the way he is communicating?

A. "You live in a dump!"
or
B. "You must have something wrong with you, that you have to talk to people like that."

413. When you respond to criticism, it's good to have all these possibilities in your repertoire. You also have all the Ida Craft options as possibilities: ignoring, differential reinforcement, assertion, conflict-resolution, criticism responses, rule of law, relaxation, away from the situation, apologizing, friendliness, force of a nonviolent type, and tones of voice. A very useful exercise is to look at the sample criticisms in Appendix 3 of this book and to carefully consider what options may work out best.

The exercise that is suggested is to

A. think about criticisms people could receive, and carefully think about what options would work best,
or
B. pick one option for handling criticism and use that option whenever you are criticized?

Chapter 13: Sources of Nonpunitive Power

414. "I can't stop losing my temper with people: they'll walk all over me." This idea is a common reason why people fail at learning anger control, or why they never try it in the first place. All people want to influence other people. They want to be able to get people to do the things they want, and to stop doing the things they don't like. The ability to influence other people is called power. This chapter is about the question, "How can I have the power to influence people, without being angry and mean to them?"

This section implies that one reason people don't learn anger control is that they are

A. just too accustomed to losing their tempers,
or
B. afraid of giving up the power that they get by angry behavior?

415. Power and influence are at work during nearly every moment that people are together. As soon as someone sees you, that person either does or does not give you gestures of attention, respect, and friendliness. The instant you say something, the other person's tone of voice often shows approval or disapproval. Whether people act nice or mean to you depends partly on the other person's social habits, and partly on your own power.

This section makes the point that:

A. Power is seldom an issue for most people.
or
B. Power is an issue during almost every moment that people interact.

416. When I refer to power here, I mean something a little different than what people sometimes mean by this word. Sometimes, when people speak of power, they think of making people do things they don't want to do, by force or threats. This is the meaning of the word *power* that is suggested by the phrases *power struggle* or *power trip*. Here, I'm referring to that type of power, but I'm also referring to a different type of power as well: the ability to influence people to *want* to do certain things, to be *happy* doing certain things, not resentful. People often use this "positive power," without even thinking of it as power.

An implication of this section is that power

A. should not be used with people you love,
or

165

B. should, if possible, be used in a way that the other person actually welcomes?

417. Here's an example. Two kids both want other kids to treat them with friendliness and respect. One of the two does this by force and threats. He says to other kids, "If you don't smile and say hi to me, I'll remember it, and I'll hurt you for it later." The other kids fear his punishment, and smile and say hi to him. But they really hate him. The second kid is friendly and talks pleasantly with the other kids. He does fun things with them and likes to joke around with them. The other kids also smile and say hi to this kid, but they don't feel compelled to. They do it because they like him.

Both kids have the "power" to gain friendliness and respect from others. But the type of power that the second kid uses, works much better in the long run.

Influencing people to treat you respectfully because they like you is

A. not really the use of power, as defined here,
or
B. the use of positive power?

418. It's true that anger, unpleasant behavior, violence, and punishment have been very important sources of power among people. "If you do things

I don't like, I'll punish you with angry looks and words, or punitive actions," is the basis of lots of power. If you stand on someone's foot, you may receive angry looks and tones of voice, until you get off and apologize. If someone drives drunk, he loses his driver's license. If someone hurts people, he gets locked up in jail. If someone insults someone, the insulted person speaks back with punitive tones. If someone doesn't do homework, he is punished by a bad grade. If an elected leader gets rid of people's freedom, the people vote him out of office or have him impeached. People do lots of things in order to avoid other people's doing unpleasant things to them. When you can punish someone if the person doesn't do what you want, you have power to influence that person.

The examples chosen for this section illustrate that:

A. The power to punish should never be used.
or
B. Sometimes the power to punish is useful and good?

419. When people use threats of punishment to get things that aren't reasonable from other people, we call that *extortion*. For example, someone from the Mafia says to a restaurant owner, "Unless you pay me a thousand dollars a month, your restaurant will get burned down." Sometimes people use

milder examples of extortion in everyday life with each other. For example, one child says, "If you don't give me that toy, I'll tell everybody that you wet your pants." Obviously, extortion is a very quick way of getting someone to dislike you and to wish that you were out of the way. And as we've discussed before, any use of punishment or threat of punishment is an invitation to the other person to punish you back.

The point of this section is that:

A. Punishment should occur as soon after the behavior as possible, if it is to be most effective.
or
B. Using threats of punishment to demand unreasonable things is called extortion, and it often stirs up hatred in the person being extorted.

420. Fortunately, there are lots of ways to get power other than by punishment or threats of punishment. Non-punitive ways of getting power work much better than the punitive ways, all other things being equal. In the rest of this chapter we will discuss several of the sources of power other than the power to punish.

The rest of this chapter will concern itself with

A. ways to influence people other than by threatening to punish them,
or

B. problems with the use of punishment?

421. A wise person said, "You can get almost anything you want, if you can help enough other people get what they want." In other words, power does not come only from the ability to punish and hurt. It also comes from the ability to help, to meet people's needs and wants, to be useful and pleasant and positive to others. One of the most important bases of power is *reciprocity*. The word reciprocity means that people tend to act toward others in the way that others act toward them. If someone treats you kindly and helps you, you are much more likely to treat that person kindly and help that person in return.

The point of this section is that:

A. Useful, helpful behavior tends to spur other people to reciprocate with the same sort of behavior.
or
B. "No good deed goes unpunished."

422. The exchange of friendly and kind behavior is one example of the type of power that people want you to use with them. What's another example of such positive power? A very obvious example is buying and selling. "If you give me the screwdriver, I'll give you the amount of money that's on the price tag, but if you don't, I won't." This is the basis of your power to influence the hardware store owner to give you the

screwdriver. Your money gives you power to change the store person's behavior. But of course, this is exactly the power he wants you to exert over him. In the same way, he has power over you, to get you to hand over your money. If you need a screwdriver and he needs money, both of you come out ahead in the exchange, and both of you are happy about the sort of power that was "used upon you." Using this sort of language to talk about a simple purchase sounds strange, because usually we don't even think of such an exchange as an exercise of power. But it certainly is. Both people have influenced the other's behavior.

In the example of a sale at a store,

A. the buyer is influencing the seller, but the seller isn't influencing the buyer,
or
B. both people are influencing each other's behavior?

423. This example illustrates that power and influence work in both directions: both people influence each other. The same thing is true in less obvious exchanges. Suppose that a child will do what his mother asks him to do only when she yells angrily at him. She is influencing him to do what she wants, by yelling. But because he does what she wants only when she yells, he is also influencing her. He is using his power to teach her to be an angry yeller.

The way in which the child exerted power to make the mom yell was by

A. doing what she wanted only after she yelled,
or
B. punishing her for yelling?

424. Here's another example: a kid gets power in the form of social status from peers by being a good athlete and bringing glory to his school. But the peers also have the power over him, to make him train and practice and spend huge amounts of time on his sport.

Here's an example of the idea that power involves exchanges, that I saw once in a cartoon. A psychologist has taught a rat to press a bar to get food. The rat is saying to another rat, "I've really got this psychologist trained. Each time I press the bar, she gives me food!" The psychologist couldn't have the *power* to get the rat to press the bar, without giving the rat the *power* to make her give food each time the rat pressed the bar!

The examples in this section demonstrate that:

A. People don't have as much power as they think they do.
or
B. Because power involves exchanges, often two people both have power to influence each other.

168

425. Money was a very smart invention of the human race. It helps people to use power with one another by exchanging rewards rather than by threatening punishments. It helps people use power with each other in ways that both of them willingly agree to. It is said that "Money is power," and it is a very important source of nonviolent power.

The attitude of the author appears to be that:

A. Money is the root of all evil.
or
B. Money is a very important way in which people can influence each other without threatening violence.

426. Two kids are in high school. One puts huge amounts of time into trying to figure out cool clothes to buy and wear, to earn the respect of other kids. The other puts huge amounts of time into learning skills that will let her get a very high-paying job. She also works and saves money. She also reads and learns about how to invest money so that the money she has earned will make her more money without her even having to work for it. Both kids are really striving for sources of power. The second kid will have power that will last even when the clothes she has purchased go out of style or get worn out.

The author's attitude seems to be that:

A. The search for money is the root of all evil.
or
B. Making and saving money is a more effective way to get power than buying clothes is.

427. The next power source on our list is also a very important source of money: the power of competence. Competence means developing skills and abilities that other people highly value or find useful. A person who knows very well how to do difficult surgical operations, how to run a company, how to expertly teach people engineering or reading, how to fix things that are broken, or how to do any of the many other things that people want and need, will have much more power than the person who has no competences to offer people.

The point of this section is that:

A. Competence in doing things that help people gives you power.
or
B. Knowing how to make friends gives you power.

428. Many groups of people value certain skills. Among players on a basketball team, the best basketball player will have power to get the respect of the other players. Among a math team, however, the basketball player may find himself less respected and powerful than someone else with

more math skill. Among a dancing group, the best dancers tend to be the ones people speak to most respectfully, and so forth.

The point of this section is that, if you want respect and power, one way to get it is to

A. cultivate skills that people value, and get into the groups that value those skills,
or
B. be friendly and kind to everyone in your group, and it won't matter how skilled you are?

429. Having competence to do useful or valued things for others does not result in power unless people are willing and able to work to use those competences. Thus the power of competence must be complemented by the "power of work capacity." If you are able to work patiently, day after day, toward achieving your goals, your power is vastly increased.

The point of this section is that if your competence is to give you power, you will need to have

A. the ability to sell your competence rather than give it away,
or
B. the ability to keep working long enough that your competence produces results?

430. One person catches on to math and science ideas very quickly, because he has a very high talent in these areas. But he has very low talent in getting himself to work. He can't even get himself to show up on time for any job he has. A second person has less talent, but is willing to work many long hours on math and science. The second person eventually learns more than the first, and is very successful in a job that gives him a great deal of power.

This example is a sales pitch for developing

A. great talent,
or
B. great work capacity?

431. Exchanges are central to all power. Even the power gained from punishment is a sort of exchange: for example, "If you don't disrupt the class, then in exchange for that, I won't give you a detention." Or, "If you turn down that music, I'll stop yelling at you."

The ability to exchange positive, useful goods or services is the basis for a great deal of the power that people have. Sometimes exchanges are obvious and concrete, as in buying and selling. Sometimes exchanges are less obvious, but are present nevertheless.

Friendship is a long series of exchanges: I listen to you and make you feel understood, and, in exchange, you say funny things that make me feel good; I provide some pleasant companionship when you want it, and in exchange you take my side when someone else spreads false rumors about me, etc.

The point of this section is that:

A. Friendship usually involves a series of exchanges between people.
or
B. Many golf games are played so that people's friendships can help them have power.

432. Of course, when people are friends, they do not usually make deals with each other. They do not usually say, "If you will make me happy by going skating with me, I will make you feel good by lending you the book you forgot to take home." Friendship is the type of relationship where people don't have to keep track of a scorecard as to who has done the most for the other. Despite this, it's true that the more one person has to offer that makes the second person feel good, the more the first person will be able to influence the second. The person who can very competently offer pleasant conversation, pleasant activities, access to other positive relationships, help in doing tasks, emotional support, and the other things that friends give, will have more "friendship power." That person will be able to ask friends for help when needed, and friends will be more likely

to say yes. So the ability to build friendships is a very important source of positive power, the type of power that people don't mind being used with them.

The main point of this section is that:

A. Much power comes from the ability to punish people.
or
B. Much power to influence people comes from making friends with them.

433. Let's give an example of the difference between the power of extortion and punishment, and the power of friendship. Imagine that two adolescents feel that their mothers are too preoccupied with work and other activities, and don't pay enough attention to them. One tries the use of punishment: she gruffly orders her mom to quit doing what she is doing; she sulks; she refuses to listen when her mother talks; all are an effort to punish her mom for not being attentive. The other tries the use of friendship: she listens very carefully when her mom speaks, speaks in a pleasant tone of voice to her, helps her with tasks she is doing, and is emotionally supportive when her mom is feeling down. Which one do you think will be more successful – more "powerful" – in getting her mom to be more attentive to her? Almost all the time, the second strategy will work better.

The point of this section is that:

A. Although friendship sometimes works, it is a weaker power than extortion.
or
B. Friendship is often much more effective than extortion.

434. In a fable by Aesop, the winter wind and the sun once had a contest to see who was more powerful. "Let's see who can get that traveler to take his coat off," they decided. The winter wind took the first turn. He blew strongly on the man, trying to blow the coat off him. But the stronger the wind blew, the more tightly the man resisted, clutching his coat around him. Next it was the sun's turn. The sun shone down with friendliness and warmth upon the man, warming him until the man *wanted* to take off his coat. The sun won the contest.

The moral of this story is that:

A. The power of friendship is often greater than the power of force.
or
B. To exert power, you have to take stands against people that show them they're defeated.

435. Acting kind and pleasant to someone produces positive power with that person, partly because the person does not want to lose your pleasant and friendly behavior. If you consistently act unfriendly long enough, the other person tends to give up on ever getting your friendly behavior. The power of friendship gets lost.

A woman is angry at her husband because he is too gruff and disapproving of her. Because she is angry at him, she is never affectionate with him, almost always speaks disapprovingly to him, and avoids him. He tries being nicer to her, but she is so angry that she cannot be friendly to him. Eventually he gives up on regaining her friendship, and they divorce.

The woman in this example

A. gave and withheld friendly behavior depending on how nice her husband acted,
or
B. withheld her friendly behavior, no matter what her husband did?

436. If the woman had been willing or able to be friendly to her husband when he was nice to her, she would have had a great deal of power to change his behavior. Because he enjoyed her friendly behavior, he may have been willing to change in order to get that friendly behavior. But when she started being consistently unfriendly to him, she gave up the power of friendship – she gave up that source of ability to influence him.

The point of this section is that:

A. No power comes from friendly behavior if you aren't ever willing to be friendly.
or
B. The ability to do skillfully whatever your group is trying to do gives you status and power in that group.

437. We are talking about the power that comes from being friendly to another person, and being willing to stop acting friendly when the other person does something you don't like. Most people don't consciously think about this power. But people use it frequently, and when it is used well, it is a very good way for people to influence one another. When it's used well, people act friendly and approving to each other almost all the time. But when the other person swings toward selfishness or thoughtless unpleasant behavior, the other stops acting in an approving way and looks and sounds disappointed with the other person.

The author's attitude is that:

A. You should always try to be friendly and approving of other people, no matter what they do.
or
B. It is reasonable and good that, although you most often approve of other people, at carefully selected times, you act disapproving.

438. It has been said that with your family members, students, employees, or other important relationships, you should try to give approval at least four times as often as you give disapproval. This means that you say things such as, "I like that!" "Thanks for doing that!" "That's a good point!" and "That makes me feel good!" at least four times as often as you say things such as, "Please don't do that!" Similarly, when you are teaching someone something, you want to say, "Good job!" or "You got it right!" at least four times as often as you say, "No, that's not it."

The author implies that family members

A. keep organized, so that people will find it more pleasant to increase their work capacity,
or
B. find something to approve of with one another at least four times as often as they disapprove?

439. Why four times as much approval as disapproval? The withdrawal of friendly behavior is a form of power that should not be used too often or too intensely. Withdrawing of friendly behavior should only be used when the other person is getting out of line. The withdrawal of friendly behavior should be as mild and as temporary as possible. This is because friendship is delicate, and withdrawal of friendly behavior for too long or too much intensity can destroy it. People can give up on getting

the other's approval and seek it elsewhere.

This section and the previous one indicate that the author thinks that:

A. If you want to belong to a group where a certain skill is important, it pays to practice over and over in that skill.
or
B. The positive power of friendship works best when lots of approval is exchanged often.

440. There's another way in which kind and friendly behavior wields very positive power: the power of modeling. Most people have a tendency to imitate the behavior that comes toward them. When people act gruff and disapproving to others, others tend to act that way back to them. When they speak with kind and approving tones of voice, others tend to reciprocate. Since almost all people want to be spoken to with politeness and approval, they greatly increase their power to achieve this goal if they model this behavior to the people they deal with.

Because of the power of modeling, often the positive power of friendship works without either person's ever having to be disapproving or having to withdraw friendly behavior! Each of them is kind to the other; each of them through models influences the other to continue being friendly; and all they

want from the other is the friendly behavior they are getting.

The point of this section is that:

A. Because of the power of modeling, people sometimes enjoy the power of friendship without ever needing to withdraw friendly behavior from each other.
or
B. Friendly behavior has no power unless you sometimes withdraw it.

441. When people have lots of friends and admirers, they get power in another way. People other than their friends will want to become their friends, because they are known as a person of influence. People want to get the benefits of that person's power, and they want to get access to that person's friends and make friends with them too. For many millennia, people probably formed such bands of friends (and relatives) in this way to defend themselves from one another in life-or-death battles. Now, fortunately, the stakes are usually lower. But people still seem to strongly want to ally with people who have other allies. This may be called the power of prestige and social status.

The point of this section is that:

A. Having friends or allies gives someone the power of social status, and allows her to get more allies more easily.

or
B. There is a certain limit to the number of people you have time to be friends with.

442. The power to withhold your rewards from someone when you are negotiating about a "deal" is sometimes called "walk-away power." Suppose that you are buying a car. The person you are bargaining with knows that you feel you must have this particular car. Furthermore, suppose the car-seller knows that there are several other people who would buy the car at the price he is asking. No amount of "negotiating skill" on your part can get the price lower than the level that others would be willing to pay. The owner of the car has "walk-away power," and you don't. The situation would be reversed if there were several other lower-priced cars that suited you just as well, and the seller felt that he needed to sell the car to you.

The point of this section is that:

A. Some people tend to be more giving to others, whereas others tend to be "takers."
or
B. Power comes from having the ability to "walk away" from a deal.

443. Power also comes from the ability to let other people know exactly what you want from them, in ways that are as gentle and non-bossy as they can be and still get the job done. The ability to let people know what you want, and to withhold rewards if necessary to stick up for yourself, is the power of assertion skills.

The point of this section is that:

A. Power also comes from being able to be assertive.
or
B. Power comes from having great work capacity.

444. A man is very interested in maps. He frequently calls his son to him, saying, "Come and look at this map." Then he speaks at length, saying, "Here's where we were, and then we went this way, and we could have gone over here instead . . . " and so forth. For many years his son puts up with this, but he finds it boring and resents it. But he loves his father and does not want to hurt him, so he keeps looking at the maps.

One day the son decides he's had enough. His father says, "Come and look at this map." The son replies, "No, I don't really want to look at the map." The father is not angry or hurt, but continues to study the map himself. The son thinks, "Is that all I needed to do!"

In this example, the son's putting up with the explanations of maps for many years

A. was necessary to keep the father in good spirits,

or

B. was unnecessary, but the son was not assertive enough to find this out until after a long time?

445. Assertion is usually carried out in words. Sometimes the exercise of assertion skills is as simple as saying, "I want this," or "No, I won't do that." But at other times, the person who can skillfully speak and interact, who can use persuasion well, who knows what to say and when to say it, can be of much more influence. This is the power of verbal ability and the power to persuade.

The point of this section is that power sometimes comes from

A. giving persuasive reasons for taking a certain course of action,

or

B. not speaking much?

446. The power to make persuasive arguments sometimes backfires. Suppose a parent makes certain reasonable rules for a teenaged daughter. The daughter enjoys arguing, and is able to argue endlessly against the parents, no matter how reasonable and persuasive their arguments. The parents end up spending huge amounts of unpleasant time trying to argue their daughter into accepting their point of view. They don't grasp that they are wasting their time, and that they should abandon hopes for winning the arguments through verbal persuasion. They should use other sources of power.

In this example,

A. the use of verbal persuasion power was very effective,

or

B. trying to use verbal persuasion power got some parents into a trap?

447. How many times have you ever seen the following happen? Two people are arguing angrily with each other. They are each loudly pointing out why the other is wrong. All of the sudden, one of them makes a very persuasive point. The other stops and says, "I never thought of it that way. You're right. I was wrong!"

You are likely to go a lifetime without seeing that happen. Perhaps, when a debate is public, an excellent point made in a forceful and angry tone may persuade the *listeners*. But the person one is arguing against? Not likely.

The point of this is that:

A. You should not try to persuade people that your point of view is correct.

or

B. Once people are in an angry argument, they very seldom are persuaded of anything.

448. On the other hand, it happens very often that, when people are *not* angry, when their minds are not fully made up, and when they discuss an issue in a friendly or neutral tone, one person will think of a persuasive point that the other will take seriously.

The conclusion from these observations about arguments is that no matter how great your verbal ability and reasoning power are, you are usually wasting your energy trying to persuade, if the conversation is conducted in an angry tone of voice. Persuasive points you make will usually only stimulate the other person to oppose you more strongly. Save your persuasive power for times when the person you are speaking to is receptive.

The point about the power of persuasion is that:

A. It never works.
or
B. It works best when people are not angry at each other.

449. A skill related to assertion and persuasion is the skill of leadership. By this I mean the willingness and ability to decide on the direction that a group of people should go, to make that opinion known, and to get other people to join in.

A group of kids is given a task to do together. One person says, "I think we should do it this way, with these steps." Other people see that the plan sounds workable, and they join in. They look to the same person to guide them when they are uncertain what to do.

One kid in this example used the power of leadership by

A. being willing to propose a plan for the group to follow,
or
B. studying possible plans until she was absolutely sure that the proposed plan was best?

450. People who like power and influence often enjoy "leadership jobs," or jobs where they are the bosses.

Rhonda and Sally work for a company that makes software. Sally is the smartest and most competent software writer in the company. She spends most of her time figuring out the code for the products the company makes. Rhonda is the president of the company. She decides who gets hired and fired, how much everyone gets paid, how long people work, which products the company makes, and whose ideas get accepted and whose do not.

The person in more of a "leadership job" in this company is

A. Sally,

or
B. Rhonda?

451. In the long run, people are more willing to be led when they see that they are being led in a good direction! In the short run, a leader can persuade people to follow if he is very self-confident, forceful, and charismatic. But the best source of loyalty to a leader comes when the leader demonstrates the ability to make good decisions, over and over. This is the power of decision-making skill.

The point of this section is that the power of leadership comes partly from

A. knowing how to speak in a way that is acceptable to the group you are in,
or
B. making and proposing plans that people find are good decisions?

452. Here is perhaps the most important source of power. No matter how persuasive you are, how assertive you are, how many friends you have, how rich you are, or how competent you are, it is much more difficult to be powerful if you are trying to do something that is ethically wrong. When you have ethics and morality on your side, your power is increased. I wish I could say that "good always triumphs." It does not. But when you use power, you should always ask yourself whether what you are trying to do is right, fair, and good.

The author believes that:

A. If you are working for what is right, you will always have the power to win any power struggle.
or
B. If you are working for what is right, you have a major advantage, even though right doesn't always win.

453. One of the most amazing events of history occurred when Mohandas Gandhi, the leader of India, led a nonviolent revolution resulting in India's gaining independence from England. Gandhi's strategy was to persuade his followers not to cooperate with the British government, but not to be violent against it. The ethical power of nonviolence was recognized by people all over the world as good and right and a model for how disputes should best be settled. This ethical power gave Gandhi the "moral high ground," and it contributed immensely to the success of his cause.

This section gives an example of

A. legal power, or doing something with the law behind you,
or
B. ethical power, or using strategies and having goals that are good and right?

454. Gandhi's strategies were carefully studied by Martin Luther King, and were used in gaining civil rights for African-American people in the U.S. At

the time there were restaurants and lunch counters whose owners refused to serve African Americans. Groups of King's followers sat down at these restaurants, but refused to use violence, even when they were forcibly dragged away from the restaurant by police. In response to African Americans' having to sit at the back of buses, civil rights leaders organized a strike in which people walked long distances and refused to take the bus – but again they avoided violence. By avoiding violence, the civil rights movement kept the moral high ground. They made it very difficult for people to feel righteous and good about denying them equal rights. Keeping ethics on their side contributed greatly to the success of the struggle.

This is another example of

A. the power that can come from studying how to gain wealth,
or
B. the power that comes from striving for good goals in ethical ways?

455. The colleagues of King and Gandhi needed to use another very important type of power: the courage to tolerate other people's anger toward them. Nonviolent activists often face hostility from two sides: from the authorities they are resisting, and from those who would like to use violence against those authorities. If their wish to be liked and appreciated is greater than their confidence in their own

convictions, they will cave in to what others want.

The source of power this section talks about is

A. the ability to make other people respect you,
or
B. the ability to stick to your convictions even when others are hostile to you?

456. Suppose that James goes to a school where everyone is very excited about the football team. As the football team approaches its championship game, someone makes up a cheer that goes, "Rip 'em up, grind 'em up, eat 'em for lunch!" People make a T-shirt with a picture of people grinding up and eating the animal that is the mascot for the other team. Someone makes enough T-shirts for everyone in the school to have one, and everyone starts wearing them, even the principal and teachers of the school. They hold rallies in which they wear their T-shirts and chant the cheer.

James has very strong beliefs in nonviolence and in animal rights. He organizes a small group of students who refuse to wear the shirt and chant the cheer. In fact, they wear peace shirts and animal rights shirts instead. They do this predicting that there will be a tremendous amount of hostility toward him, and they are right. They endure taunting and jeering every day, and they are sometimes shoved and hit. But they support one another through this ordeal. They insist on their right to protection from violence, and when they can't persuade their principal, they take their case to the school superintendent. The superintendent sides with them, and gradually more and more students come to appreciate their courage. Eventually they teach their whole school an important lesson about not giving in to tribalism.

This story illustrates that an important source of power is

A. the ability to raise money for your cause,
or
B. the ability to tolerate other people's hostility?

457. The stories of Martin Luther King, Mohandas Gandhi, and the imaginary story of James illustrate another principle regarding power. If you have a strong conviction, there are likely to be others with the same conviction. It's usually better to find those people and to organize into a group than to attempt to take on the world all by yourself. It is very courageous to take a lone stand and be totally rejected by everyone around you, but. if you're interested in the power to get things done, form a group if possible.

This section speaks about the power that comes from

A. taking a stand even if the whole world opposes you,
or
B. forming a group of people who share your goals and convictions?

458. A woman goes to her son's school and sees that the roof leaks, the textbooks are torn up, and the bathroom toilets don't work. The classes are very large and the teachers are poorly paid. She is aware that there are other schools in her state where the buildings are kept in good repair, the students have up-to-date textbooks, and the teachers are paid very well.

She talks to the school officials to try to understand the situation better. She writes to her state representatives and her governor, and arranges personal meetings with them. But her individual efforts have no effect.

Then she starts to communicate with other parents. She forms an organization of parents whose children go to poorly-funded schools. She asks other people to help by recruiting more people through emails and personal contacts. She finds someone who will assemble a many photos showing the differences between schools. Then a student who is good with video equipment makes a movie about how some schools have so much more than others. Someone offers to organize a group to make many copies of this video. After a while the video shows up on TV, and then a TV station does a documentary. Meanwhile the woman continues to organize people, and now, instead of her going to see her state representative all by herself, she organizes a rally at the state capitol with thousands of people. Changes start to take place in the schools!

This story illustrates the principle that, if you want to have power,

A. you have to be able to handle it when people are mad at you,
or
B. people are more powerful when organized into groups than when working separately?

459. What is right and what is legal are not always the same thing. (The segregation laws that King's followers broke provide a very good example of this.) But having the law is on your side is another very important source of power, especially if you are in a country or a group where the rule of law is respected.

This section is about

A. legal power, or having the law on your side,
or
B. the power of social status, or having lots of admirers, friends, and allies?

460. Suppose a leader of a country decides to listen secretly to the phone conversations of citizens, to try to prevent criminal activity. The leader has many sources of power. But if the laws of that country clearly state that the leader does not have the authority to do this, then the leader's opponents have a very important source of power. On the other hand, if the leader carries out the spying program in such a way that he obeys the law, his power is increased.

This section provides an example where a leader would be wise to

A. make sure that what he is doing is on the side of the law,
or
B. make sure that he has enough of the power that money gives him?

461. Power is the ability to accomplish your goals. It is the ability to influence other people to act in a way that helps you get what you want. If your use of power is ethical and good, other people will get what they want and what is good for them in the process. But, if you don't have goals, if you don't know what you want, it's hard to have power.

The point of this section is that:

A. There are many nonviolent sources of power.
or

B. If you are clueless as to what you want, power doesn't do you any good?

462. Imagine two people. One says, "I want to set up an organization that will help people learn to be nonviolent. I want to lead this organization. I want the organization to have enough money to operate for a long time. I want to prove that the work it does is actually effective, and to persuade other people to do similar things. I want to make it true that. because of my work, fewer people are hurt and killed."

When the second person is asked, "What are your goals?" he replies, "I don't know." The second person is pressed: "Can't you think of anything that you would like to make happen?" He replies, "Not really, no."

The first person has a very ambitious goal. He may or not be able to get the power to attain his goal. But the second person is powerless unless he figures out something that he wants to accomplish. Thus another important source of power is the power of clear goals.

The point of this section is that you increase your power by

A. forming clear goals,
or
B. getting highly-developed work skills?

463. Let's summarize. Here are sources of nonviolent, nonpunitive power discussed in this chapter:

1. reciprocity
2. money
3. competence in valued skills
4. work capacity
5. friendship
6. modeling
7. prestige and social status
8. walk-away power
9. assertion
10. verbal persuasion
11. leadership
12. leadership jobs
13. decision-making skill
14. ethics
15. tolerance of others' hostility to you
16. organizing groups
17. the law
18. clear goals

The more someone cultivates these sources of nonviolent, nonpunitive power, the less the person ever needs to raise his voice in anger or to fight. The need to scream or hit is often a sign that a person has not developed thoroughly enough the more positive sources of power discussed in this chapter. We can develop these sources of power through careful study, practice, and work.

The point of this section is that:

A. Violence and punishment should be used only as a last resort.
or

B. Violence and punishment are often
signs that someone has not worked hard
enough, or cleverly enough, at getting
the positive sources of power?

Chapter 14: Beyond Provocations: Improving the Emotional Climate

464. This book devotes lots of attention to the question of how to respond to provocations. But it could well be that the most important part of anger control, conflict resolution, and nonviolence happens at times other than when you are experiencing provocations. If you create a feeling of friendliness and good will among the people you deal with, there will be fewer provocations. It will also be easier to deal with the provocations that do come up.

This section is saying that:

A. The only important thing about anger control is dealing well with provocations.
or
B. When you're not dealing with provocations, it's very important to create a feeling of friendliness and good will.

465. How people feel about each other in general is called the emotional climate. If you are continuously working toward a good emotional climate, provocations are not nearly so much of a problem.

Here's an example of this idea. Imagine that there are two sisters. When they see each other in the morning, they don't say anything. When they speak to each other, they sound a little grumpy most of the time. When one of them does something, the other never offers to help. When one does a good job at something, the other never says anything about it. Now imagine that one of them accidentally breaks something that belongs to the other one. What do you imagine as the response to this provocation? How much anger is there?

Now please imagine two other sisters. When they see each other in the morning, they say, "Good morning!" in a cheerful voice. They do a lot of laughing as they talk with each other. When one of them does a good job on something, the others says, "Hey, good job on that!" Now please imagine that one of them accidentally breaks something that belongs to the other one. What do you imagine as the response to this provocation? How much anger is there?

The point of this section is that:

A. People will always respond the same to the same provocation.
or
B. If there's a good emotional climate, provocations will create less anger.

466. Here's another example. Two people are in a class at a school. The first one usually comes in with a grumpy look. This person doesn't say "hi" to anybody. This person occasionally glares at other people in the class when they make too much noise.

When the second person comes into class, this person looks all around and smiles and says, "Good morning," to anyone who gives eye contact. When someone drops his pencil, this person picks it up and returns it to the other person with a smile. When someone answers a question well in class, this person sometimes says, after class, "Hey, that was a good point you made when the prof asked that question!" People feel friendly to this person.

Suppose that someone in the class decides to entertain himself by making insulting remarks to a classmate.

Which person do you think he will pick to be the target of his insults?

A. the grumpy person,
or
B. the more cheerful person?

467. This example illustrates that, when you create a better emotional climate, not only is it easier to deal with the provocations that come up; you also receive fewer provocations.

Creating a positive emotional environment results in fewer provocations because

A. people don't often provoke people they feel friendly toward,
or
B. if you act mean enough, people will be too scared to provoke you?

468. What are the things people say that create a positive emotional climate? Please study the following list, and please consider saying these very sentences, often, to the people you know.

Things To Say To Create a Good Emotional Climate

Expressing gladness that the other person is here:

Good morning! Good afternoon! Good evening! I'm glad to see you! It's good to see you! Welcome home! Hi! I'm glad you're here!

Expressing gratitude and appreciation:

Thanks for doing that for me! I really appreciate what you did. I'm glad you told me that! Yes, please! That's nice of you to do that for me! This is a big help to me. Thanks for saying that!

Reinforcing a good performance of the other person:

You did a good job! That's interesting! Good going! Good point! Good job! Congratulations to you! You did well on that! That's pretty smart!

Positive feelings about the world and the things and events in it:

Wonderful! That's really great! Wow! Hooray! I'm so glad it happened like that! Sounds good! Look how beautiful that is!

Wishing well for the other person's future:

I hope you have a good day. Have a nice day! Good luck to you! I wish you the best on (the thing you're doing).

Offering help or accepting a request for help:

May I help you with that? I'd like to help you with that. I'll do that for you! I'm going to do this job so that you won't have to do it! Would you like me to show you how I do that? I'd be happy to do that for you! I'd love to help you in that way!

Positive feelings about oneself:

I feel good about something I did. Want to hear about it? Hooray, I'm glad I did this!

Being forgiving and tolerating frustration:

That's OK; don't worry about it. It's no problem. I can handle it. I can take it. It's not the end of the world.

Expressing interest in the other person:

How was your day today? How are you? How have you been doing? How have things been going? So let me see if I understand you right. You feel that _____. So, in other words you're saying _____. I'd like to hear more about that! I'm curious about that. Tell me more. Uh huh . . . Yes . . . Oh?

Consoling the other person:

I'm sorry you had to go through that. I'm sorry that happened to you.

Apologizing or giving in:

I'm sorry I said that. I apologize for doing that. I think you're right about that. Upon thinking about it more, I've decided I was wrong. I'll go along with what you want on that.

Being assertive in a nice way:

Here's another option. Here's the option I would favor. An advantage of this plan is . . . A disadvantage of that option is . . . Unfortunately I can't do it. I'd prefer not to. No, I'm sorry, I don't want to do that. It's very important that you do this.

Humor:

Saying or doing funny things, retelling funny things, or laughing when the other person is trying to entertain you by being funny - but avoiding sarcasm or making fun of the other person.

* * *

What does the author recommend that you do with the things to say that are listed above?

A. not really say them, but see them as examples of a complicated point,
or
B. actually say these things, often, to other people in your life?

469. If you would like to try an experiment, you may find that it changes your life. Here it is: Read the list of things to say to improve the emotional climate, every day. Imagine any opportunities you may have to say these things. Imagine yourself saying these things to the people in your life, with enthusiastic tones of voice. Then actually say these things, as often as you get the chance, with enthusiasm. Notice, over time, the effect on the emotional climate. Does it make you happier? Does it make others happier? Does it reduce provocations, and reduce

the need for anger control? Try it and see.

The author's suggestion in this section involves

A. fantasy rehearsing and enthusiastically saying the things that improve the emotional climate,
or
B. trying to make other people happy in as many ways as possible?

Chapter 15: Self-Monitoring and Celebrations

470. Let's review the strategy we've talked about so far for improving anger control and conflict-resolution. You set a clear goal. You create an internal sales pitch, a set of reasons for wanting to achieve that goal. You list choice points, the types of situations in which you want to use good anger control and conflict-resolution. You decide what thoughts, emotions, and behaviors you want to use in those choice points. (In doing so, you use the concepts this book has defined, in order to think better about the options.) Then you do many fantasy rehearsals of the desirable patterns. You also fantasy rehearse and say the sorts of things that improve the emotional climate and prevent provocations before they happen.

What next? You want the desirable patterns of thought, emotion, and behavior you have decided upon to transfer from fantasy rehearsal to real life. You want to examine your real-life behaviors to see if the patterns you have decided upon really are working. You want to celebrate and feel very good whenever you have an "anger control triumph" or a "conflict-resolution triumph" in which you carry out, in real life, a good example of these skills. These tasks are the subject of this chapter.

This chapter is about

A. making good anger control and conflict-resolution happen in real life as well as fantasy,
or
B. setting goals for anger control and conflict-resolution?

471. One of the tasks to do in order to make the good behaviors transfer to real life is called self-monitoring. Self-monitoring means that you measure how well you do in your real life behavior. You do this not just once, but regularly, over and over again.

Here's an example. Every night before Tom goes to bed, he asks himself, "How well did I do at anger control and conflict-resolution today? How well did I create a positive emotional climate?" He uses the following scale:

0 = Very bad
2 = Bad
4 = So-so
6 = Pretty good
8 = Good
10 = Very good

He makes an entry on a spreadsheet, and occasionally he looks at the graph of how well he is doing over time.

What Tom is doing is called

A. self-monitoring,
or
B. self-interest?

472. Every Sunday afternoon Pat thinks back over how well he has done in conflict-resolution, anger control, and creating a positive emotional climate in the past week. Pat also asks his spouse what she thinks about how he has done. He assigns himself a weekly rating on a 0 to 10 scale, and writes it down in a notebook.

Pat is using another form of

A. the Four-thought Exercise,
or
B. self-monitoring?

473. As you self-monitor, you ask yourself, "Am I succeeding? If so, what am I doing that is making me succeed? What is important for me to keep on doing?" When I am not succeeding, I want to ask, "What could I be doing, that would make it more likely for me to succeed?" In other words, self-monitoring helps me know whether I'm on the right track or not, and how to get on the right track and stay on it.

The point of this section is that:

A. Once you enter a number in a graph or table, you're done with all you need to do about self-monitoring.
or

B. You use your self-monitoring results to think about why you are on the right track or the wrong track.

474. Another very important way of making positive patterns happen more often in real life is called the celebrations exercise. This exercise is very similar to a fantasy rehearsal. In a sense, it's a type of fantasy rehearsal. The difference is that rather than *imagining* something smart or good you *would like to do* in a choice point, you *remember* something smart or good you have *already done*. As with other fantasy rehearsals, you run through your mind very vividly the image of your doing something smart or good, and you try to celebrate and feel good about having done it.

Answering which of these questions leads someone to do the celebrations exercise?

A. What have you done lately that you are glad you have done?
or
B. What have you done lately that you wish you hadn't done?

475. Here's an example of someone's doing the celebrations exercise.

"A kid in my neighborhood came up to me on the sidewalk and said, 'Why did you mess up that fort we built in the woods?'

"I quickly thought to myself something like, 'I'm getting accused of something I didn't do. But this isn't the end of the world. I want to remind myself that I don't need to feel on trial. I don't need to persuade this person of anything. My goal is to stay cool.'

"I felt pretty cool and calculating, and determined to stay cool.

"I said, 'I didn't mess up any fort.' The kid rolled his eyes like he didn't believe me.

"I said, 'You're rolling your eyes as if you think I'm lying.'

"The kid said, 'It wouldn't surprise me.'

"I said, 'Think whatever you want to, then.' I walked on.

"I feel really good about how I handled this! I stuck up for myself, but I didn't lose my cool!"

In recounting this, the person talked about which of the following?

A. the situation, thoughts, emotions, behavior, and celebration,
or
B. the reflection, agreeing with part of criticism, and the asking for more specific criticism?

476. As the example above illustrates, when you recount a celebration, you can tell the situation, thoughts, emotions, and behavior, and you can celebrate what you have done. Or you can leave out any of these. For example, you can just tell the situation and what you did.

There are two big reasons to do the celebrations exercise. When you recall something good that you did and feel good about it, the good feelings you have reinforce the good behavior. That means that you are more likely to do something like that again. You have rewarded yourself for doing the thing you're glad you've done.

The second reason for doing the celebrations exercise is that when you often feel proud and happy about the things you've done, you feel happier overall, and this is a good thing too!

The two reasons for doing the celebrations exercise are that it

A. reinforces good patterns and makes you happier,
or
B. gets your feelings out and teaches you to learn new words?

477. If you are particularly strongly working on anger control, conflict-resolution, and/or nonviolence skills, you will want to pick every possible opportunity to celebrate doing something good in these areas. Almost every day you will find some little (or big) provocation that you have a chance

to practice handling well, leading to a possible celebration. If there is no such situation, you almost always have the chance to say one of the things that make a better emotional climate. About the only days you won't get a chance to practice are days when you don't see or speak to one person!

Opportunities to celebrate choice points having to do with the goals of this book will probably come

A. at least every day, usually many times,
or
B. once a month or so?

478. If you have energy and motivation to devote to the goals of conflict-resolution and anger control, an excellent way to use that energy is to make a *celebrations diary*. To do this, you write down your celebrations regularly. The best schedule is the one that you can sustain over time, can keep doing. Perhaps it involves writing every day; perhaps every week. The big advantage of writing down the celebrations is that you can review them repeatedly, long after you do them. (If you don't write them down, you'll forget most of them.) Each time you run them through the circuitry of your brain, you are practicing the good patterns and making them more likely to happen again. Thus not only writing the celebrations, but also reading and vividly imagining what you have

written, are habits that will help you achieve your goals.

This section makes a case for

A. sharing your celebrations with someone else,
or
B. writing down your celebrations and often reviewing what you have written?

479. Can you find someone else who is also interested in your achieving your goals, or someone who is working on the same goals? If so, it is good to start a ritual of regularly sharing celebrations. It often works best if two people take turns. One tells a celebration, and the other listens and congratulates the other; then the other tells a celebration. If the other person is genuinely happy about your accomplishments, sharing your celebrations can make a huge difference in accomplishing your goal. When the other person says, "Good job," that is called social reinforcement. When you say "Good job" to yourself, that is called self-reinforcement. You have the best chance of succeeding when you have both social reinforcement and self-reinforcement working for you.

This section makes a case for

A. writing down your celebrations,
or
B. sharing your celebrations with someone else?

480. The various options for motives, thoughts, emotions, and behaviors that this book has defined are possibilities to choose from. Sometimes one option works much better than another. You will need to observe what happens in real life as you try out options, to see what makes things turn out best in the long run.

Marta has a friend who often criticizes her. Marta decides that rather than defending herself and arguing back and forth, she will simply try apologizing. She does this for a while, but she finds that this leads her friend to become even more dominating and critical. She shifts her strategy. She uses assertion, and if the friend keeps on criticizing, Marta occasionally "criticizes the critic." This turns out to keep the friend's wish for dominance in check enough that Marta doesn't have to use her last resort strategy, which is moving "away from the situation" by ending the relationship.

The point of this section is that:

A. You have to observe the real-life results of the options you pick, to know what works the best.
or
B. You should make your best choice and stick with it, even if it doesn't seem to be working out well.

481. If you are able to have an "anger control triumph" or a "conflict-resolution triumph" or an "emotional climate triumph" in even one situation, that is cause for great celebration. If you are able to make your overall pattern of dealing with people more peaceful, you've done something truly heroic. Not many people are able to accomplish this, and if you are able to, you deserve to feel very proud.

The point of this section is that:

A. You should not stop working on this goal.
or
B. If you are able to accomplish this goal, you have reason to feel very proud.

Chapter 16: More Ways To End Violence

482. This book has described a detailed and useful way for people to improve their anger control and conflict-resolution skills, and to create more positive interpersonal climates. One very important way to reduce violence in the world would be for everyone to practice these techniques, starting from a very early age.

But there are still other ways of reducing the amount of violence in the world. Let's review them in this chapter.

The author's point of view is that:

A. The only way to reduce violence is for each person to do what has already been described in this book.
or
B. There are more ways of reducing violence that we haven't talked about yet.

Having Fewer Guns

483. One important way to reduce violence is to have fewer guns available. Imagine that two people get into a conflict where they are moving closer and closer to violence. Even if they have no weapons, there is a chance that one will kill the other. Fists and feet and almost anything you can pick up and swing can be lethal weapons. But the chance of a killing is far lower than if there is a gun in the picture.

If one person has a gun, or if both have guns, each one of them may think, "If I don't shoot him first, I am likely to get shot." The situation is drastically changed.

The main point of this section is that:

A. When guns are in the picture, people tend to use them out of fear that others will use them first.
or
B. People can kill each other, even without weapons.

484. Unfortunately, having better weapons than the other tribe has aided human beings in survival for centuries. The tribe who used slingshots probably had a survival advantage over the tribe who threw rocks. The tribe who had bows and arrows tended to wipe out the other tribe who had spears only. Thus it is not surprising that people, particularly males, tend to be fascinated with guns and weapons. But, even if there is an inborn tendency to be thrilled by weapons, we can eventually train ourselves to feel differently.

The author's point of view is that:

A. Fascination with weapons is built into the brain, and there is nothing to be done about that.
or
B. Even if there is an attraction to weapons built into the brain, people can overcome that through training.

485. Why do people want to own weapons? One reason is for self-defense. The more afraid someone is that people will come and terrorize him, the more that person will want to be able to get his hands on a gun quickly. On the other hand, if there is little or no violence in the person's neighborhood, and if there is trust in police and in the rule of law, there is less reason for someone to feel the need to have a gun. Thus the less violent a certain region is, the fewer guns there are.

The idea of this section is that:

A. Once a neighborhood has become nonviolent, it is easier for it to stay that way, because people have fewer guns.
or
B. People should be required to own guns, because then there would be less crime.

486. As humanity becomes more and more civilized, there will be less and less need for guns for self-defense. People hopefully will be able to come around to the attitude of the philosopher Lao-Tsu, whose words were recorded many centuries ago::

"Weapons are the tools of violence;
all decent people detest them.
Weapons are the tools of fear;
decent people will avoid them
except in the direst necessity
and, if compelled, will use them
only with the utmost restraint.
Peace is their highest value.
If the peace has been shattered,
how can they be content?
Their enemies are not demons,
but human beings like themselves.
They do not wish them personal harm.
Nor do they rejoice in victory.
How could they rejoice in victory
and delight in the slaughter of others?"

Lao-Tsu believed that:

A. A good warrior should take pleasure in conquering his enemy.
or
B. People should not enjoy violence or using weapons, even they have to use them.

Avoiding Alcohol

487. Hundreds of research studies have examined the relation of alcohol to violence. In one study of nearly two thousand killings, in about half of them the killer had been drinking alcohol at the time. In another study, researchers interviewed 268 people who had killed

someone else. Thirty-two percent reported having been drunk on alcohol at the time of the killing.

The author seems to feel that:

A. People are more likely to be violent when they have been drinking alcohol.
or
B. Lots of people are violent without having drunk alcohol, so there isn't any connection between alcohol and violence.

488. The town of Barrow, Alaska, passed a law totally banning alcohol sales. Shortly after that, the ban was lifted, so that alcohol was allowed again for a while. Then the citizens put the ban back in place, getting rid of alcohol again.

Researchers realized that this gave a chance to study how having alcohol available affects violence. They looked at the records of emergency rooms of hospitals. They counted those visits caused by one person's hurting another. These visits for assault went down when alcohol was banned, went back up when alcohol came back, and went down again when alcohol was banned again!

The author reports this study as evidence that:

A. Changing laws has bad effects.
or

B. When alcohol is less available, people hurt each other less often.

489. In many laboratory studies, scientists have tested people's abilities to use self-control (to resist an impulse) and particularly to keep their tempers. In order to test the effects of alcohol, some people have been given alcohol, and others something else to drink.

The conclusion is very strong that alcohol makes it harder for people to use self-control and to control their tempers.

The author seems to feel that:

A. People should be able to control themselves, alcohol or no alcohol.
or
B. Alcohol makes it harder for people to control themselves.

Stopping the Trade of Illegal Drugs

490. Among the jobs where violent death is most likely, the job of illegal drug dealer has to rank near the top. With no legal means for drug dealers to decide who gets to sell to which markets, the favorite method seems to be drive-by shootings and other violence.

When people are addicted to illegal drugs, they can be motivated to hold up stores or carry out muggings to get the money to keep from going into withdrawal.

If the illegal drug trade were somehow stopped, lots of lives would be saved.

The point of this section is that:

A. Buying and selling of illegal drugs is criminal, but it has nothing to do with violence.
or
B. Buying and selling illegal drugs has a lot to do with violence.

491. What's the best way to stop the buying and selling of illegal drugs? Is it penalties for drug dealers? Penalties for drug users? More testing for drug use? Better education about the harmful effects of illegal drugs? More and better drug treatment? Methadone maintenance programs and others where people addicted to drugs get them from clinics and not drug dealers? Legalizing certain drugs? There is not space here to discuss the pros and cons of different options. The drug problem is very difficult to solve.

However, anyone who wants to solve the problem should at least not contribute to it. That means never, ever, buying a drug illegally, and trying to persuade others to follow this rule also.

One of the only definite recommendations the author can make about the illegal drug trade is that:

A. All drugs of abuse should be dispensed in clinics so that people won't have to buy them from dealers.
or
B. If you want to help solve this problem, you can start by never buying a drug illegally, and also asking your friends not to.

Achievement Versus Aggression

492. One great way of helping people not to be aggressive is to help them to be successful, to achieve. For children, a most important area of success is school achievement. It's frustrating to feel like a failure in school, and perhaps this is one reason why people who feel like they're failing tend to be more aggressive. On the other hand, someone who is learning interesting things, taking on challenges, and getting the good feeling of succeeding in those challenges, tends to be happier and less angry. Tutoring and other ways of helping people be more successful are important ways of reducing aggression and violence.

The point of this section is that:

A. Such things as learning to read and learning math are fine, but they don't have anything to do with anger control and nonviolence.
or

B. Becoming more successful at reading and math helps people with anger control and nonviolence.

Stopping Bullying by the Rule of Law

493. When students have been surveyed in schools, it is sometimes found that more than one in every five children either bullies others or gets bullied. Thus there is much meanness and hostility going on. The mean behavior of bullies is a way of practicing for later violence: bullies become criminals more often than other students do.

The best solution to bullying is for schools to have very clear-cut rules against one person's victimizing another, and for those rules to be very strictly enforced. In other words, the best solution is summarized by a phrase we have studied before: *the rule of law*.

The author's conclusion is that bullying is best ended by

A. establishing clear rules and enforcing them thoroughly,
or
B. teaching martial arts skills to the victims, so they can defend themselves against bullies?

494. In some schools, adults have taken the attitude, "Let them work it out for themselves." When children have reported to teachers that other children

are victimizing them, they have been called "tattletales." When kids have been seen fighting, some adults have said, "Boys will be boys." And some kids have been afraid to report being victimized, for fear of the disapproval of both adults and peers.

All of this must come to a halt if we are to deal effectively with the bullying problem. People need to talk openly about bullying and to take seriously children's reports about being victimized. Kids need to know whom to report it to when they are being bullied. Adults need to be able to monitor children's behavior closely enough that all kids are protected from anyone who would bully others.

The author makes the point in this section that:

A. Children learn responsibility by being able to handle bullying on their own.
or
B. Adults should bear responsibility for making and enforcing rules against bullying.

Ending Abusive Relationships

495. There are, unfortunately, relationships where one person repeatedly hits or kicks or hurts another. There are also relationships where one person frequently says hostile and

insulting things to another. Sometimes both people are hostile and violent to each other! When the level of hostility reaches a certain level – and no one can say exactly where the border is – we begin to speak of an "abusive relationship." Often these abusive relationships are based on power and control: the abuser wants to keep close control over what the other person does and thinks and feels.

Sometimes the person being abused thinks, "I should be loyal. It's my fault that the other person acts this way. Maybe I can change him if I act better. I'll try this other way." Or, "I'll just keep trying."

This section makes the point that people sometimes abuse someone else

A. because they want to control the other person,
or
B. because they just have a chemical imbalance that makes them lose control at times.

496. Particularly when the people in an abusive relationship are adults, the simplest solution to the problem is usually the best: leave. The technique of "away from the situation – permanently" was particularly designed for abusive relationships. The abuser should get out of the relationship and then work on anger control. The person abused should get out of the

relationship and then work on whatever skills are necessary to avoid abusive relationships in the future.

Which of these statements would the author tend to agree with?

A. Divorce is a sin and should be avoided at all costs.
or
B. It is much better to end a relationship than to risk ending a life.

497. When the abuser is a parent, or a child, it still remains true that when physical violence or hostility and rejection reach a certain level, parent and child should be separated. Perhaps they can have a relationship later on when the abuser has mastered the skill of anger control.

The author feels that the solution of "away from the situation"

A. applies only when the people in an abusive relationship are both adults,
or
B. applies to all abusive relationships?

498. It's easier for people to get out of abusive relationships if they have some other place to go. If our society supports shelters for people to live in while they are regrouping after leaving an abusive relationship, then it is helping to prevent violence. Some shelters, for example, let women come and live there when

they escape from an abusive relationship.

This section makes the point that:

A. Not so many people would be abusive if people studied the ideas in this book.
or
B. Shelters where people can go when they escape abusive relationships help to reduce violence.

Reducing Violent Entertainment

499. Throughout this book, I have emphasized the technique of fantasy rehearsal. If you want to keep cool in provocations, practice doing this in your imagination as often as you can.

It makes sense that fantasy rehearsal can work in the other direction, also. What if people often imagine kicking and shooting and hurting other people? Such negative fantasy rehearsal will not necessarily make these behaviors come to pass in real life. But it makes them more likely, and the more fantasy rehearsals there are, the higher the likelihood climbs.

The point of this section is that:

A. Fantasy rehearsal can increase anger and violence as well as decrease it.
or

B. Violence usually has bad effects upon the person who carries it out as well as the victim.

500. The theory of fantasy rehearsal suggests that, if someone watches television shows and movies, and plays video games that have almost nonstop hostility and violence, that person is getting lots of negative fantasy rehearsal. Such practice works in just the opposite direction from that which this book recommends.

The author is suggesting that:

A. Violent movies, TV shows, and video games have very little effect.
or
B. Violent movies, TV shows, and video games have bad effects.

501. You sometimes hear people say, "Do we really know whether violent television and movies and video games affect real-life behavior?" The answer to that is, "Yes!" We do know the answer to that. Literally hundreds of studies have been done on this subject. There have been at least several dozen articles or books reviewing the studies that have been done.

In 2003, a group of prominent scientists reviewed the evidence on this question. They wrote: "The scientific debate over whether media violence increases aggression and violence is essentially over." In other words, we have enough evidence to answer the question.

The point the author is making is that:

A. More research is needed before we can settle the question of whether violent shows are harmful.
or
B. The question is really settled.

502. What is the answer? The evidence is very strong that violent television, films, video games, and music increase the likelihood of aggressive behavior in real life.

How did researchers find this out? There are four main ways. They looked at a group of kids and measured how aggressive they were and what shows they watched. Then they came back years later, and did the same measurements on the same people. They found that the ones who watched more violence were not only more aggressive to begin with, but they became more aggressive over time. They increased their aggression more than the ones who watched less violence.

The second way is that researchers studied how much violence there was in communities before and after a big change in fantasy violence exposures, for example, after the introduction of television. They found that, as television was introduced into various

places, the rate of violence went up. Furthermore, the violence rate went up soonest in those places where television was introduced soonest.

A third way that researchers have used is to randomly assign people to watch violent or nonviolent shows, and then study their behavior immediately afterwards. They have found that seeing violence leads to more aggressive attitudes and behavior shortly afterward.

A fourth way of researching this question is very promising in a world where nearly everyone has a high exposure to entertainment violence. You ask some parents to restrict entertainment violence carefully for their children, and you see if these children become less aggressive as compared to other children. The answer to this question has been "Yes!"

This section tells four ways that:

A. Researchers have found that violent entertainment makes people more aggressive.
or
B. Researchers have tried to get people to become aware of their findings.

503. There are literally billions of dollars spent each year on producing violent entertainment. This is money that our society could be using to promote peace and anger control and conflict-resolution.

Violent entertainment is a problem throughout our whole culture. Almost everywhere you look, you see violent entertainment. If you turn on any television and surf the channels, you can usually see a killing acted out within a very short time. Many video games have fantasy killings not only watched, but also directed, by the player. Video game fantasy killings can occur at extremely high rates, yielding more fantasy practice than television.

What can any one person do about this problem? First, you can let people know what the research findings are. Second, you can avoid contributing your own time, energy, and money to violent entertainment.

The point of this section is that:

A. The problem is so widespread that people must act together – there is nothing any one person can do.
or
B. As only one person, at least you can help educate other people, and you can boycott violent entertainment yourself.

Peace through International Law

504. What's the best solution to the violence of warfare, the violence that threatens the whole human race? A major answer surely must lie in providing ways for groups of people to settle their disputes through law rather than through violence. Many careful thinkers have realized that the best the human race has to end war lies in international laws, international organizations to enforce those laws, and international courts to settle disputes. In other words, individual countries have to surrender some of their power to some form of world government. This is very difficult to do. But when it can be achieved, nations can settle their disputes in courtrooms rather than through bombs and bullets.

The author's point is that world peace will come when

A. all people of the world learn to have love in their hearts,
or
B. there is a system of international courts and laws and law enforcement that works as well as that of a well-run country?

505. When did the United States of America become a country? Most people would say 1776, the year of the Declaration of Independence. But from 1776 until 1788, there was not one country – there were thirteen former colonies that could make their own rules, without being subject to a central government. Each of them was like a little country unto itself. When the fishermen of one state had a dispute with those of another, they didn't go to federal court, because there was no

federal court – they fought with each other. Some of these thirteen states came close to war with one another at least half a dozen times. Things were a mess – sort of like the way they are now between countries. What straightened out the mess was making a government that had higher authority than any single state. After that happened in 1788, when two states had disputes with each other, they could take their dispute to the government of the country, and people could figure out the answer according to law and not by having a war.

The point of this section is that:

A. When the states of the U.S.A. formed themselves into a country, they created a way to resolve disputes among each other without violence.
or
B. When the states of the U.S.A. formed themselves into a country, they found a way to resolve disputes with other countries without violence.

506. Albert Einstein, the brilliant scientist, applied his mind not only to physics, but also to the problem of world peace. He wrote that the only way to world peace is to form a "legislative and judicial body to settle every conflict arising between nations." This means a world congress and a world court.

But Einstein also pointed out that this requires that the nations have to agree that they will accept it when decisions don't go their way. This means giving up some of their power to decide things for themselves.

Nations don't want anyone from any other nation telling them what to do. This is why world government hasn't taken hold yet. But it was also tough for Pennsylvania and New York and Delaware and the others to give up some of their power to a government of the U.S.A. Perhaps some day a world government will be able to enforce nonviolent resolutions to the disputes between nations.

People are having more and more contact with each other across the world. They are buying and selling all over the world. There is more and more mixing of races in marriage. Language barriers are falling. The Internet makes communication among people all over the world almost instantaneous. Perhaps it will not be long before enough people see themselves as citizens of one planet, that they can form a world government.

Albert Einstein believed that:

A. World peace would be achieved only when all people became good.
or
B. World peace would be achieved only when countries gave up some of their

power, by letting an international court settle disputes.

Please Find the Missing Ideas

507. What big ideas on promoting nonviolence are left out by this chapter? Teaching parents better ways to deal with their children? Departments of peace in governments? More mediation centers, where people can take their disputes and get help from a mediator who seeks a just solution? An international language? More foreign exchanges that help people get to know people from other countries? School tests on nonviolence skills and knowledge as well as reading and mathematics? Inventing ways of measuring people's anger control and conflict-resolution skills? Peace academies, where scholars can devote large efforts to the question of nonviolence? More public rewards and awards for the efforts of "nonviolence heroes?"

Let's try to imagine a world in which people spent even a tenth as much time and energy wondering about how to produce nonviolence as they do on other less useful or even harmful pursuits. It would be a very different world.

But you don't have to wait for that world to come. You can start now spending time thinking about ideas that will help reduce violence. Perhaps you can be one of the people who can really make a difference by reducing violence.

The attitude of the author is that:

A. This book provides all the answers, and other people should just put them into effect.
or
B. People should always keep asking the question of how to reduce violence, and always look for what this book has left out.

Appendix 1: Conflicts for Practice

How to Use the Practice Choice Points

1. You can role-play both parts of a conflict-resolution conversation, trying to meet all seven of the guidelines of "Dr. L.W. Aap": defining, reflecting, listing, waiting, advantages, agreement, and politeness. Or, you can play one of the parts and role-play such a conversation with someone else.

2. You can give yourself concentrated practice in listing options. Think of options for what the two people in these situations could do to solve their problem. If two people do this exercise together, it's often most fun to take turns listing options.

3. You can imagine yourself in the role of first one, and then the other, of the two people, and do the Four-thought Exercise (or the Twelve-thought Exercise) about the situation. (In the Four-thought Exercise, you practice not awfulizing, goal-setting, listing options and choosing, and celebrating your own choice.)

4. You can imagine yourself in the role of first one, and then the other, of the two people, and do a fantasy rehearsal of handling the situation. (Remember - situation, thoughts, emotions, behaviors, and celebration.)

5. You can imagine yourself in both roles and practice coming up with goal-setting thoughts that lead to the motives most connected with peace: avoiding harm, self-discipline, problem-solving, empathy and understanding, and kindness and friendship-building. (ASPEK).

Please remember that you benefit from practicing with situations that involve people very different from you! If you are forty years old, you'll benefit from taking the perspective of children who need to share a toy. If you are eight years old, you will benefit from taking the perspective of married people who are trying to figure out how to share their money. Getting outside your own world view and seeing things from others' perspectives is one of the benefits of these exercises.

* * *

508. One person in a family likes to listen to a certain type of music. The other hates it.

509. Pat and Lee live together. Pat's favorite food is a dish made of fish and sauerkraut. When Pat cooks it, it makes a smell all through the place that Lee thinks is horrible.

510. One person in a family wants to study. The other wants to practice playing his drum. The drum-playing bothers the studier.

511. Two people want to go out to a restaurant together and eat. One person wants to go to the pizza place, and the other person wants to go to the vegetarian restaurant.

512. You and another family member share a room. The other family member (the fresh-air lover) likes to leave the window open to get fresh air. You (the noise-hater) don't, because you don't like the noise from the street.

513. You are in a boat with a friend who keeps fooling around, rocking the boat. The water is very deep, and while your friend says not to worry, you are afraid the boat will tip over. The friend (the boat-rocker) feels that what he is doing is safe enough.

514. Someone has a dog who barks at night so much that the next-door neighbor can't sleep.

515. One person in the family is taking a shower, and sometimes, when another person turns water on or off somewhere else, or flushes a toilet, it can make the water in the shower too hot or too cold.

516. A family has a rule that everyone will begin eating supper only when everyone has come to the table. One person in the family (the latecomer) often shows up late, and everyone else has to wait for that person.

517. Two people are in the library trying to read and study, sitting across the table from each other. One of them (the tapper) is tapping his pen on the table, and this keeps the other one (the distracted one) from being able to concentrate on what he is doing. The tapper has such a strong habit of tapping that he may not be able to concentrate well if he doesn't tap.

518. Two people are friends. One of them (the interrupter) grew up in a big family where, if you wanted to talk, you usually had to interrupt other people. The other of them (the pauser) grew up as an only child in a family where you could think for a long time before you talk, and still have people listen. The pauser is irritated when the interrupter interrupts; the interrupter is irritated when the pauser pauses and thinks too long before speaking.

519. One person ("the talker") likes to talk for a long time without stopping. The other person ("the talker's" friend) gets bored with this and wishes the other wouldn't hog the conversation so much.

520. A girl's dad has met her at a swimming pool, and has taken her home. Just as they are walking in the

door, they realize that the girl left something she owned at the swimming pool. She is interested in going back immediately to try to get it. But the dad has things to do, and also thinks the pool may be closed by now.

521. Some parents buy a new thing that a brother and sister both want to play with and look at very much. But they can't both play with it at the same time.

522. You share the responsibility of caring for your dog with your brother. For the last few days, however, he hasn't been doing his share, even though you've reminded him about it, and you've had to do all the work.

523. You and your brother/sister have something at home that you both want to take to school to show your class, on the same day, at the same time, in different classrooms.

524. Ted comes over to visit at Jack's house. Jack wants to play with video games, but Ted thinks video games are a big waste of time and would like to practice throwing a baseball outside, or be by himself and read a book, more than playing with video games.

525. Some boys are playing tackle football. One person (the softer-tackle wisher) says that another one (the hard tackler) is tackling too hard.

526. Jane and Sara are friends at school, and they sit beside each other. Jane keeps talking to Sara, and Sara talks back to her, and the teacher gets mad at both of them when this happens.

527. There are two brothers. One has lots of trouble with his schoolwork, so his parents spend a lot of time helping that brother. But the other brother feels that he is getting the short end of the stick and that his parents don't spend enough time with him.

528. Tracy and Michael are playing a computer game. When Tracy is playing, Michael is too bossy and directive; for example he is constantly saying things such as, "No, don't do it that way. Put it there! Now go over there. The other direction. You don't have enough to do that." Tracy doesn't have much fun when Michael does this.

529. Three people are together. Two of them are hungry and want to go to a restaurant and get something to eat. The third (the non-hungry one) doesn't feel like eating at all.

530. You have a hard decision to make, and you want to be alone in your room to think things out. A family member wants to talk with you or play a game.

531. A father thinks his teenaged daughter should brush her teeth every time she eats, and keeps asking her if she has done so. The daughter thinks

that she is old enough to make her own decision on that.

532. A man and a woman are married. The woman suggests that they see a certain movie, but the man doesn't like movies.

533. It is a very snowy day. Mr. Smith has worked very hard to shovel out a place by the side of the road to park. When he gets through shoveling, he goes and gets his car to park in the place. When he gets back to the place with his car, Mr. Jones has just parked in it. Both people feel that they have a right to park in the place. Part of the problem is that Mr. Jones doesn't know whether to believe that Mr. Smith really did all the work.

534. A person agrees to give a speech for an organization, where a couple of hundred people will come and hear the speaker. The time of the speech is planned several months in advance. Just three days before the speech is scheduled, the speaker's mother gets very sick, in a town far from where the speech will be, and the speaker wants to look after her rather than give the speech. The organization people want to have their speech.

535. Two people are married. One likes things to be put away, so that things in the house are not out of place and lying around. The other thinks it isn't so

important to be neat, and leaves lots of things lying around.

536. One spouse thinks that they should spend a lot of money to go someplace exotic for a vacation. The other spouse thinks they should save the money for the future, such as for education.

537. A kid's mother likes to visit graveyards. She takes the kid along, because the kid is too young to stay home alone. Graveyards give the kid a creepy feeling.

538. There is a mouse in the house. One person wants to kill the mouse, but the other is an animal lover.

539. A kid feels that he has worked very hard during the school year and wants to take the summer off just to relax. His parent thinks that this would be lazy.

540. One person in a family likes the custom that people get very nice presents for one another on birthdays and holidays. The other person thinks that this wastes money and creates too much clutter.

541. A person has a younger brother who treats the family's cat too roughly. The person has talked with the brother about this, but it has done no good. The person talks with a parent about what to do about this problem.

542. A kid wants to get a small tattoo, and the parent thinks that this is a bad idea.

543. A girl wants to get her ears pierced with two holes, not just one. The girl's parent thinks that one hole is enough.

544. A girl wants to get her belly button pierced. Her dad thinks this looks really bad.

545. A teenager has a boyfriend or girlfriend. Her parent thinks that, because the friend smokes, the friend must be a real loser, and the parent doesn't want the child to see this friend.

546. Someone is trying to lose weight. He wants to eat a little bit, quickly, and then get away from food so that he won't be tempted to eat more. But his family member thinks it's important to have long conversations at the dinner table, for the sake of family closeness.

547. Someone is on a basketball team with someone else. The second one hardly ever passes the ball to the first one, even when the first one is open.

548. One person in a family wants to recycle everything that can be recycled. But the other wants not to be bothered by recyclable trash but to put some recyclables in the regular trash.

549. One person nods his head in time with music when she hears it. The other person finds this annoying.

550. A kid wants his mom or dad to homeschool him. But they feel they wouldn't be good enough teachers.

551. When the first kid strikes out in baseball, the second kid says things such as, "You struck out! You made an out for us!" in a disapproving tone. The first doesn't like this.

552. The first person has a good friend. A second person teases that good friend for being a little overweight.

553. A child's divorced parents say to the child, "You decide which of us you want to be with on the holiday." The child doesn't like this plan and wants to work out a different one.

554. A boy wanted to sign up for soccer. But once he got started doing it, he very much disliked it. His parents feel that he should finish what he started.

555. A person likes his privacy, but his brother comes into his room uninvited.

556. Some parents want a child and his brother to fly on a plane by themselves. They are afraid to fly by themselves. But it will cost a lot of money for someone to fly with them.

557. A kid has a brother who seems to like to make him mad just for the fun of it. The brother gets a bored feeling and wants to stir up something interesting.

558. The first person likes to play games. But when the second person loses, that person gets really angry.

559. A girl at school likes a boy, and tries to sit next to him and walk to places beside him. But he doesn't like this, because the other boys tease him about it.

560. A boy and his mom yell at each other when they argue, and this makes both of them feel bad.

561. A boy's older sisters tease him. They think he is too sensitive, but he doesn't like it.

562. A girl has a friend who tells people she is on a gymnastics team and that she wins meets. But the girl knows that the friend is lying. This makes the girl uncomfortable.

563. There is a fad toy that all the kids seem to want. A girl wants to have several of them, to be like her friends. But her parents think these things are a waste of money and the world would be better off without fads like this.

564. One person in the family likes to lie on the couch, but the other one feels that he has a right to sit on it too.

565. One person likes to have raw broccoli dipped in mustard. The second person thinks that this is gross.

566. Two people play basketball together, but one plays too roughly to suit the other.

567. There is a custom in the family for people to buy each other presents for birthdays and several other holidays. But this family has enough money that they buy anything they really want right away. So most of the presents get wasted.

568. The first person has promised that the second could use his computer game when the second is home recovering from an operation. But it turns out that the first person really needs money for something else, and wants to take the computer game back and get his money back.

569. The first person believes that the war his country is fighting is immoral. The second person thinks the war is just and good.

570. One family member wants to keep things private, and thinks the other is too nosy. The second family member thinks that people should share with one another what's on their minds.

571. A parent wants her teenaged daughter not to get involved with any

boyfriend, but the girl is interested in boys.

572. A boy's father wants him to do really well in sports. But the boy is not nearly as interested in sports as his father seems to want him to be.

573. A boy likes to play video games, and doesn't see anything wrong with them. But his parents feel that the games are too violent.

574. The first kid acts nice to the second kid during the week when they go to school together, but the first ignores the second on weekends.

575. Two family members both want to sit in a certain seat of the car.

576. A person has a family member who irritates their dog.

577. When a kid wakes up at night, he gets out of bed and tells his parents that he woke up. He is lonely and wants to be with someone. But his habit interferes with his parents' sleep.

578. A boy wants to work toward becoming a professional basketball player. His dad thinks that his chances for success in this field are very small, and he should put his efforts elsewhere.

579. A piano teacher wants a kid to practice between lessons. But the kid doesn't like practicing, and doesn't do it very much.

580. A younger sister doesn't like how her older sister acts very conceited at times.

581. There is a new kid in school. When a second kid looks at the new kid to say "Hi," the new kid says, "What are you looking at?" The second kid just wants to be friendly, but it seems that the new kid suspects malice.

582. The people next door have a dog who barks ferociously when someone comes out into his yard. The person is worried that the dog might jump over the fence.

583. When two people have an argument, they act sullen and don't talk with each other for a long time. They would like to get over feeling angry sooner.

584. Two siblings are in the habit of trying to get each other in trouble with their parents.

585. One person in a family likes pasta sauce very spicy, but for the other person this ruins the whole dish.

586. One person roots for a certain team to win, and his friend roots for a different team. They feel uncomfortable with each other about this.

587. A younger kid needs more sleep than his older brother, so he has to go to bed earlier. But the older brother gets time alone with the parent after he goes to bed, and he feels he's missing out.

588. One friend believes very strongly in a religion, and the other friend doesn't.

589. The family owns a dog. But two siblings are jealous about which of them the dog likes best. When one of them starts sweet-talking with the dog, the other asks him to stop. This makes the first one angry.

590. A kid is a very good swimmer, and her parents think she could go to the Olympics. But the kid thinks too much of life is being taken up with swimming practice, and would like to get into other activities.

591. A kid has a friend who doesn't like one of the kid's other friends. The first kid doesn't want to have to choose.

592. One pen pal writes long letters, but the other just writes a few words.

593. One sibling pesters the other one too much. The problem is discussed by the two siblings.

594. One sibling pesters the other too much. The problem is discussed by the pestered sibling and a parent.

595. An older sibling wants to have things in her room that are dangerous for the two-year-old sibling. But the younger sibling wanders into the room a lot. The problem is discussed between the older sibling and a parent.

596. A parent wants a boy to let his younger brother play on his team in the neighborhood baseball games. But the younger brother is not a very good player yet, and he makes the team lose.

597. A sister puts her things on another sister's bed.

598. The computer is in the first brother's room. The second brother comes in to use the computer while the first is still in bed and wakes him up.

599. A brother and sister have fallen into the habit of purposely getting each other in trouble with their parents.

600. There are two friends. The first of them gets jealous and angry when the second tells about fun and interesting things she did with a third friend.

601. A kid thinks her mom is too soft on her when she does something wrong.

602. A kid thinks her mom is too hard on her and too soft on her brother when they do something wrong.

603. Two kids sit next to each other in school. They get into conflicts because

one puts his books and papers into the other person's space.

604. A boy finds that often when some important event is coming up, such as a going-away party for his best friend who's moving away, his parents have planned a trip out of town and he has to go too.

605. A kid has so many music lessons and sports lessons that he doesn't have time to relax. But his parents want him to become competent at many things.

606. A boy agrees to trade toys with another kid. But then the other kid demands to trade back again whenever he feels like it.

607. Two friends are able to spend some time playing together. They need to decide together what to do.

608. A child is supposed to go to bed at a certain time. But it takes so long for the child to get ready for bed that it usually ends up being much later when the child actually goes to bed. The parent and child talk this over.

609. A kid's sister always wants to sleep in her bed. The sister is scared of being alone at night. The kid talks this problem over with a parent.

610. A kid would like her father to spend more time with her and pay more attention to her.

611. A kid's friend always wants to make everything a contest. He wants to see who can do things fastest or best and to see who wins. The kid would rather not be competing all the time.

612. A parent tells people outside the family things about the child that the child wishes were kept private, such as the child's problems with school subjects. The parent just tends to talk about whatever problem is on her mind.

613. A kid hates broccoli, and her parents want her to eat it.

614. A kid has a brother who is a stimulus-seeker. The brother likes to stir up trouble just for the fun of it. He does things like marking on the kid's homework paper just to create some excitement.

615. Two family members like to play chess. But one is much better at the game than the other. If both play as well as they can, one will always win and the other will always lose.

616. One person has the habit of looking over the other's shoulder at what the person is writing, on paper or on the computer. The second person wants privacy when he is writing.

617. A kid gets asked to clean up a lot, even when it was her little brother who made the mess. She is asked because

she is older and can do a better job of cleaning up than the little brother can. She talks with her parent about this.

618. A kid is hit by the ball when up at bat in baseball. After that he is afraid of the ball. But another family member thinks he should be brave and tough.

619. A kid likes to play tennis with his friend in a relaxed way, doing a lot of chatting, and not trying terribly hard. His dad feels that he should be working very hard to play well, so that he can be good enough at tennis that it will help him get into college.

620. Someone borrows a book from a friend, but loses it.

621. One parent wants to sign a child up for many lessons in art and sports and music. The other parent feels that children are raised to be too selfish, and should be more involved in activities that help people, such as volunteering for a tutoring project.

622. One parent thinks that the child should be taught as many foreign languages as possible. The other thinks that learning languages is a waste of time and that the time would be better spent in learning other subjects.

623. One parent thinks that it is important to go to a baby and see what the problem is whenever the baby cries. The other parent thinks that to do this

wouldn't give the parent enough rest and also would not particularly help the child.

624. One parent thinks that it's OK for the child to ride a bike on the street. The other thinks that this is too dangerous.

625. One person in a family is trying to lose weight. He doesn't want any cookies or cakes or other sweets in the house to tempt him. Another family member wants to have those foods in the house.

626. One person wants no alcohol in the house, because he believes that alcohol does huge harm to society. Another person sees nothing wrong with drinking alcohol and wants to keep it in the house.

627. One person thinks that, when a thunderstorm comes, you should turn off everything electric in the house. The other thinks that this is being too cautious without good reason.

628. Two people own a very old dog who has lots of health problems. One thinks the dog should be put to sleep, and the other thinks the dog should be able to live as long as possible.

629. One person in a family is in the habit of drinking milk right out of the carton. Another person thinks this is unsanitary.

630. One person is very concerned with clothes and the appearance of rooms and how things look; the other person thinks that these are superficial concerns and that people should think of more important things.

631. One person who is allergic to wool is moving into the same house with someone who really likes wool clothes.

632. The first person feels that the second doesn't drive carefully enough; the second thinks that the first drives too slowly.

633. One person has a burglar alarm on his house that often goes off for false alarms. The neighbor has been awakened by this two or three times.

634. One person in a family thinks that the inside of the house should be painted again, to make the house look better. The other thinks that this is unnecessary and a waste of money.

635. A student thinks that a tutor wants him to work too long without resting. The tutor wants the student not to be lazy.

636. One parent thinks that kids should be able to have junk food when they want it, so that they won't value it too highly. The other parent thinks that junk food should be saved and used for a reward, to motivate self-disciplined behavior.

637. One family member gets the second an expensive present for a birthday. But the one who received the present feels that the family can't afford to spend its money on things like this.

638. A teenager goes to school with kids who make fun of any kids who are seen with their parents. The teenager doesn't want to get picked on by his friends. The parents of this teenager think that the other kids are ungrateful brats for feeling this way, and that their child should have more courage in resisting them.

639. One parent feels that their child is too entitled and spoiled and needs to be treated with stricter discipline. The other feels that the child acts negatively because he hears too much negativity, and the best way to improve the child's behavior would be to act more joyous and upbeat.

640. One person in a family feels that watching TV is a good way to relax and have fun. Another feels that the television watcher is being lazy, wasting time, and avoiding doing more beneficial activities.

641. One person in the family feels that violent entertainment is bad for people in general and that everyone in the family should boycott it. The other person has the point of view that lots of people can handle violent entertainment

without getting violent, and that he shouldn't have to give it up because of some other people who get violent.

642. One neighbor hires someone to build a shed. The neighbor finds that the builder has crossed over the dividing line of their property; some of the shed is on the neighbor's property. But the shed is already built.

643. A man is adamant about not having anyone who smokes in the house, and in asking anyone who does smoke to go outside. This embarrasses his wife. She would like to have some people over who smoke. She fears that he would embarrass her.

644. A woman quits her job. Her husband doesn't like it that she didn't tell him beforehand so they could make the decision together. She thinks that what he really minds is that she quit the job and that his complaint about her not consulting him is just an excuse for his being angry.

645. A man thinks his wife should get a job and support the family. She thinks that the job of child-rearing is an important one and that he should value it more than money alone.

646. A woman invites people over, but if her husband does not find the conversation interesting, or if a good TV show comes on, he has been known

to leave and not return, leaving her with the guests. She does not like this.

647. A woman wants to go back to school. Her husband resists, because he fears that she will think he is not good enough for her if she becomes educated.

648. A man doesn't like it that his wife fixes special meals only when they have company and not just for the two of them.

649. A woman becomes preoccupied with work and other things and often seems to be "in the clouds," not paying attention to people and things around her. Her husband feels unloved because she ignores him at these times.

650. When a man and his wife are with other people, she gives him displeased looks or kicks under the table when he's not behaving in a way that she thinks is appropriate. He doesn't like this.

651. A woman makes a particular purchase that her husband disapproves of. The real issue is how much she can make up her own mind without consulting him before spending money.

652. One member of a couple wants more affection, concern, and tenderness from the other.

653. A man has some children from a previous marriage. He doesn't want his wife to discipline the children. When

she's alone with them, a situation arises where she thinks she should discipline them.

654. A husband and wife don't have projects or activities they like to do together. Each does her or his own thing. They feel that they are drifting apart.

655. A man watches TV more than his wife would like him to.

656. A man spends so much time on work that his wife thinks he doesn't care about her.

657. A man watches Sunday night football. His wife dislikes being neglected on Sunday nights.

658. A man dislikes his wife's parents. But she likes to spend time with them often.

659. A man doesn't want his wife to contradict or criticize him when they are out in social gatherings. His wife thinks that free interchange of ideas is desirable.

660. A woman wants her husband simply to listen to her concerns and feelings without trying to fix the problems or give her solutions. He is in the habit of quickly advising solutions.

661. One member of a couple resents the amount of time the other spends on the telephone.

662. A woman gets the feeling she is boring to her husband because she's always taking care of little children and doesn't have worldly things to talk about.

663. A woman takes on a school or job project that her husband supports. However, he seems to expect her to keep up with all her former jobs around the house.

664. A man and a woman dance together. The woman wants to lead, and the man finds this irritating.

665. A woman criticizes her husband often for not picking up around the house, not saying nice things to her and so forth. He says that the criticism just makes him feel like doing nice things less often. She says that he doesn't do the things unless she criticizes him.

666. A man believes in laying down the law in an authoritarian manner with the children. His wife believes in hearing the children out and negotiating with them.

667. A woman wants her husband to put in equal time on chores. The man resents her score-keeping.

668. When a man and his wife take vacations, she always wants to be on the go. He likes to take it easy.

669. A man has a tendency to run up bills on their credit cards. His wife prefers to buy only what they can pay for at the time.

670. A woman doesn't want her husband to intervene when she is disciplining the children. He tends to break in and take over.

671. A man likes to play golf on weekends and wants his wife to learn how to play, so they can do this together. His wife is not interested in playing golf.

672. A woman saves up problems with the children for her husband to reopen and solve when he comes home. He doesn't like this custom.

673. A man is rigidly moral about the use of language, drinking, and so forth, and he corrects his wife in front of the children when he sees her stepping out of line. She resents this.

674. A woman is gaining weight and this bothers her husband. She thinks he should love her anyway and is hurt by the suggestion that he would not be as attracted to her if she were fat.

675. A man tries to help his wife with tasks such as moving things, opening doors, opening jars, navigating in the car, and other tasks he has regarded as examples of what a man should do. His wife wants him to let her do these things herself. She feels insulted when he implies that she can't do them. He feels insulted when she won't let him help.

676. A husband and wife belong to a church where he likes the people and is liked. She doesn't like the church or the people. It has been important to both of them that they go to church together.

677. When a man and his wife are at a party, she talks to other men in a way that he thinks is flirting. She thinks that he is silly to be jealous.

678. A woman spends a lot of time putting her children to bed. Her husband wants her to spend time with him.

679. A man and his wife dance together. He just wants to dance naturally and have a good time. She wants to perform all the steps perfectly, and she comments often on whether they did something right or not. He thinks this habit spoils his fun.

680. A woman talks for a long time at a stretch when she gets talking. Her husband finds it difficult to listen to her for this reason. She is offended by his not listening.

681. One spouse is involved in political causes in a big way. The other gets tired of hearing about them.

682. A man likes to go to movies and often decides to go on the spur of the moment. His wife is unwilling to go on the spur of the moment without spending some time getting made up and looking good. The result is that he usually goes alone. This is OK with him, but she feels left out and neglected.

683. When a man goes to parties, he starts acting uninhibited and silly in a way that seems to entertain the other guests, but embarrasses his wife.

Appendix 2: Provocations for Practice

How To Use the Practice Choice Points

1. Go through the options of Ida Craft (ignoring, differential reinforcement, assertion, conflict-resolution, criticism-response, rule of law, relaxation, away from the situation, apologizing, friendliness, force that is nonviolent, and tones of voice). Think about the advantages and disadvantages of each of these in the situation, and decide which ones you would favor.

2. Do a fantasy rehearsal of handling the provocation well. (STEBC = situation, thoughts, emotions, behaviors, celebration).

3. Practice the Four-thought Exercise with the provocation (not awfulizing, goal-setting, listing options and choosing, and celebrating your own choice.) Or practice the Twelve-thought Exercise.

4. Role play a conflict-resolution conversation about the provocation, trying to fulfill each of the seven guidelines.

5. Practice goal-setting thoughts that lead to the ASPEK motives: avoiding harm, self-discipline, problem-solving, empathy, and kindness.

6. Practice thoughts that lead to emotions other than anger: determined, curious, cool and calculating, sympathetic, humble, proud.

Here's another reminder that can help you greatly when a situation involves people who are very different from you. Taking the perspective of someone older or younger or in a very different role gives mental flexibility that is a great asset in anger control and conflict resolution.

* * *

684. A family member sings a lot, without trying to sing well, and the sound grates on you.

685. A family member keeps asking you whether you have done something that you have promised to do, when there's no urgency to the task and you have definite plans to do it.

686. A family member keeps reminding you to brush your teeth.

687. You are playing baseball and you make an error. A teammate says to you, "You blew it. If we lose the game, it will be your fault."

688. You are trying to concentrate on something, and someone interrupts you.

689. You pay a cashier in change rather than in bills, and the cashier speaks to you in a very disrespectful way.

690. You tell someone about a conflict that you had with someone else, hoping to get some support, but instead you get a morality lesson about how not to do what you did again.

691. You are getting off a bus and someone, trying to be funny, grabs onto your backpack and pulls back on it as you go down the steps.

692. You are driving, and at an intersection, someone turns in front of you, without having signaled.

693. You are at a restaurant and a waitperson spills water on you.

694. You have an appointment with someone, but the person doesn't show.

695. You ask someone to turn down the loud music, and they do, but fifteen minutes later it's loud again.

696. You are at a party and you hear someone you know say behind your back something critical of you.

697. You are trying to explain something to someone, and you think you're explaining it very clearly. But the person keeps saying, "I don't know what you're talking about."

698. Someone comes up to you with a friendly smile and makes a teasing remark about the clothes you are wearing. The remark is actually fairly insulting.

699. You are driving, and someone pulls out from a side street in front of you, causing you to slam on the brakes.

700. You are walking in a shopping area, and a group of kids comes by laughing and making lots of noise. One of them looks at you and says, "Hey, elephant-head!" and the others laugh loudly.

701. A friend says something to you that is insulting about a better friend.

702. Someone assumes that, because of your age, you never clean up your room. The person teases you about this, when in fact you clean up your room very conscientiously.

703. You are in a conversation, and the other person keeps talking on and on without giving you a chance to talk.

704. You would like to do something fun and interesting with a friend, but the friend comes up with all sorts of reasons, which don't strike you as good ones, why it would not be a good idea.

705. You go to a lecture, but the lecturer goes on and on about boring stuff that is off the subject.

706. You are working on a computer, and it crashes in the middle of what you are doing.

707. You spend time making a clay pot. Someone brushes it with their coat, knocking it off the table and breaking it into many pieces.

708. There is one piece left of a food you like on a plate on the table. You start to get it, but a family member grabs it first and puts it into his mouth, then looks at you and laughs.

709. You live in an apartment. The neighbors have a loud argument with each other, waking you up with their yelling just after you had gone to sleep.

710. You're outside on a cold day. A kid grabs your hat off your head and runs away with it, laughing.

711. You're playing football, and someone you're playing with tackles you too hard.

712. In a card game, someone is trying to look at your cards.

713. In basketball, someone says the ball bounced out of bounds; you think it didn't.

714. There's a climbing toy at a park that only one person can get on at a time. You move to get on it, but someone else runs to get on it first.

715. You take a certain medicine to improve your behavior. Whenever you do anything that someone in your family doesn't like, that person says, "Did you not have your medicine today?"

716. Someone in your family smokes, even though the person knows you don't like it.

717. You're at a park, and some kids you don't know are standing around together. When you walk by, one of them says, "Hey, bone-brain."

718. The way you talk is a little different from most other people. You see and overhear someone imitating the way you talk, smiling as he does it.

719. Someone spills grape juice on your book.

720. Someone is speaking to you, with very long pauses while the person is thinking of what to say next.

721. Someone makes a joke about "your mother," trying to get you mad.

722. Your teacher gives you a very long homework assignment.

723. You lost a book that belonged to the library. The librarian says, "You were really irresponsible," in a very disapproving voice.

724. You are waiting your turn to do an activity during a class session at school. Just as it's about to be your turn, the teacher says, "It's time to stop this and go on to something else. Everyone go back to your seats."

725. A kid who is purposely trying to make you angry draws on your arm with a pen.

726. You tell someone about a mistake you made, hoping that you can confide in the other person, but the other person said, "How stupid was that!"

727. You're a parent. You have your child with you at a park. You say it's time to go home, but the child ignores you.

728. You're trying to read, and people in your family interrupt you.

729. You are a lifeguard at a pool. There is a swimming lesson, and no one can swim in the pool until the lesson is over. Some kids start swimming there anyway, even after you told them not to.

730. A young child asks you to read a book to him. But soon after you start reading, he wanders off and gets interested in something else.

731. It's a summer day, and you go into a restaurant or library or store. The air conditioning makes it so cold that it's very unpleasant to be inside.

732. You are drawing. Someone spills a drink on your drawing.

733. You want to have a conversation with your dad, but your step-mom butts into the conversation, as she almost always does.

734. You're sitting on a bus. Someone steps on your foot. The person then looks at you with an angry face and says, "Why don't you keep your feet out of the aisle?"

735. You lend a book to someone, and get it back. Later you find a page torn out of the book.

736. You have very strong opinions about a war that your country fought. Someone else tells you that you are all wrong and that anybody should be able to see that the opposite of what you think is the best opinion.

737. You take a test at school. The teacher has put on the test a question that wasn't covered in class or in your textbook.

738. You have to take a course in school that you have no interest in at all.

739. You have someone over to visit. The visitor frequently says things like, "I bet I can do that faster than you," and "Mine is better than yours is."

740. You're a parent. You have lots of work to do in the house. You ask your child to help, and the child says OK but does nothing but watch TV.

741. After you are married, your spouse lets his or her appearance go downhill, so that your spouse is less attractive to you.

742. Your neighbors put a lot of chemicals on their lawns. You think these chemicals are harmful to your health.

743. Some kids in your school call you by name and say hi to you in an overly friendly way that you think is not sincere, but teasing.

744. You're playing a game against someone who is more skilled at it than you are. The person lets you almost win, but then each time comes from behind and wins himself.

745. You live in a neighborhood where kids like to play in the street. An older teenager drives a car very fast down your street.

746. You have a boyfriend or girlfriend or spouse who likes to flirt with other people when you go out together.

747. You have a boyfriend or girlfriend or spouse, and some other person is flirting with your partner when you go out together.

748. You know a lot about astronomy. You point out to someone that Jupiter is visible in the sky. The person says, "No, that's a star."

749. You think you've left a quarter on your desk, but it isn't there. You think a certain person in your family took it.

750. You're talking with your mom about some accomplishment you made. Your brother butts in and talks about something good that he did, distracting the attention from you.

751. Some people you know have caught a lizard, and they are keeping it in captivity. You think they are not treating the animal right and should let it go.

752. The contract for your apartment says that you get charged a penalty if you pay the rent late. You pay it only one day late, and you get charged the penalty anyway.

753. You have strong opinions about whether it is right or wrong to go hunting. Someone else tells you that you are totally wrong in thinking that way.

754. You have some strong beliefs about whether there is a God who intervenes in human affairs. Someone else says that your ideas are ridiculous.

755. Your parents weren't married to each other. Someone else brings this up and says that you are not as good as he or she is because of this.

756. One person says to another person, "I heard your father was a drunk."

757. One person makes good grades, and the other person tries to tease him and pick on him because of that, calling him a nerd.

758. You are looking forward to buying something at a store. When you get there, the person is locking the door and won't let you in, even though there are still a couple of minutes till closing time.

759. You are cleaning up your room. Your mom yells up to you in a nagging voice, "Don't forget to clean up your room! You promised that you would do it."

760. People in your family often don't come to the room you're in when they want to speak to you, but instead yell from other parts of the house, and most of the time you can't understand what they are saying.

761. You show a parent some homework, proud of how much work you've done. But your parent, instead of praising your work, checks it and finds a couple of little mistakes and points them out in a disapproving way.

762. You have a brother who likes to put on piano concerts for guests when they come over. The brother plays really badly.

763. Some guests come over to visit. One of them is sick. The person gives the sickness to everyone in your family.

764. Someone says that his dog doesn't bite. But one day the dog nips you for almost no reason, and the bite hurts.

765. Your family is very short of money. You find out that your spouse has spent a lot of money on expensive pictures to put on the walls.

766. Your family is very short of money. You find out that your spouse has bought a very expensive computer, even though the spouse already has one that has worked well.

767. Your family is moving. You have some strong opinions about when you should get packed up to move and whether you should start ahead of time, or wait until the last minute. Another family member thinks that you are all wrong on this, and lets you know.

768. Your family is moving. You have opinions about how necessary it is to pack everything very carefully in a well-cushioned way. Another family member strongly disagrees with what you think.

769. You have strong opinions about whether it is OK to enjoy a lot of junk food, or whether it is bad for anyone to do this. Another family member disagrees strongly with you about this.

770. You find out that some people have planted marijuana plants on your property.

771. You make a move in a chess game. Someone else watching the game says, "That was a wimpy move."

772. You say something, and someone else repeats what you've said in a mocking tone of voice.

773. You have strong feelings about whether there is life after death, and someone else says that your opinion is ridiculous.

774. You're a piano teacher, and a student keeps coming for lessons without ever having done any practicing at all.

775. You are working with a scientist. You come up with a good idea, which you suggest. The scientist further explores it, and it turns out to be a great discovery. But the scientist does not give credit for the idea to you.

776. You are a parent, and your child asks you for something, and you say no. Your child screams at you and calls you bad names.

777. You are a parent. You find out that, while you were out of the house, your child burned paper in a trash can.

778. You are walking at night. Someone shines a flashlight in your eyes; this temporarily blinds you.

779. You try out for a sport. On the first day, the coach makes you run a lot more than you think you should have to.

780. You sing a song in front of people. Most people say you did a great job. One person says you were off pitch three or four times, and tells you the words that you didn't sing right.

781. You have a spouse who spends so much time at work that you hardly ever see him or her.

782. Your spouse complains about your spending too much time at work, but you notice that your spouse does not mind the family's having the money you make by working a lot.

783. You are a teenager. Your parent doesn't just listen when you talk about

something, but almost always gives you advice or commands about what to do.

784. You are walking with someone who has a habit of getting in front of you and then slowing down.

785. You are a parent. You have made many sacrifices for your child. Your child does not want his friends to see you with him or her, because for some reason the teenagers in your child's culture think that it is shameful to do things with your parents.

786. You are trying to sleep, because you have to get up early tomorrow morning to work. The neighbors in your apartment building have a very loud party that is keeping you awake.

787. You are trying to study, and a sibling walks by and touches you on the head, just to get the stimulation of your response. When you don't respond, he does it again.

788. You tell a doctor about something that was wrong with you, and the doctor says, "Here, take this; it will make you better." The doctor gives you a prescription. Later you read about the medicine that the doctor prescribed, and it looks to you as if the medicine is harmful and shouldn't be given for what you complained about.

Some Provocations for Kids in School

789. You are laughing to yourself as you walk down the hall in school, thinking about something that was funny that happened. An assistant principal thinks you are laughing in a disrespectful way and reprimands you in a very bossy manner.

790. You speak very quietly in school to someone, in a way that doesn't disturb anyone. A teacher who sees your lips moving yells at you and reprimands you.

791. You work very hard on a written essay with good ideas. The teacher sees it and criticizes the quality of your handwriting.

792. You are working at a desk and humming. Someone tells you, in a very bossy tone, to quit humming and work quietly.

793. You are a kid at school, and you are sent out into the hall as punishment. You take something with you to draw on while you are in the hall. The teacher tells you in a mean tone of voice to hand over your pencil and the drawing paper.

794. You're in a classroom and a kid takes something of yours away. You get it back from him and say something to

him. The teacher sees this, and you get in trouble, but the other kid doesn't.

795. You are a kid at school, playing on the playground with another kid, in a way that a teacher thinks is too rough. The teacher tells you to not touch the other kid.

796. Someone sees a grade on your homework assignment and says, "Ha, ha, ha! I did better than you did!"

797. A kid is bored and very restless in class and starts running around giving little pushes to other kids to keep from being bored. The teacher tells him to sit by himself, to regain control.

798. A kid comes to school and is told he is going to have to spend time being punished for what he did the previous day, because there was not time to finish his punishment the previous day. The kid thinks that it is not fair that he has to be punished for something he did the previous day.

799. A kid has to wait outside. He thinks that it is too hot outside. But he is not permitted to go inside, because he is waiting for a bus or a cab to take him home.

800. You are getting ready to listen to an audio recording, but you can't get the player to work right.

801. Someone at school curses when frustrated by a machine's not working right. The teacher assigns a punishment.

802. Someone at school is playing a game, but he has to stop it and put it away because it is time for lunch.

803. A person at school wants to listen to a recording. The teacher says that the person isn't allowed to use the player because the person mistreated this piece of equipment in the past.

804. A school kid refuses to recite the pledge of allegiance and is told that all people who don't recite it have to write it.

805. A person in a group is trying to ask a question, but another person is talking over him.

806. It is recess and a kid wants to play in the puddles. The teacher says that this is not allowed, and that the kid will have to stay inside for recess if he does.

807. A kid is not allowed to go in the puddles. He goes near the puddles. The teacher says that he disobeyed, even though he was not in the puddles.

808. A kid is going out for recess. The teacher says he has to put his jacket on before he goes out. He feels hot, and he doesn't feel like putting his jacket on.

809. A kid has been antsy all day and has been having trouble following directions. He is looking forward to gym. He is told that he won't be able to go to gym because he has not been able to follow directions.

810. A kid gets in an argument with a bus driver, and he is directed by the bus driver to sit quietly for two minutes. He considers this unfair because he thinks that the bus driver was arguing just as much as he was.

811. A person in a class is given some instructions on schoolwork. The instructions are very confusing, leaving it very unclear what is to be done.

812. A kid is playing on a jungle gym. A teacher thinks that he is playing dangerously on it. He is given a punishment for this. He thinks that this is unfair because he thinks the jungle gyms were put there to play on in any way you want.

813. A kid is told to write sentences. He finds this hard and boring, and he doesn't want to do it.

814. A kid has a music CD and is playing it in the computer. The teacher tells him that it is inappropriate music and that he will have to turn it off.

815. A kid is told to turn off a music CD. He is beginning to do so when the teacher pulls the plug on the CD.

816. A kid has received a punishment. When he returns from punishment to be with the other kids in the classroom, they seem to be laughing at him and teasing him.

817. A person wants to work on a computer, but someone else is already working on it. Then the person would like to stand and watch what the other person is doing, but the other person resents this and says so.

818. A person in school is given some homework to do that the person doesn't know how to do.

819. A kid has been doing something in the hall that the teacher does not know about. When they get into the class another kid tells on him, and the teacher reprimands the other kid for telling.

820. A kid is being very loud outside at recess, but he feels that he has a right to do this. The teacher then punishes him.

821. A kid has some math work that is hard. He is told that he can't go to recess until he finishes his math. He feels that he doesn't know how to finish it.

822. There is a playground with wood chips. A kid throws some wood chips and is given a punishment for this. He feels that this is unfair because he feels that he wasn't doing any harm.

823. A kid has a friend. Some other kid accidentally hurts the friend.

824. A person gets threatened by another person who is irritated by something the person did.

825. A person has a yo-yo on his finger; the string gets stuck.

826. A person sees two other people start to argue or fight with each other and tries to break it up, but one of the people turns on him.

827. A kid is arguing with another kid. A teacher directs him to stop arguing with the kid. The teacher tells him to turn his chair around and not talk to the kid. He turns his chair around. But he does not like the tone of voice in which the teacher told him.

828. A school kid is in the library picking out a book. Before he has made his choice, the teacher tells the group that they have to go back to class, and that those who haven't picked a book will have to wait till next time.

829. A kid's parents are having a meeting with teachers. The kid is not allowed to go into the meeting.

830. You are playing a game with someone else, and there is a disagreement about the rules.

831. There is a reward that school kids earn if they have behaved well - they get to go to super kid's club. A kid finds out that he will not be able to go because the teachers think that he has not behaved well.

832. A school kid comes back to class from an outside activity that he was asked to go to. He is told that he will have to make up what he missed, even though all the other kids are playing.

833. A kid is asked to make puppets in class. He doesn't want to do this activity. The teacher tells him that if he doesn't do the activity, he will have to sit in his chair.

834. A kid thinks that a teacher is being too bossy, so he talks back to the teacher. The teacher threatens punishment.

835. There is a store where you can buy things with points that you earn. A teacher tells a kid that he cannot go to the store today, because he was too out of control.

836. A kid is in line, but feels that the other kids are crowding him too much. He tells the other kids to get away from him in a tone of voice that the teacher doesn't like. The teacher threatens punishment.

837. A kid wants to play with a certain other kid. However, the teacher says

that he can't because recently he and the other kid got into some conflict.

838. A kid has some extra money. He asks one of the staff members working in the kitchen if he can buy some extra food. He is told no.

839. There is a scooter at school. A kid sees it and thinks that it would be great fun to ride on. He does so, but the teacher gives him a punishment because he did not get permission.

840. A kid sees a shower in the bathroom. Out of curiosity he turns it on. A staff member gives him a punishment for this.

841. You are at a school, and another person keeps staring at you.

842. You talk with a teacher about the fact that someone is staring at you. The teacher tells you to ignore the person.

843. A kid has been playing with some toys that you stick together to make things. The time for the activity ends, and everything has to be taken apart. The boy doesn't want his creation to be disassembled.

844. A kid is told that he can earn some extra time outside if he can get some "caught you being good cards" from the teachers. This makes him mad because he figures that other people will probably get them and he won't.

845. A kid has his shoes off and is just about ready to go to the computers. The teacher tells him to put his shoes on. He doesn't see why he has to do this.

846. It is art project time. A kid has worked on his project as much as he wants to, and wants to do something else. The teacher tells him that he is not allowed to put his project away and start something else.

847. A kid is feeling very agitated. A staff member tells him to sit down and calm down. He doesn't want to do this because he is so restless.

848. There is a point system where you earn privileges depending on how much you do. Some other kids get to go outside, but one kid doesn't, because he isn't at that level.

849. A kid is getting a punishment of having to stay in a certain room. He has to go to the bathroom. When in the bathroom, he wants to stay there just to cool down, but the staff members say that he has to come back to the room.

850. It is computer time. There are some really cool computer games. Just as a kid is playing a fun computer game, the teacher tells him that he has to do keyboarding.

851. Another kid at school calls a kid a "dummy."

852. A kid is talking about his favorite movies. A staff member tells him that it is inappropriate to talk about this at school and that he has to stop.

853. There is a school spring festival during after-school hours. A kid finds out that he won't be able to go because his parents can't take him.

854. A kid is told to sit in a certain place. But there is a kid next to him he doesn't like.

855. A kid is asked to wash his hands. He thinks that the teacher said this in too bossy a way.

856. A kid teases another kid. He is told that he needs to apologize or sit out of the activity that they are doing.

857. A kid sees that another kid has something that he lost. He thinks that the kid stole it from him, so he tries to grab it back. The teacher and the kid scold for this.

858. A kid normally sits at a certain seat during an activity. Today, however, the teacher tells him that the seats are being reassigned.

859. A kid is tapping on his desk. The teacher tells him to stop doing this.

860. There is a point system for how much you do in academics. A kid does not get as many points as he thinks that he deserves.

861. A kid is asked to sit calmly for ten minutes. He gets a really strong urge to go to the bathroom. He asks the teacher if he can go, but she says that he has to wait and listen to directions for five more minutes before he can go.

862. A kid brings a CD player to school. He is told that he can't have that at school, and it is taken away from him to be stored for the school day.

863. A kid is being picked on by other kids. He breaks a yo-yo. He is told that he can not have another yo-yo because he intentionally broke the first one.

864. A kid is doing schoolwork. He feels that he needs a break. He wanders over to another area and begins to play with blocks, but the teacher gives him the count of five to get back to his work.

865. A kid is saying the phrase "mother chucker." He feels that he is not saying anything wrong, but the teacher tells him that he will be punished if he says it again.

866. A kid is spinning a necklace around his finger. The string breaks and the beads hit another kid. The kid is given a punishment for this, but he thinks that this is unfair because it was an accident.

867. A kid is doing something in class that he thinks is interesting, but he is told that he has to line up to go to the next activity.

868. There is a certain reward a kid will get if he earns 100 points. He gets 98 points and does not get the prize.

869. A kid throws an orange peel to see if he can get it into the trash can. Instead of making it, he accidentally hits a teacher and gets punished.

870. During game time a kid wants to play a certain game, but he can't because he is being punished for something he did previously that day.

871. A kid is asked to write a journal entry. He doesn't want to do this.

872. A kid wants to play Uno with a certain teacher, but the teacher is unavailable.

873. Point sheets are being reviewed. A kid finds out that points have been taken off because a teacher thought he was mean on the playground.

874. A kid is playing a board game, and he begins to lose at it.

875. There are two groups to go outside. A kid wants to go with the first group, but he finds that he has to go in the second group.

876. A kid is doing a group activity with other kids. Another kid gets into the space that he thinks should be his.

877. A kid is playing with a toy. He is told that he has to stop or he will not get points toward the things he is working for.

878. A kid is doing a project in woodshop, but he can't get it to work right.

879. A kid has finished his academic work, but he has to wait for the other kids to finish before he can start something else. He has to sit without anything to do in one area. He moves to another area but is told to come back to his seat.

880. A kid goes to woodshop, but at the end, he is told that he did not earn any points on the point system.

881. There is a game where, if you make a mistake, you are out. A kid makes a mistake and is out. Some kids laugh at him.

882. A kid is talking to peers. He finds out later that he does not get a prize because of too much talking.

883. A kid comes back to class. Because other kids are having trouble, more time is added to quiet time. The

kid thinks that this is unfair because he did not do anything.

884. A kid finds out that a teacher sent a note to his mom telling about some bad behavior.

885. While walking back from breakfast, a kid gets a piece of food thrown at him by another kid.

886. A kid makes a paper plane, but it does not fly as far as another kid's paper plane.

887. A kid gets a breakfast bagel, but it is not as soft as he wanted it.

888. A kid comes to school with some items that the teacher thinks he stole. The teacher questions him about it.

889. A kid is taking a walk with some staff members. He asks for a magazine, but is told no.

890. A kid has an appointment with a psychologist. He finds out that it is postponed, and gets upset.

891. A kid is playing with a classmate. The classmate refuses to share with him.

892. A kid has yelled something loudly, and is given a punishment for this.

893. A kid is making noises to get another kid's attention, and the kid throws a pencil at him.

894. There is a seat where a kid normally sits during a certain class, but another kid is already sitting there.

895. A kid is talking, and the teacher tells him to be quiet in a way that he doesn't like.

896. A kid is having trouble doing some work. He is told that he will have to finish his work before he can move on to the next activity. He is looking forward to the next activity.

897. A kid gets too close to another kid's personal space, and the other kid shows it.

898. A kid notices that another kid is copying him.

899. In a cooking class a kid wants to eat the thing that he has mixed up immediately after he made it. The teacher tells him that he has to wait for it to bake.

900. A kid is using the computer. He is told that he has to get off the computer because he did not get permission to use it.

901. A kid is standing close to the oven. A teacher tells him to get away from the oven and to go back to his seat.

902. A kid is asked to go to a special class that he does not like and that he does not want to go to.

903. After a certain activity, a kid is asked to clean up. He does not like the tone in which the teacher asked this.

904. A kid is told he may not go to the restrooms with other students. Instead he will have to go with staff.

905. A kid is mad. Some staff members ask him what is wrong, but he does not want to tell. They keep asking him and won't let him alone.

906. A kid is playing a game with a peer. Another peer walks by and steps on the game.

907. A kid sees another kid get a treat bag from the staff. He thinks that the amount of stuff in the other kid's bag is considerably greater than the amount that his bag held.

908. A kid sees a rubber band lying on a teacher's desk. He can't keep himself from flipping it across the room. He gets punished for this.

909. A student is punished for making too much noise during a test.

910. A kid has a lunch buddy. His lunch buddy leaves earlier than he wanted him to.

911. A kid is full of energy, but he has to sit in his seat.

912. A kid is asked to listen to a story in the library. He is not interested in the story and does not want to listen to it.

913. A kid gets hit by a snowball.

914. A kid throws snowballs at another kid. He gets punished for this. He feels that this is unfair because snowballs wouldn't hurt anybody.

915. A kid is talking loudly in the breakfast line, and a staff person asks him why he is talking so loudly.

916. A kid is called a name by another kid.

917. A kid is arguing with another kid. The kid gets a punishment, but the other kid is not punished as much. The kid doesn't think this is fair.

918. A kid hopes to get a new puppy, but he finds out that he will not get one.

919. A kid wants to help a peer clean up sand. However, the peer refuses his help.

920. The rule is that there are only two people allowed in the bathroom at a time. A kid has to go, but he has to wait for the other two to come out.

921. A staff member comes into the room to get two helpers. A certain kid is not high enough on the point system to be eligible to be a helper, so he wasn't selected. He gets upset because he thinks that this is unfair.

922. A kid makes a threatening remark to a teacher, and, as a consequence for this, he has to be scanned by a metal detector each time he comes into the building.

923. A kid lines up for something, but he doesn't get as close to the front of the line as he wanted to.

924. There is a certain activity where a kid could earn more points. Because he is already being punished for something else, he does not get the chance.

925. A kid is given a math workbook to work in. He does not like the one he is given, and he wants a different one.

926. Another kid gets too close to a kid.

927. When a kid gets too close to another kid, the kid screams at him.

Appendix 3: Criticisms for Practice

How to Practice with These Choice Points

1. Go through each of the following responses to criticism: "thank you," planning to ponder or problem-solve, agreeing with part of criticism, asking for more specific criticism, reflection, silent eye contact, explanation and debate, and criticizing the critic. Imagine what each of these would be like, and think about the advantages and disadvantages and which ones you would favor.

2. Consider the Ida Craft options for responding to provocations (ignoring, differential reinforcement, assertion, conflict-resolution, criticism-response, rule of law, relaxation, away from the situation, apologizing, friendliness, force of a nonviolent nature, and tones of voice). Imagine each of these and decide which, if any, would be appropriate.

3. Practice the Four-thought Exercise (or the Twelve-thought Exercise).

4. Do a fantasy rehearsal.

5. Practice the ASPEK motives (avoiding harm, self-discipline, problem-solving, empathy, and kindness).

6. Practice non-angry emotions (determination, curiosity, coolness and calculation, sympathy, humility, and pride).

* * *

928. You are taking singing lessons, and your voice teacher says, "You need to hold your larynx lower in your neck. When you hold it too high, the tone sounds too whiny."

929. You are doing schoolwork, and someone says, "That's baby work."

930. Someone is explaining something, and you don't quite get it. The person says, "What's the matter with you?"

931. Someone passes you and says, "Hey, pea-brain."

932. A family member says, "Could you please not interrupt me when I'm in the middle of work that I'm trying to concentrate on? I think you can tell when those times are, can't you?"

933. Your boss says to you, "Your work seems to be of good enough quality, but you aren't fast enough. You need to learn to do more work in a shorter time."

934. You answer a question about a math problem, and the instructor says, "No! No! No!" in a very critical tone.

935. A student asks a question in class, and a teacher says, "Why do you ask so many questions? Do you think you're going to go to Harvard or something?"

936. Someone else is harassing you, and you report it to a teacher or supervisor, who says to you, "Aren't you a little tattletale."

937. You're a student reading aloud, and, when you read a word wrong, your instructor stops you and says "Wait, correct that misread please!"

938. You're a boy, and you get dressed up for a special occasion. Someone says, "You look like a girl."

939. You're a fifty-five-year-old man, and you have a wife who looks younger than you. Someone says to you, "You're her husband? I thought you were her father."

940. You are at a dance. Someone says to you, "Are you waiting for someone to dance with you? Just don't hold your breath."

941. You have written an essay, and an instructor says, "You need to organize the thoughts better. You need to divide the essay into parts, using an outline, before you start writing."

942. Someone in your family says, "I think you would be better off if you would get more into the habit of putting things away."

943. Someone says, "I don't think you're getting enough exercise. You need to get into better shape."

944. You are driving a car, and someone passes you, looking at you and making an angry gesture with his hand.

945. Someone is giving you a tennis lesson. The person says, "You need to swing the racket more level. You've got way too much upward movement."

946. A teacher says, "This is shabby work."

947. You are telling a story to some people, and one of them says, "Come on, get to the point! You don't have to keep going over and over the same thing!"

948. You are playing soccer. A teammate of yours makes a good play, and another teammate says to him, "Good move! You really know what you're doing in this game!" Then, with a glance in your direction, he says, "Unlike some other people I know!"

949. You are on a basketball team. One of your teammates says to you, "I think you dribble the ball too much when you'd do better to pass it to someone else. You miss opportunities when someone is open."

950. A kid says to another, "Congratulations!" The other kid says, "For what?" The first kid says, "For getting into the Book of World Records for being the world's stupidest person!" Then he and another kid start laughing.

951. You are getting a lesson in how to do something. You are getting so much information so fast that you can't remember it. The person teaching you keeps quizzing you, and, when you miss a question, he says with lots of impatience and irritation, "Come on! I've already told you that, three times!"

952. You are in a typing class, where you are a good bit slower than other people in the class. You are typing an assignment that other people have finished. Someone in your class looks at your work and says, "Hey, Speedy! What's the matter, do you have constipation of the fingers today?"

953. You have written several songs, and you finally get to play a recording of them for someone at a music publishing company. He listens to about two or three seconds of each song, and then says to you, "There's nothing there. Your songs are tiresome and trite.

My advice is to try to find something else you can do."

954. Someone used to be the head of a company, but then he got fired by the board of directors. Someone who used to work for him sees him at a party. He says, "You used to be the big kahuna, didn't you? I guess the bigger they are, the harder they fall."

955. You are learning dancing. An instructor sees you and says, "Try standing up straighter. You'll be amazed how much better dancing looks if you use good posture."

956. You are from a certain ethnic group. Someone says to you, "Of course, all ____ (members of that group) are lazy."

957. You joke around, and the other person says, "Oh, that's REALLY FUNNY," in a very sarcastic tone.

958. You've written a book. Someone says, "It was too boring."

959. You've written a book. Someone says, "I think it would be easier to understand if you made the sentences shorter."

Bibliography

Chapter 1: What We're Trying To Do, and Why

The phrase, "The Law of Club and Fang" was taken from Jack London's novel, *The Call of the Wild*.

The study mentioned in which children played with different types of toys was:
Feshbach, S. (1956) The catharsis hypothesis and some consequences of interaction with aggressive and neutral play objects. *Journal of Personality*, 24, 449-462.

The study mentioned about exit interviews when workers were laid off their jobs was:
Ebbesen, E., Duncan, B, and Konecni, V. (1973). Effects of content of verbal aggression on future verbal aggression: a field experiment. *Journal of Experimental Social Psychology*, 11, 192-204.

The survey finding that people who yelled more hit others more was:
Straus, M. (1974). Leveling, civility, and violence in the family. *Journal of Marriage and the Family*, 36, 13-29.

The study finding that women were more attracted to men who acted unselfish was:
Urbaniak, G., and Kilmann, P. (2003). Physical attractiveness and the "nice guy paradox." *Sex Roles: A Journal of Research*, 49, 413-426.

There are several studies confirming the idea that aggressive children don't do as well in our society as non-aggressive children. One is:
Kokko, K., and Pulkkinen, L. (2000). Aggression in childhood and long-term unemployment in adulthood: a cycle of mal-adaptation and some protective factors. *Developmental Psychology*, 36, 463-472.

Another study on how aggressive children don't do well is:
Loeber, R., Green, S. M., Lahey, B. B., and Kalb, L. (2000). Physical fighting in childhood as a risk factor for later mental health problems. *Journal of the American Academy of Child and Adolescent Psychiatry*, 39, 421-428.

A third study on poor outcome for aggressive children is:
Loeber, R., Green, S. M., Keenan, K., and Lahey, B. B. (1995). Which boys will fare worse? Early predictors of the onset of conduct disorder in a six-year longitudinal study. *Journal of the American Academy of Child and Adolescent Psychiatry*, 34, 499-509.

A study finding that aggression predicts the breakup of marriages is:

Rogge, R. D., and Bradbury, T. N. (1999) Till violence does us part: the differing roles of communication and aggression in predicting adverse marital outcomes. *Journal of Consulting and Clinical Psychology*, 67, 340-351.

Another study finding that aggression reduces marital satisfaction is: Testa, M., and Leonard, K. E. (2001). The impact of husband physical aggression and alcohol use on marital functioning: does alcohol "excuse" the violence? *Violence and Victims* ,16, 507-516.

The following article reviews work showing that aggressive behavior by parents toward children tends to make children more aggressive, whereas training parents to use better discipline methods makes children less aggressive. This article also reviews many other influences on children that lead to aggression or the lack of it. The article is: Rappaport, N., and Thomas, C. (2004). Recent research findings on aggressive and violent behavior in youth: implications for clinical assessment and intervention. *Journal of Adolescent Health*, 35, 260-277.

Statistics on the number of U.S. homicides in 2001 were obtained from the web site of the FBI: www.fbi.gov. (The exact number this site reported for 2001 was 16,037.) Statistics on the number of homicides plus assaults in

the U.S. in 2001 were obtained from the web site of the U.S. Bureau of Justice Statistics: www.ojp.usdoj.gov/bjs.

Chapter 4: Fantasy Rehearsal

The study I mentioned by Suinn was: Suinn, R. M; (1972) Behavior rehearsal training for ski racers. *Behavior Therapy*, 3, 519-520.

Three more of the many studies on fantasy rehearsal are as follows: Berthoz, A. (1996). The role of inhibition in the hierarchical gating of executed and imagined movements. *Brain Research: Cognitive Brain Research*, 3: 101-113.
Kazdin, A.E. (1982). The separate and combined effects of covert and overt rehearsal in developing assertive behavior. *Behaviour Research and Therapy*, 20: 17-25.
Wieselberg, N., Dyckman, J.M., Abramowitz, S.I.(1979). The desensitization derby: in vivo down the backstretch, imaginal at the wire? *Journal of Clinical Psychology*, 35: 647-650.

Chapter 16: More Ways of Ending Violence

Regarding the relationship between alcohol and violence, the studies I cited were summarized in: U.S. Department of Health and Human Services (2000). *10th Special Report to the U.S. Congress on Alcohol and*

Health, Highlights from Current Research. U.S. Department of Health and Human Services.

Another article on the relation of alcohol to physical fighting between spouses is:
Leonard, K. E., Bromet, E. J., Parkinson, D. K., Day, N. L., and Ryan, C. M. (1985). Patterns of alcohol use and physically aggressive behavior in men. *Journal of Studies on Alcohol*, 46, 279-282.

Several studies support the idea that greater achievement in school is related to less aggression. Some of these are:
Stanton, W. R., Feehan, M., McGee, R., and Silva, P. A. (1990). The relative value of reading ability and IQ as predictors of teacher-reported behavior problems. *Journal of Learning Disabilities*, 23, 514-517.
Dishion, T. J., Loeber, R., Stoutthamer-Loeber, M., and Patterson, G. R. (1984). Skill deficits and male adolescent delinquency. *Journal of Abnormal Child Psychology*, 12, 37-54.
Miles, S. B., and Stipek, D. (2006). Contemporaneous and longitudinal associations between social behavior and literacy achievement in a sample of low-income elementary school children. *Child Development*, 77, 103-117.

The article I cited regarding entertainment violence was:
Anderson, C. A., Berkowitz, L., Donnerstein, E., Huesmann, L. R.,

Johnson, J. D., Linz, D., Malamuth, N. M., and Wartella, E. (2003). The influence of media violence on youth. *Psychological Science in the Public Interest*, 4: 81-110.

An article on the usefulness of restricting the exposure to violent entertainment is:
Robinson, T. N., Wilde, M. L., Navracruz, L. C., Haydel, K. F., and Varady, A. (2001). Effects of reducing children's television and video game use on aggressive behavior: a randomized controlled trial. *Archives of Pediatric and Adolescent Medicine*, 155, 17-23.

One of the studies finding that about 20 percent of school children are involved in bullying was:
Juvonen, J., Graham, S., and Schuster, M. A. (2003). Bullying among young adolescents: the strong, the weak, and the troubled. *Pediatrics*, 112, 1421-1422.

Regarding world peace through international law and world government, a very useful source is
Ferencz, B. B., and Keyes, K. (1991). *Planethood: The Key to Your Survival and Prosperity*. Coos Bay, Oregon: Love Line Books.

An article reviewing the risk factors for violent behavior that are currently known is:

Loeber, R., Pardini, D., Homish, L.,
Wei, E. H., Crawford, A. M.,
Farrington, D. P., Stouthamer-Loeber,
M., Creemers, J., Koehler, S.A., and
Rosenfeld, R. (2005) The prediction of
violence and homicide in young men.
*Journal of Consulting and Clinical
Psychology*, 73, 1074-1088.

Index

Printed in the United States
88742LV00004B/80/A